Fodor's

KAUA'I

3rd Edition

Fodor's Travel Publications   New York, Toronto, London, Sydney, Auckland
www.fodors.com

Be a Fodor's Correspondent

Your opinion matters. It matters to us. It matters to your fellow Fodor's travelers, too. And we'd like to hear it. In fact, we need to hear it.

When you share your experiences and opinions, you become an active member of the Fodor's community. That means we'll not only use your feedback to make our books better, but we'll publish your names and comments whenever possible. Throughout our guides, look for "Word of Mouth," excerpts of your unvarnished feedback.

Here's how you can help improve Fodor's for all of us.

Tell us when we're right. We rely on local writers to give you an insider's perspective. But our writers and staff editors—who are the best in the business—depend on you. Your positive feedback is a vote to renew our recommendations for the next edition.

Tell us when we're wrong. We're proud that we update most of our guides every year. But we're not perfect. Things change. Hotels cut services. Museums change hours. Charming cafés lose charm. If our writer didn't quite capture the essence of a place, tell us how you'd do it differently. If any of our descriptions are inaccurate or inadequate, we'll incorporate your changes in the next edition and will correct factual errors at fodors.com immediately.

Tell us what to include. You probably have had fantastic travel experiences that aren't yet in Fodor's. Why not share them with a community of like-minded travelers? Maybe you chanced upon a beach or bistro or B&B that you don't want to keep to yourself. Tell us why we should include it. And share your discoveries and experiences with everyone directly at fodors.com. Your input may lead us to add a new listing or highlight a place we cover with a "Highly Recommended" star or with our highest rating, "Fodor's Choice."

Give us your opinion instantly at our feedback center at www.fodors. com/feedback. You may also e-mail editors@fodors.com with the subject line "Kaua'i Editor." Or send your nominations, comments, and complaints by mail to Kaua'i Editor, Fodor's, 1745 Broadway, New York, NY 10019.

You and travelers like you are the heart of the Fodor's community. Make our community richer by sharing your experiences. Be a Fodor's correspondent. Aloha!

Tim Jarrell, Publisher

FODOR'S KAUA'I
Editor: Jess Moss
Writers: Lois Ann Ell, Michael Levine, Charles E. Roessler, and Kim Steutermann Rogers

Production Editor: Evangelos Vasilakis
Maps & Illustrations: Henry Colomb and Mark Stroud, Moon Street Cartography; David Lindroth, Inc., *cartographers;* Bob Blake, Rebecca Baer, *map editors;* William Wu, *information graphics*
Design: Fabrizio La Rocca, *creative director;* Guido Caroti, Siobhan O'Hare, *art directors;* Tina Malaney, Chie Ushio, Ann McBride, Jessica Walsh, *designers;* Melanie Marin, *senior picture editor*
Cover Photo: (Na Pali Coast): Mark A. Johnson/Corbis
Production Manager: Angela L. McLean

3rd Edition

ISBN 978-1-4000-0440-9

ISSN 1934-550X

SPECIAL SALES
This book is available at special discounts for bulk purchases for sales promotions or premiums. Special editions, including personalized covers, excerpts of existing books, and corporate imprints, can be created in large quantities for special needs. For more information, write to Special Markets/Premium Sales, 1745 Broadway, MD 6-2, New York, New York 10019, or e-mail specialmarkets@randomhouse.com.

AN IMPORTANT TIP & AN INVITATION
Although all prices, opening times, and other details in this book are based on information supplied to us at press time, changes occur all the time in the travel world, and Fodor's cannot accept responsibility for facts that become outdated or for inadvertent errors or omissions. So **always confirm information when it matters,** especially if you're making a detour to visit a specific place. Your experiences—positive and negative—matter to us. If we have missed or misstated something, **please write to us.** We follow up on all suggestions. Contact the Kaua'i editor at editors@fodors.com or c/o Fodor's at 1745 Broadway, New York, NY 10019.

PRINTED IN CHINA

10 9 8 7 6 5 4 3 2 1

CONTENTS

ABOUT
THIS BOOK

Our Ratings

Sometimes you find terrific travel experiences and sometimes they just find you. But usually the burden is on you to select. That's where our ratings come in.

As travelers we've all discovered a place so wonderful that its worthiness is obvious. And sometimes that place is so unique that superlatives don't do it justice. These sights, properties, and experiences get our highest rating, **Fodor's Choice**, indicated by orange stars throughout this book. Black stars highlight sights and properties we deem **Highly Recommended**, places that our writers, editors, and readers praise for consistency and excellence.

By default, there's another category: any place we include in this book is by definition worth your time, unless we say otherwise. And we will.

Disagere with any of our choices? Care to nominate a place or suggest that we rate one more highly? Visit our feedback center at www.fodors.com/feedback.

Budget Well

Hotel and restaurant price categories from ¢ to $$$$ are defined in the opening pages of each chapter. For attractions, we always give standard adult admission fees; reductions are usually available for children, students, and senior citizens. Want to pay with plastic? **AE, D, DC, MC, V** following restaurant and hotel listings indicate whether American Express, Discover, Diners Club, MasterCard, and Visa are accepted.

Restaurants

Unless we state otherwise, restaurants are open for lunch and dinner daily. We mention dress only when there's a specific requirement and reservations only when they're essential or not accepted—it's always best to book ahead.

Hotels

Hotels have private bath, phone, TV, and air-conditioning and operate on the European Plan, meaning without meals, unless we specify that they use the Continental Plan (CP, with a continental breakfast), Breakfast Plan (BP, with a full breakfast), or Modified American Plan (MAP, with breakfast and dinner), or are all-inclusive (AI, including all meals and most activities). We always list facilities but not whether you'll be charged an extra fee to use them, so when pricing accommodations, find out what's included.

Listings

★	Fodor's Choice
★	Highly recommended
⊠	Physical address
⊹	Directions or Map coordinates
⟟	Mailing address
☎	Telephone
🖷	Fax
⊕	On the Web
✉	E-mail
🖾	Admission fee
☉	Open/closed times
Ⓜ	Metro stations
⊟	Credit cards

Hotels & Restaurants

🏨	Hotel
⟿	Number of rooms
⟁	Facilities
⦿	Meal plans
✕	Restaurant
⟿	Reservations
⟁	Dress code
↘	Smoking
⌐	BYOB

Outdoors

⚘	Golf
⚑	Camping

Other

☺	Family-friendly
⊠	Branch address
☞	Take note

Experience
Kaua'i

WHAT'S WHERE

1 North Shore. Dreamy beaches, green mountains, breathtaking scenery, and abundant rain, waterfalls, and rainbows characterize the North Shore, which includes the communities of Kīlauea, Princeville, and Hanalei.

2 East Side. This is Kaua'i's commercial and residential hub, dominated by the island's largest town, Kapa'a. The airport, harbor, and government offices are found in the county seat of Līhu'e.

3 South Shore. Peaceful landscapes, sunny weather, and beaches that rank among the best in the world make the South Shore the resort capital of Kaua'i. The Po'ipū resort area is here, along with the main towns of Kōloa, Lāwa'i, and Kalāheo.

4 West Side. Dry, sunny, and sleepy, the West Side includes the historic towns of Hanapēpē, Waimea, and Kekaha. This area is ideal for outdoor adventurers because it's the entryway to the Waimea Canyon and Kōke'e State Park, and the departure point for most Nāpali Coast boat trips.

■ TIP→ On Kaua'i, the directions "mauka" (toward the mountains) and "makai" (toward the ocean) are often used. Locals tend to refer to highways by name rather than by number.

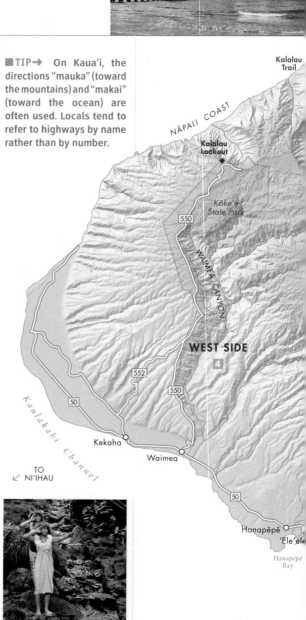

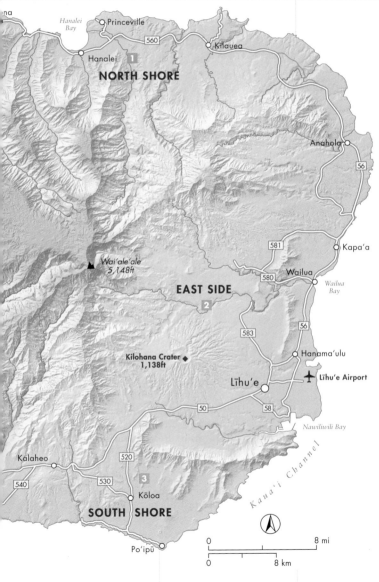

Hanalei
Bay

Princeville

560

Kīlauea

Hanalei

1

NORTH SHORE

Anahola

56

581

Kapa'a

Wai'ale'ale
5,148ft

580

Wailua

EAST SIDE

Wailua
Bay

2

583

56

Kilohana Crater
1,138ft

Hanama'ulu

Līhu'e Airport

Līhu'e

50

58

Nawiliwili Bay

Kalaheo

520

Kaua'i Channel

540

530

3

Kōloa

SOUTH SHORE

Po'ipū

0   8 mi

0   8 km

KAUA'I AND HAWAI'I TODAY

Despite its small size—about 550 square mi—Kaua'i has four distinct regions, each with its own unique characteristics. The windward coast, which catches the prevailing trade winds, consists of the North Shore and East Side, while the drier, leeward coast encompasses the South Shore and West Side. One main road nearly encircles the island, except for a 15-mi stretch of sheer cliffs called the Nāpali Coast.

The center of the island—Mt. Wai'ale'ale, completely inaccessible by car and rarely viewable except from above due to nearly year-round cloud cover—is the wettest spot on earth, getting about 450 inches of rain per year.

Hawaiian culture and tradition here have experienced a renaissance over the last few decades. There's a real effort to revive traditions and to respect history as the Islands go through major changes. New developments often have a Hawaiian cultural expert on staff to ensure cultural sensitivity and to educate newcomers.

Nonetheless, development remains a huge issue for all Islanders—land prices are skyrocketing, putting many areas out of reach for the native population. Traffic is becoming a problem on roads that were not designed to accommodate all the new drivers, and the Islands' limited natural resources are being seriously tapped. The government, though sluggish to respond at first, is trying to make development in Hawai'i as sustainable as possible.

Sustainability

Prior to Western contact, Hawai'i's native dwellers were 100% sustainable. For a place so well endowed with the richest natural resources, contemporary Hawai'i is a far cry from its past. This great challenge also presents a great opportunity. Hawai'i's climate and renewable resources—the sun, the wind, and the waves—can be developed for the greater good and provide almost every conceivable kind of alternative energy.

Although sustainability is an effective buzzword and authentic direction for the island's dining establishments, 90% of Hawai'i's food and energy is imported. Most of the land is used for monocropping of pineapples or sugarcane, which have both severely declined in the past decades. Sugarcane is now only produced commercially on Maui, while pineapple production has dropped by half. Dole, once the largest pineapple company in Hawai'i, closed its plants in 1991, and after 90 years, Del Monte stopped pineapple production in 2008. The next year, Maui Land and Pineapple Company also ceased its Maui Gold pineapple operation although about one-third of its crop was taken over in early 2010 by a group of execs who created a new company. Low cost of labor and transportation from Latin American and Southeast Asian countries are factors for the industry's demise. Although this proves daunting, it also sets the stage for great agricultural change to be explored.

Back to Basics Agriculture

Emulating how the Hawaiian ancestors lived and returning to their simple ways of growing and sharing a variety of foods has become a statewide initiative. Hawai'i has the natural conditions and talent to produce far more diversity in agriculture than it currently does.

The seed of this movement thrives through various farmers' markets and partnerships between restaurants and local farmers. Localized efforts such as the Hawai'i Farm Bureau Federation are collectively leading the organic and sustainable agricultural

renaissance. From home-cooked meals to casual plate lunches to fine-dining cuisine, these sustainable trailblazers enrich the culinary tapestry of Hawai'i and uplift the island's overall quality of life.

Tourism and the Economy

The over-$10 billion tourism industry represents a third of Hawai'i's state income. Naturally, this dependency causes economic hardship as the financial meltdown of recent years affects tourists' ability to visit and consume. One way the industry has made changes has been to adopt more eco-conscious practices, as many Hawaiians feel that planning shouldn't happen without regard for impact to local communities and their natural environment.

Belief that an industry based on the Hawaiians' *aloha* should protect, promote, and empower local culture and provide more entrepreneurial opportunities for local people has become more important to tourism businesses. More companies are incorporating authentic Hawaiiana in their programs and aim not only to provide a commercially viable tour but also to ensure that the visitor leaves feeling connected to his or her host. The concept of *kuleana*, a word for both privilege and responsibility, is upheld. Having the privilege to live in such a sublime place comes with the responsibility to protect it.

Sovereignty

Political issues of sovereignty continue to divide the natives of Hawai'i with myriad organizations, each operating with separate agendas but collectively lacking one defined goal. Ranging from achieving complete and utter independence to solidifying a nation within a nation, existing sovereignty models remain fractured and their future unresolved. The introduction of the Native Hawaiian Government Reorganization Act of 2009 attempts to set up a legal framework in which Native Hawaiians can attain federal recognition and coexist as a self-governed entity. Also known as the Akaka Bill after Senator Daniel Akaka of Hawai'i, this pending bill has been presented before Congress and is still evolving at the time of this writing.

Rise of Hawaiian Pride

After Hawai'i received statehood in 1959, a process of Americanization transpired. Traditions were duly silenced in the name of citizenship. Hawaiian language and arts were banned from schools and children were distanced from their local customs. But Hawaiians are resilient people, and with the rise of the civil rights movement they began to reflect on their own national identity, bringing an astonishing renaissance of the Hawaiian culture to fruition. The people rediscovered language, the hula, the chant or *mele*, and even the traditional Polynesian art of canoe building and wayfinding (navigation by the stars without use of instruments). This cultural resurrection is now firmly established in today's Hawaiian culture, with a palpable pride that exudes from Hawaiians young and old.

The election of President Barack Obama has definitely done its share of fueling not only Hawaiian pride but also ubiquitous hope for a better future. The president's strong connection and commitment to Hawaiian values of diversity, spirituality, family, and conservation have restored confidence that Hawai'i can inspire a more peaceful, tolerant, and environmentally conscious world.

KAUA'I PLANNER

When You Arrive

All commercial and cargo flights use the Līhu'e Airport, 2 mi east of the town of Līhu'e. It has just two baggage-claim areas, each with a visitor information center.

A rental car is the best way to get to your hotel, though taxis and some hotel shuttles are available. From the airport it will take you about 15 to 25 minutes to drive to Wailua or Kapa'a, 30 to 40 minutes to reach Po'ipū, and 45 minutes to an hour to get to Princeville or Hanalei.

Visitor Information

Information Hawai'i Beach Safety (⊕ www. hawaiibeachsafety.org). **Hawai'i Department of Land and Natural Resources** (⊕ www.state.hi.us/dlnr). **Kaua'i Vacation Explorer** (⊕ www.kauaiexplorer.com). **Kaua'i Visitors Bureau** (4334 Rice St., Suite 101, Līhu'e ☏ 808/245–3971 or 800/262–1400 ⊕ www. kauaidiscovery.com). **Po'ipū Beach Resort Association** (✉ Box 730, Kōloa 96756 ☏ 808/742–7444 or 888/744–0888 ⊕ www. poipu-beach.org).

Getting Here and Around

Unless you plan to stay strictly at a resort or do all of your sightseeing as part of guided tours, you'll need a rental car. There is bus service on the island, but the buses tend to be slow and run limited hours.

You most likely won't need a four-wheel-drive vehicle anywhere on the island, so save yourself the money. And while convertibles look fun, the frequent, intermittent rain showers and intense tropical sun make hardtops a better (and cheaper) choice.

If possible, avoid the "rush" hours when the local workers go to and from their jobs. Kaua'i has some of the highest gas prices in the Islands. *See "Travel Smart Kaua'i" for more information on renting a car and driving.*

Island Driving Times

It might not seem as if driving from the North Shore to the West Side, say, would take very much time, as Kaua'i is smaller than O'ahu, Maui, and certainly the Big Island. But it will take longer than you'd expect, and Kaua'i roads are subject to some pretty heavy traffic, especially going through Kapa'a and Līhu'e. Here are average driving times that will help you plan your excursions accordingly.

Hā'ena to Hanalei	5 mi/15 min.
Hanalei to Princeville	4 mi/10 min.
Princeville to Kīlauea	5 mi/12 min.
Kīlauea to Anahola	8 mi/15 min.
Anahola to Kapa'a	5 mi/10 min.
Kapa'a to Līhu'e	10 mi/20 min.
Līhu'e to Po'ipū	13 mi/25 min.
Po'ipū to Kalaheo	8 mi/20 min.
Kalaheo to Hanapepe	4 mi/10 min.
Hanapepe to Waimea	7 mi/10 min.

Money-Saving Tips

There are ways to travel to paradise even on a budget. Pick up free publications at the airport and at racks all over the island; many of them are filled with money-saving coupons. Access to beaches and most hiking trails on the island is free to the public. Grocery stores and Wal-Mart generally stock postcards and souvenirs; they can be less expensive here than at hotel gift shops. For inexpensive fresh fruit and produce, check out farmers markets and farm stands along the road—they'll often let you try before you buy.

Dining and Lodging on Kaua'i

Hawai'i is a melting pot of cultures, and nowhere is this more apparent than in its cuisine. From lū'au and "plate lunch" to sushi and steak, there's no shortage of interesting flavors and presentations.

Whether you're looking for a quick snack or a multicourse meal, we'll help you find the best eating experiences the island has to offer.

There are several top-notch resorts on Kaua'i, as well as a wide variety of condos, vacation rentals, and bed-and-breakfasts to choose from. Selecting vacation lodging is a tough decision, but fret not—our expert writers and editors have done most of the legwork.

Looking for a tropical forest retreat, a big resort, or a private vacation rental? We'll give you all the details you need to book a place that suits your style. Quick tips: Reserve your room far in advance. Be sure to ask about discounts and special packages (hotel Web sites often have Internet-only deals).

WHAT IT COSTS

	¢	$	$$	$$$	$$$$
Restaurants	under $10	$10–$17	$18–$26	$27–$35	over $35
Hotels		under $100	$100–$180	$181–$260	$261–$340	over $340

Restaurant prices are for a main course at dinner. Hotel prices are for two people in a standard double room in high season. Condo price categories reflect studio and one-bedroom rates.

Seeing Nāpali

Let's put this in perspective: Even if you had only one day on Kaua'i, we'd still recommend heading to the Nāpali Coast on Kaua'i's northwest side. Once you're there, you'll soon realize why no road traverses this series of folding-fan cliffs. That leaves three ways to experience the coastline—by air, by water, or on foot. We recommend all three, in this order: air, water, foot. Each one gets progressively more sensory.

Nāpali Coast runs 15 mi from Kē'ē Beach, one of Kaua'i's more popular snorkeling spots, on the island's North Shore to Polihale State Park, the longest stretch of beach in the state, on the West Side of the island.

If you can't squeeze in all three methods—air, water, and foot—or you can't afford all three, we recommend the helicopter tour for those strapped for time and the hiking for those with a very low budget. The boat tours are great for family fun.

Whatever way you choose to visit Nāpali, you might want to keep this awe-inspiring fact in mind: At one time, thousands of Hawaiians lived self-sufficiently in these valleys.

TOP KAUA'I EXPERIENCES

Nāpali

(A) Some things defy words, and the Nāpali Coast is one of them. Besides, *beautiful, verdant, spectacular,* and *amazing* lose their meaning after repeated usage, so forget trying to think of words to describe it, but don't forget to experience Kaua'i's remote, northwest coastline any which way—by air, water, or trail, preferably all three.

Waimea Canyon Drive

(B) From its start in the west Kaua'i town of Waimea to the road's end some 20 mi uphill later, at Pu'u O Kila Lookout, you'll pass through several microclimates—from hot, desertlike conditions at sea level to the cool, deciduous forest of Koke'e—and navigate through the traditional Hawaiian system of land division called *ahupua'a.*

Hanalei Bay

(C) Families. Honeymooners. Retirees. Surfers. Sunbathers. Hanalei Bay attracts all kinds, for good reason—placid water in the summers; epic surf in the winters; the wide, 2-mi-long crescent-shape beach year-round; and the green mountain backdrop striated with waterfalls—also year-round but definitely in full force in winter. And did we mention the atmosphere? Decidedly laid-back.

Spas, Spas, Spas

(D) Kaua'i is characterized by its rural nature (read: quiet and peaceful), which lends itself nicely to the spa scene on the island. The vast majority of spas could be called rural, too, as they invite the outside in—or would that be the inside out? For a resort spa, ANARA Spa is not only decadent but set in a garden. A Hideaway Spa sits in a grove of old-style plantation homes, and Angeline's traditional Hawaiian spa, Mu'olaulani, is in her home.

Highway 560
(E) This 10-mi stretch of road start-ing at the Hanalei Scenic Overlook in Princeville rivals all in Hawai'i and in 2003 was listed on the National Regis-ter of Historic Places, one of only about one hundred roads nationwide to meet the criteria. Indeed, the road itself is said to follow an ancient Hawaiian walking trail that skirts the ocean. Today, Route 560 includes thirteen historic bridges and culverts, most of which are one lane wide. Be patient.

River Kayaking
(F) The best part about kayaking Kaua'i's rivers is that you don't have to be expe-rienced. There are no rapids to run, no waterfalls to jump and, therefore, no excuses for not enjoying the scenic sights from the water. On the East Side, try the Wailua River; if you're on the North Shore, don't miss the Hanalei River. But if you have some experience and are in reasonably good shape, you may choose to create a few lifetime memories and kayak the Nāpali Coast.

Sunshine Markets
(G) Bananas. Mangos. Papayas. Lem-ons. Limes. Lychees. The best and fresh-est fruits, vegetables, flowers—and goat cheese—are found at various farmers' markets around the island. Just don't get there too late in the day—all the best stuff goes early.

GREAT ITINERARIES

As small as Kaua'i may be, you still can't do it all in one day: hiking Kalalau Trail, kayaking Wailua River, showering in a waterfall, watching whales at Kīlauea Lighthouse, waking to the sunrise above Keālia, touring underwater lava tubes at Tunnels, and shopping for gifts at Kōloa Town shops. Rather than trying to check everything off your list in one fell swoop, we recommend choosing your absolute favorite and devoting a full day to the experience.

A Bit of History

Because Hawaiian beliefs were traditionally rooted in nature, much of what you see in Kaua'i today is built on sacred ground. If you're interested in archaeological remains where sacred ceremonies were held, focus on the Wailua River area. Your best bet is to take a riverboat tour—it's full of kitsch, but you'll definitely walk away with a deeper understanding of ancient Hawai'i. Then, head to Līhu'e's Kaua'i Museum, where you can pick up a memento of authentic Hawaiian artistry at the gift shop. End your day at Gaylord's restaurant and meander through the historic Kilohana Plantation sugar estate.

Adventure Galore

For big-time adventure, kayak Nāpali Coast or spend a day learning to fly a microlight. For those whose idea of adventure is a good walk, take the flat, coastal trail along the East Side—you can pick it up just about anywhere starting at the southern end of Lydgate Park, heading north. It'll take you all the way to Anahola, if you desire. After it's all over, recuperate with a massage by the ocean—or in the comfort of your own room, so you can crash immediately afterward.

A Day on the Water

Start your day before sunrise and head west to Port Allen Marina. Check in with one of the tour-boat operators—who will provide you with plenty of coffee to jump-start your day—and cruise Nāpali Coast before heading across the Kaulakahi Channel to snorkel the fish-rich waters of Ni'ihau. Slather up with sunscreen and be prepared for a long—and sometimes big—day on the water; you can enjoy a couple of mai tais on the return trip. Something about the sun and the salt air conspires to induce a powerful sense of fatigue—so don't plan anything in the evening. The trip also helps build a huge appetite, so stop at Grinds in Hanapēpē on the way home.

Coastal Drives

If you're staying on the East Side or North Shore, the best drive for ocean vistas is, hands down, Highway 560, which begins at Princeville on the main highway where Highway 56 ends. Stop at the first lookout overseeing Hanalei River valley for a few snapshots; then head down the hill, across the one-lane bridge—taking in the taro fields—and through the town of Hanalei and on to the end of the road at Kē'ē Beach. If you're up for it, enjoy a bit of unparalleled hiking on the Kalalau Trail, go snorkeling at Kē'ē, or simply soak up the sun on the beach, if it's not too crowded. If you're staying on the South Shore or West Side, follow Highway 50 west. You'll start to catch distant ocean vistas from the highway as you head out of the town of Kalāheo and from the coffee fields of Kaua'i Coffee. Stop here for a sample. You'll come closer to the ocean—and practically reach out and touch it—after you pass through Waimea en route to Kekaha. Although this isn't great swimming water—it's unprotected,

with no reef—there is a long stretch of beach here perfect for walking, running, and purely meandering. Once the paved road ends—if you're brave and your car-rental agreement allows—keep going and you'll eventually come to Polihale, a huge, deserted beach. It'll feel like the end of the world here, so it's a great place to spend a quiet afternoon and witness a spectacular sunset. Just be sure to pack plenty of food, water, and sunscreen before you depart Kekaha—and gas up the car.

Shop Till You Drop

You could actually see a good many of the island's sights by browsing in our favorite island shops. Of course, you can't see the entire island, but this itinerary will take you through Kapa'a and north to Hanalei. Don't miss Marta's Boat—high-end clothing for mom and child—across from Foodland in Waipouli. Just a few blocks north, Kela's Glass has great art pieces. From there, a leisurely drive north will reveal the rural side of Kaua'i. If you enjoy tea, sake, or sushi, stop at Kīlauea's Kong Lung, where you can stock up on complete place settings for each. Then, head down the road to Hanalei. If you're inspired by surf, stop in Hanalei Surf Company. Our favorite for one-of-a-kind keepsakes—actually antiques and authentic memorabilia—is Yellow Fish Trading Company, and we never head into Hanalei without stopping at On the Road to Hanalei.

Relax Kaua'i-Style

If you're headed to Kaua'i for some peace and quiet, you'll want to start your day with yoga at Yoga Hanalei or Kapa'a's Bikram Yoga Kaua'i. If you're staying on the South Shore, try yoga on the beach (actually a grassy spot just off the beach) with longtime yoga instructor Joy Zepeda

(⊕ www.aloha-yoga.com). If it happens to be the second or last Sunday of the month, you might then head to the Lāwa'i International Center (⊕ www.lawaicenter.org) for an afternoon stroll among 88 Buddhist shrines. On the North Shore, Limahuli Gardens is the perfect place to wander among native plants. Then watch the sun slip into the sea on any west-facing beach and call it a day with a glass of wine.

Have a Little Romance

We can't think of a better way to ensure a romantic vacation for two than to pop a bottle of champagne and walk the Māhā'ulepū shoreline at sunrise, hand in hand with a loved one. Make this a Sunday and follow your walk with brunch at the Grand Hyatt. Then spend the afternoon luxuriating with facials, body scrubs, and massage in the Hyatt ANARA Spa's Garden Treatment Village, in a private, thatched hut just for couples. That'll put you in the mood for a wedding ceremony or renewal of vows on the beach followed by a sunset dinner overlooking the ocean at the Beach House restaurant. Can it get any more romantic than this?

WHEN TO GO

Long days of sunshine and fairly mild year-round temperatures make Hawai'i an all-season destination. Most resort areas are at sea level, with average afternoon temperatures of 75°F–80°F during the coldest months of December and January; during the hottest months of August and September the temperature often reaches 90°F. Only at high elevations does the temperature drop into the colder realms, and only at mountain summits does it reach freezing.

Kaua'i is beautiful in every season, but if you must have good beach weather, you should plan to visit between June and October. The rainy season runs from November through February, with the windward or east and north areas of the island receiving most of the rainfall. Nights can be chilly from November through March. Rain is possible throughout the year, of course, but it rarely rains everywhere on the island at once. If it's raining where you are, the best thing to do is head to another side of the island, usually south or west.

If you're a beach lover, keep in mind that big surf can make many North Shore beaches unswimmable during winter months, while the South Shore gets its large swells in summer. If you want to see the humpback whales, February is the best month, though they arrive as early as December and a few may still be around in early April. In the winter, Nāpali Coast boat tours can be rerouted due to high seas, the Kalalau Trail can become very wet and muddy or, at times, impassable, and sea kayaking is not an option. If you have your heart set on visiting Kaua'i's famed coast you may want to visit in the drier, warmer months (May–September).

Hawaiian Holidays

If you happen to be in the Islands on March 26 or June 11, you'll notice light traffic and busy beaches—these are state holidays not celebrated anywhere else. March 26 recognizes the birthday of Prince Jonah Kūhiō Kalaniana'ole, a member of the royal line who served as a delegate to Congress and spearheaded the effort to set aside homelands for Hawaiian people. June 11 honors the first island-wide monarch, Kamehameha I; locals drape his statues with lei and stage elaborate parades. May 1 isn't an official holiday, but it's the day when schools and civic groups celebrate the quintessential Island gift, the flower lei. Statehood Day is celebrated on the third Friday in August (admission to the Union was August 21, 1959). In October, the Queen Emma festival in Kōke'e meadow commemorates the queen's famous horseback ride to the uplands in 1871. Check the local daily paper for upcoming events.

Climate

Moist trade winds drop their precipitation on the North Shore and East Side of the island, creating tropical climates, while the South Shore and West Side remain hot and dry.

Average maximum and minimum temperatures for Kaua'i are listed at left; the temperatures throughout the Hawaiian Islands are similar.

HAWAIIAN HISTORY

Hawaiian history is long and complex; a brief survey can put into context the ongoing renaissance of native arts and culture.

The Polynesians

Long before both Christopher Columbus and the Vikings, Polynesian seafarers set out to explore the vast stretches of the open ocean in double-hulled canoes. From western Polynesia, they traveled back and forth between Samoa, Fiji, Tahiti, the Marquesas, and the Society Isles, settling on the outer reaches of the Pacific, Hawai'i, and Easter Island, as early as AD 300. The golden era of Polynesian voyaging peaked around AD 1200, after which the distant Hawaiian Islands were left to develop their own unique cultural practices and subsistence in relative isolation.

The island's symbiotic society was deeply intertwined with religion, mythology, science, and artistry. Ruled by an *ali'i*, or chief, each settlement was nestled in an *ahupua'a*, a pyramid-like land division from the uplands where the ali'i lived, through the valleys and down to the shores where the commoners resided. Everyone contributed, whether it was by building canoes, catching fish, making tools, or farming land.

A United Kingdom

When the British explorer Captain James Cook arrived in 1778, he was revered as a god upon his arrival and later killed over a stolen boat. With guns and ammunition purchased from Cook, the Big Island chief, Kamehameha, gained a significant advantage over the other ali'i. He united Hawai'i into one kingdom in 1810, bringing an end to the frequent interisland battles that dominated Hawaiian life.

Tragically, the new kingdom was beset with troubles. Native religion was abandoned, and *kapu* (laws and regulations) were eventually abolished. The European explorers brought foreign diseases with them, and within a few short years the Hawaiian population was cut in half.

New laws regarding land ownership and religious practices eroded the underpinnings of precontact Hawaii. Each successor to the Hawaiian throne sacrificed more control over the island kingdom. As Westerners permeated Hawaiian culture, Hawai'i became more riddled with layers of racial issues, injustice, and social unrest.

Modern Hawai'i

Finally in 1893, the last Hawaiian monarch, Queen Lili'uokalani, was overthrown by a group of Americans and European businessmen and government officials, aided by an armed militia. This led to the creation of the Republic of Hawai'i, and it became a U.S. territory for the next 60 years. The loss of Hawaiian sovereignty and the conditions of annexation have haunted the Hawaiian people since the monarchy was toppled.

Pearl Harbor was attacked in 1941, which engaged the United States immediately into World War II. Tourism, from its beginnings in the early 1900s, flourished after the war and naturally inspired rapid real estate development in Waikīkī. In 1959, Hawai'i officially became the 50th state. Statehood paved the way for Hawaiians and Hawai'i's immigrants to participate in the American democratic process.

HAWAIIAN PEOPLE AND THEIR CULTURE

By July 2009, Hawai'i's population was more than 1.3 million with the majority of residents living on O'ahu. Twenty-five percent are Hawaiian or part Hawaiian, more than 40% are Asian-American, and about 20% Caucasian. More than a fifth of the population list two or more races, making Hawai'i the most diverse state in the United States. Among individuals 18 and older, about 89% finished high school, half attained some college, and a little shy of 30% completed a bachelor's degree or higher.

The Role of Tradition

The kingdom of Hawai'i was ruled by a spiritual class system. Although the *ali'i,* or chief, was believed to be the direct descendent of a deity or god, the high priest, known as the *kahuna,* presided over every imaginable life ceremony and *kapu* (taboos) that strictly governed the commoners. Each part of nature and ritual was connected to a deity—Kane was the highest of all deities, symbolizing sunlight and creation; Ku was the god of war; Lono represented fertility, rainfall, music, and peace; Kanaloa was the god of the underworld or darker spirits; and there is Pele, the goddess of fire. The kapu not only provided social order, they also swayed the people to act with reverence for the environment. Any abuse was met with extreme punishment, often death, as it put the land and people's *mana,* or spiritual power, in peril.

Ancient deities play a huge role in Hawaiian life today—not just in daily rituals, but in the Hawaiians' reverence for their land. Gods and goddesses tend to be associated with particular parts of the land, and most of them are connected with many places, thanks to the body of stories built up around each.

One of the most important ways the ancient Hawaiians showed respect for their gods and goddesses was through the hula. Various forms of the hula were performed as prayers to the gods and as praise to the chiefs. Performances were taken very seriously, as a mistake was thought to invalidate the prayer, or even to offend the god or chief in question. Hula is still performed both as entertainment and as prayer; it is not uncommon for a hula performance to be included in an official government ceremony.

Who Are the Hawaiians Today?

To define the Hawaiians in a page, let alone a paragraph, is nearly impossible. First, there are Hawaiians by residence, similar to Californians, New Yorkers, or Texans. Those considered to be indigenous Hawaiians are descendents of the ancient Polynesians who crossed the vast ocean and settled Hawai'i. According to the government, there are Native Hawaiians or native hawaiians (note the change in capitalization) depending on their blood makeup.

Federal and state agencies apply different methods to determine Hawaiian lineage, from measuring blood percentage to mapping genealogy. This has caused turmoil within the community for the simple fact that it excludes so many. It almost guarantees that, as races intermingle, even those considered Native Hawaiian now will eventually disappear on paper, displacing generations to come.

Modern Hawaiian Culture

Perfect weather aside, Hawai'i might be the warmest place anyone can visit. The Hawai'i experience begins and ends with *aloha,* a word that envelops love, affection, and mercy, and has become a salutation for hello and goodbye. Broken

down, *alo* means "presence" and *ha* means "breath"—the presence of breath. It's to live with love and respect for self and others with every breath. Past the manicured resorts and tour buses, aloha is a spirit and moral compass that binds all of Hawai'i's people.

Hawaiians have been blessed with some of the most unspoiled natural wonders, and aloha extends to the land, or *'aina*. Hawaiians are raised outdoors and have strong ties to nature. They realize as children that the ocean and land are the delicate source of all life. Even ancient gods were embodied by nature, and this reverence has been passed down to present generations who believe in *kuleana*, their privilege and responsibility.

Hawaiians' diverse cultures unfold in a beautiful montage of customs and arts— from music, to dance, to food. Musical genres range from slack key to *Jawaiian* (Hawaiian reggae) to *hapa-haole* (Hawaiian music with English words). From George Kahumoku's Grammy-worthy laid-back strumming, to the late Iz Kamakawiwo'ole's "Somewhere over the Rainbow," to Jack Johnson's more mainstream tunes, contemporary Hawaiian music has definitely carved its ever-evolving niche. The Merrie Monarch Festival is celebrating almost 50 years of worldwide hula competition and education. The fine-dining culinary scene, especially in Honolulu, has a rich tapestry of ethnic influences and talent. But the real gems are the humble hole-in-the-wall eateries that serve authentic cuisines of many ethnic origins in one plate, a deliciously mixed plate indeed.

And perhaps, the most striking quality in today's Hawaiian culture is the sense of family, or *ohana*. Sooner or later, almost everyone you meet becomes an uncle or auntie, and it is not uncommon for near-strangers to be welcomed into a home as a member of the family. Until the late 1950s, the practice of *hanai*, in which a family essentially adopts a child, usually a grandchild, without formalities, was still prevalent. The *hanai*, which means to feed or nourish, still resonates within most families and communities.

How to Act Like a Local

Adopting local customs is a firsthand introduction to the Islands' unique culture. So live in T-shirts and shorts. Wear cheap rubber flip-flops, but call them slippers. Wave people into your lane on the highway, and, when someone lets you in, give them a wave of thanks in return. Never, ever blow your horn, even when the pickup truck in front of you is stopped for a long session of "talk story" right in the middle of the road.

Holoholo means to go out for the fun of it—an aimless stroll, ride, or drive. "Wheah you goin', braddah?" "Oh, holoholo." It's local-speak for Sunday drive, no plan, it's not the destination but the journey. Try setting out without an itinerary. Learn to *shaka*: pinky and thumb extended, middle fingers curled in, waggle sideways. Eat white rice with everything. When someone says, "Aloha!" answer, "Aloha no!" ("And a real big aloha back to you"). And, as the locals say, "No make big body" ("Try not to act like you own the place").

KIDS
AND FAMILIES

With dozens of adventures, discoveries, and fun-filled beach days, Hawai'i is a blast with kids. Even better, the things to do here do not appeal only to small fry. The entire family, parents included, will enjoy surfing, discovering a waterfall in the rain forest, and snorkeling with sea turtles. And there are plenty of organized activities for kids that will free parents' time for a few romantic beach strolls.

Choosing a Place to Stay

Resorts: All the big resorts make kids' programs a priority, and it shows. When you are booking your room, ask about "kids eat free" deals and the number of kids' pools at the resort. Also check out the size of the groups in the children's programs, and find out whether the cost of the programs includes lunch, equipment, and activities.

On the North Shore the best bet is the St. Regis Princeville Resort, where kids can spend the day (without their parents) exploring local sea life with a marine biologist. The Kaua'i Marriott Resort is a good choice on the East Side, and on the South Shore both the Grand Hyatt Kaua'i and Sheraton Kaua'i Resort have kids' programs.

Condos: Condo and vacation rentals are a fantastic value for families vacationing in Hawai'i. You can cook your own food, which is cheaper than eating out and sometimes easier (especially if you have a finicky eater in your group), and you'll get twice the space of a hotel room for about a quarter of the price. If you decide to go the condo route, be sure to ask about the size of the complex's pool (some try to pawn a tiny soaking tub off as a pool) and whether barbecues are available. One of the best parts of staying in your own place

is having a sunset family barbecue by the pool or overlooking the ocean.

On the North Shore, there are numerous condo resort choices in Princeville. Hanalei Bay Resort even offers kids' programs. On the South Shore, Outrigger Kiahuna Plantation is a family favorite, with an excellent location that includes a very swimmable beach adjacent to a grassy field great for picnics.

Ocean Activities

Hawai'i is all about getting your kids outside—away from TV and video games. And who could resist the turquoise water, the promise of spotting dolphins or whales, and the fun of body boarding or surfing?

On the Beach: Most people like being in the water, but toddlers and school-age kids tend to be especially enamored of it. The swimming pool at your condo or hotel is always an option, but don't be afraid to hit the beach with a little one in tow. There are several beaches in Hawai'i that are nearly as safe as a pool—completely protected bays with pleasant white-sand beaches. As always, use your judgment, and heed all posted signs and lifeguard warnings.

Generally calm beaches to try include 'Anini Beach and Hanalei Bay Beach Park on the North Shore, Lydgate State Park and Kalapaki Beach on the East Side, Po'ipū Beach Park on the South Shore, and Salt Pond Beach Park on the West Side.

On the Waves: Surf lessons are a great idea for older kids, especially if Mom and Dad want a little quiet time. Beginner lessons are always on safe and easy waves and last anywhere from two to four hours.

The Blue Seas Surf School is best for beginners, and you can book your kids a 1½-hour lesson for $75.

The Underwater World: If your kids are ready to try snorkeling, Hawai'i is a great place to introduce them to the underwater world. Even without the mask and snorkel, they'll be able to see colorful fish darting this way and that, and they may also spot turtles and dolphins at many of the island beaches.

Get your kids used to the basics at Lydgate State Park on the island's East Side, where there's no threat of a current. On its guided snorkel tours, SeaFun Kaua'i will show kids of all ages how to identify marine life and gives great beginner instruction.

Land Activities

In addition to beach experiences, Hawai'i has rain forests, botanical gardens, numerous aquariums (O'ahu and Maui take the cake), and even petting zoos and hands-on children's museums that will keep your kids entertained and out of the sun for a day.

On the North Shore, kids will love Na 'Āina Kai, a garden with a 16-foot-tall Jack and the Beanstalk bronze sculpture, gecko maze, tree house, kid-size train, and tropical jungle, and on the East Side is Smith's Tropical Paradise, a 30-acre botanical garden.

Horseback riding is a popular family activity, and most of the tours on Kaua'i move slowly, so no riding experience is required. Kids as young as two can ride at Esprit de Corps.

When it rains on Kaua'i, kids don't have to stay indoors. ATV tours are the activity of choice. Try Kaua'i ATV Tours, which has two-passenger "Mud Bugs" to accommodate families with kids ages five and older.

After Dark

At night, younger kids get a kick out of lū'aus, and many of the shows incorporate young audience members, adding to the fun. The older kids might find it all a bit lame, but there are a handful of new shows in the Islands that are more modern, incorporating acrobatics, lively music, and fire dancers. If you're planning on hitting a lū'au with a teen in tow, we highly recommend going the modern route—try Lū'au Kalamaku in Līhu'e. The best lū'au for young kids on Kaua'i is Smith's Tropical Paradise, in Wailua. A tram tour takes families through the botanical garden before dinner, and the show starts with some high-tech pyrotechnics. Also, guests actually leave their dinner tables to walk to the amphitheater, which means young ones don't have to sit still the entire evening.

TOP 10 HAWAIIAN FOODS TO TRY

Food in Hawai'i is a reflection of the state's diverse cultural makeup and tropical location. Fresh seafood, organic fruits and vegetables, free-range poultry and meat, and locally grown products are the hallmarks of Hawai'i regional cuisine. Its preparations are drawn from across the Pacific Rim, including Japan, the Philippines, Korea, and Thailand—and now, "Hawaiian food" is a cuisine in its own right.

Saimin

The ultimate hangover cure and the perfect comfort food during Hawai'i's mild winters, saimin ranks at the top of the list of local favorites. In fact, it's one of the few dishes deemed truly local, having been highlighted in cookbooks since the 1930s. Saimin is an Asian-style noodle soup so ubiquitous, it's even on McDonald's menus statewide. In mom-and-pop shops, a large melamine bowl is filled with homemade dashi or chicken broth and wheat-flour noodles and then topped off with strips of omelette, green onions, bright pink fish cake and char siu (Chinese roast pork) and/or canned luncheon meat, such as SPAM. Add shoyu and chile pepper water, lift your chopsticks and slurp away.

SPAM

Speaking of SPAM, Hawai'i's most prevalent grab-and-go snack is SPAM musubi. Often displayed next to cash registers at groceries and convenience stores, the glorified rice ball is rectangluar, topped with a slice of fried SPAM and wrapped in nori (seaweed). Introduced back in the plantation days by Japanese field workers, musubi is a mini-meal in itself. But just like sushi, the rice part hardens when refrigerated. So it's best to gobble it up, right after purchase.

Hormel Company's SPAM actually deserves its own recognition—way beyond as a mere musubi topping. About five million cans are sold per year in Hawai'i and the Aloha State even hosts a festival in its honor. One local claims she can stretch a can of SPAM into three separate meals for a family of five. The spiced luncheon meat gained popularity in World War II days, when fish was rationed. Gourmets and those with aversions to salt, high cholesterol and high blood pressure may cringe at the thought of eating it, but SPAM in Hawai'i is here to stay.

Manapua

Another savory snack is manapua, fist-sized dough balls fashioned after Chinese bao and stuffed with fillings such as char siu pork and then steamed. Many mom and pop stores sell them in commercial steamer display cases along with pork hash and other dim sum. Modern-day fillings include curry chicken.

Fresh 'Ahi or Tako

There's nothing like fresh 'ahi or tako (octopus) poke to break the ice at a back-yard party, except, of course, the cold beer handed to you from the cooler. The perfect pūpū, poke (pronounced poh-kay) is basically raw seafood cut into bite-sized chunks and mixed with everything from green onions to roasted and ground kukui nuts. Other variations include round onion, sesame oil, seaweed and chile pepper water. Shoyu is the constant. These days, grocery stores sell a rainbow of varieties such as kim chee crab and anything goes, from adding mayonnaise to tobiko caviar. Fish lovers who want to take it to the next level order sashimi, the best cuts of ahi sliced and dipped in a mixture of shoyu and wasabi.

Tropical Fruits

Tropical fruits such as apple banana and strawberry papaya are plucked from trees in island neighborhoods and eaten for breakfast—plain or with a squeeze of fresh lime. Locals also love to add their own creative touches to exotic fruits. Green mangoes are pickled with Chinese five spice, and Maui Gold pineapples are topped with li hing mui powder (heck, even margarita glasses are rimmed with it). Green papaya is tossed in a Vietnamese salad with fish paste and fresh prawns.

Plate Lunch

It would be remiss not to mention the plate lunch as one of the most beloved dishes in Hawai'i. It generally always includes two scoops white steamed rice, a side of macaroni and/or macaroni-potato salad, heavy on the mayo, and perhaps kim chee or koko (salted cabbage). There are countless choices of main protein such as chicken katsu, fried mahimahi and beef tomato. The king of all plate lunches is the Hawaiian plate. The main item is laulau (pork, beef and fish or chicken with taro, or lū'au, leaves wrapped and steamed in ti leaves) or kalua pig and cabbage along with poi, lomilomi salmon, chicken long rice and steamed white rice.

Bento Box

The bento box gained popularity back in the plantation days, when workers toiled in the sugar cane fields. No one brought sandwiches to work then. Instead it was a lunch box with the ever-present steamed white rice, pickled ume (plum) to preserve the rice and main meats such as fried chicken or fish. In the Hawai'i of today, many stores sell pre-packaged bentos or you may go to an okazuya with a hot buffet counter and create your own.

Malasadas

The Portuguese have contributed much to Hawai'i cuisine in the form of sausage, soup and sweetbread. But their most revered food is malasadas, hot, deep-fried doughnuts rolled in sugar. Malasadas are crowd pleasers. Buy them by the dozen, hot from the wok, placed in brown bags to absorb the grease. Or bite into gourmet malasadas at restaurants, filled with vanilla or chocolate cream.

Shave Ice

Much more than just a snow cone, shave ice is what locals crave after a blazing day at the beach or a hot-as-Hades game of soccer. If you're lucky, you'll find a neighborhood store that hand shaves the ice, but it's rare. Either way, the counter person will ask you first if you'd like ice cream and/or azuki beans scooped into the bottom of the cone or cup. Then they shape the ice to a giant mound and add colorful fruit syrups. First timers should order the Rainbow, of course.

Crack Seed

There are dozens of varieties of crack seed in dwindling specialty shops and at the drug stores. Chinese call the preserved fruits and nuts "see mui" but somehow the pidgin English version is what Hawaiians prefer. Those who like hard candy and salty foods will love li hing mangoes and rock salt plums and those with an itchy throat will feel relief from the lemon strips. Peruse large glass jars of crack seed sold in bulk or smaller hanging bags—the latter make good gifts to give to friends back home.

ONLY IN HAWAI'I

Traveling to Hawai'i is as close as an American can get to visiting another country while staying within the United States. There's much to learn and understand about the state's indigenous culture, the hundred years of immigration that resulted in today's blended society, and the tradition of aloha that has welcomed millions of visitors over the years.

Aloha Shirt

To go to Hawai'i without taking an aloha shirt home is almost sacrilege. The first aloha shirts from the 1920s and 1930s were classic canvases of art and tailored for the tourists. Popular culture caught on in the 1950s, and they became a fashion craze. With the 1960s' more subdued designs, the Aloha Friday was born, and the shirt became appropriate clothing for work, play, and formal occasions. Because of its soaring popularity, cheaper and mass-produced versions became available.

Hawaiian Quilt

Although ancient Hawaiians were already known to produce fine *kapa* (bark) cloth, the actual art of quilting originated from the missionaries. Hawaiians have made the designs to reflect their own aesthetic, and bold patterns evolved over time. They can be pricey, but only because the quilts are intricately made by hand and can take years to finish. These masterpieces are considered precious heirlooms that reflect the history and beauty of Hawai'i.

Popular Souvenirs

Souvenir shopping can be intimidating. There's a sea of island-inspired and often kitschy merchandise, so we'd like to give you a breakdown of popular and fun gifts that you might encounter and consider bringing home.

Hula doll. The hula dancer has been immortalized and commodified in many ways, from the classic dashboard bobble hip to the newer hula girl desktop duster.

Grass skirts and coconut bras. Sometimes bought as a set and sometimes as separates, either way this costume will definitely elicit a smile or ten at a lū'au.

Home accessories. Relive your spa treatment at home with Hawaiian bath and body products, or deck out the kitchen in festive lū'au style with bottle openers, pineapple mugs, tiki glasses, shot glasses, slipper and surfboard magnets, and salt-and-pepper shakers.

Lei and shell necklaces. From silk or polyester flower lei to kukui or puka shell necklaces, lei have been traditionally used as a welcome offering to guests (although the artificial ones are more for fun, as real flowers are always preferable).

Lauhala products. Lauhala weaving is a traditional Hawaiian art. The leaves come from the Hala or Pandanus tree and handwoven to create lovely gift boxes, baskets, bags, and picture frames.

Vintage Hawai'i. You can find vintage photos, reproductions of vintage postcards or paintings, heirloom jewelry, and vintage aloha wear in many specialty stores.

Warrior helmets. Traditionally called *makaki'i* or *makini* after ancient Hawaiian warriors, these helmets are miniature masks adorned with feathers. They're popular among a younger crowd and hung on the car's rearview mirror or doorway for protection.

Lū'au

The lū'au's origin is traced back in 1819 when King Kamehameha II broke a great taboo and shared a feast with women and commoners. The name came from a traditional dish of chicken wrapped in taro leaves and baked in coconut milk. In the

olden days, lu'au were enjoyed sitting on the floor where woven lauhala mats were laid and covered with ti leaves and tropical flowers. Platters of *kalua pu'a* (pig baked in the *imu*, or underground oven), salted fish, sweet potatoes and *poi* (pounded taro and a staple in Hawaiian cuisine) were shared in the gathering.

Over time, the hula, fire knife dance and other Polynesian dances became part of the celebration. Today, the lu'au usually commemorates a child's first birthday or graduation. Offered in many elaborate presentations, it remains a Hawaiian experience that most visitors enjoy.

Nose flutes

The nose flute is an instrument used in ancient times to serenade a lover. For the Hawaiians, the nose is romantic, sacred and pure. The Hawaiian word for kiss is *honi*. Similar to an Eskimo's kiss, the noses touch on each side sharing one's spiritual energy or breath. The Hawaiian term, *'ohe hano ihu*, simply translated to "bamboo," with which the instrument is made; "breathe," because one has to gently breathe through it to make soothing music; and "nose," as it is made for the nose and not the mouth.

Slack Key Guitar and the Paniolos

Kiho'alu, or slack key music, evolved in the early 1800s when King Kamehameha III brought in Mexican and Spanish vaqueros to manage the overpopulated cattle that had run wild on the islands. The vaqueros brought their guitars and would play music around the campfire after work. When they left, supposedly leaving their guitars to their new friends, the Hawaiian *paniolos*, or cowboys, began to infuse what they learned from the vaqueros with their native music and chants, and so the art of slack key music was born.

Today, the paniolo culture thrives where ranchers have settled. Slack key music has also enjoyed international recognition and garnered Grammy Awards numerous times for the Hawaiian music genre.

'Ukulele

The 'ukulele or 'uke literally translates to the "the jumping flea" and came to Hawaii in the 1880s by way of the Portuguese and Spanish. Once a fading art form, today it brings international kudos as a solo instrument, thanks to tireless musicians and teachers who have worked hard to keep it by our fingertips.

One such teacher is Roy Sakuma. Founder of four 'ukulele schools and a legend in his own right, Sakuma and his wife Kathy produced O'ahu's first 'Ukulele Festival in 1971. Since then, they've brought the tradition to the Big Island, Kaua'i, and Maui. The free event annually draws thousands of artists and fans all over the globe.

Hula

"Hula is the language of the heart, therefore the heartbeat of the Hawaiian people."— Kalākaua I, the Merrie Monarch. Thousands—from tots to seniors—devote hours each week to hula classes. All these dancers need some place to show off their stuff. The result is a network of hula competitions (generally free or very inexpensive) and free performances in malls and other public spaces. Many resorts offer hula instruction or "hula-cise."

To watch hula, especially in the ancient style, is to understand that this was a sophisticated culture—skilled in many arts, including not only poetry, chant, and dance but also in constructing instruments and fashioning adornments.

TOP 5 KAUA'I OUTDOOR ADVENTURES

Kaua'i's spectacular scenery makes getting outdoors a must-do activity for most people.

There are endless options here for spending time outside enjoying waterfalls, rivers, coastlines, and canyons, but here are a few of our favorites.

Tour Nāpali Coast by Boat

Every one of the Hawaiian Islands possesses something spectacularly unique to it and this stretch of folding cliffs is it for Kaua'i. To see it, though, you'll want to hop aboard a boat. You may opt for a leisurely ride aboard a catamaran or a more adventurous inflatable raft. Some tours offer the opportunity to stop for snorkeling or a walk through an ancient fishing village.

Word of Mouth: "It's really spectacular to see the coast from the water (I've done helicopter tours as well), and I highly recommend a tour . . . well worth the expense and time, in my opinion. Have fun!" –nobigdeal

Kayak the Wailua River

The largest river in all Hawai'i, the Wailua River's source is the center of the island—a place known as Mt. Wai'ale'ale—the wettest spot on earth. And yet it's no Mighty Mississippi. There are no rapids to run. And that makes it a great waterway on which to learn to kayak. Guided tours will take you to a remote waterfall. Bring the whole family on this one.

Hike the Kalalau Trail

The Sierra Club allegedly rates this famous, cliffside trail a difficulty level of 9 out of 10. But don't let that stop you. You don't have to hike the entire 11 miles. A mile hike will reward you with scenic ocean views—in winter, you might see breaching whales—sights of soaring seabirds and tropical plant life dotting the trail sides.

Wear sturdy shoes, pack your camera, and be prepared to ooh and aah.

Word of Mouth: "I would say that you can see the coast after the first .75 mile and about 400 ft. elevation gain from the trailhead. If you have the legs you can hike to Hanakāpī'ai Beach, which is two miles from the trailhead. It's a hard hike but hundreds do it daily and most are not in prime condition." –wbpiii

Enjoy a Helicopter Ride

If you drive from Kē'ē Beach to Polihale, you may think you've seen all of Kaua'i, but we're here to tell you there's more scenic beauty awaiting you. Lots more. Save up for this one. It's not cheap, but a helicopter ride over The Garden Island will make you think you're watching a movie with 3D glasses. For breathtaking photos with no glass reflection, or if you just want a thrill, consider a doorless helicopter tour.

Word of Mouth: "The pilot flew very close to the canyon walls (at some points I was a little scared). However, it is absolutely incredible to be that high up and that close to the canyon with nothing in between you but air." –annabellefreddie

Zipline Over the Trees

It may not feel natural to take a running leap over the ledge of a valley, but it sure is fun. Guides clip your harness to wires and slow you down for landings, leaving you free to enjoy ocean and mountain views as you "fly" over treetops and across valleys. Most outfitters offer a shorter "express" version of their signature tours, though we recommend the full tour so you have time to catch your breath—you're sure to lose it screaming.

TOP 5 KAUA'I BEACHES

With over 50 miles of sandy shores—more than any other Hawaiian island—Kaua'i is a beach bum's dream. It's easy to give in to "Hawai'i time" and spend your trip relaxing on the sand. Here are some of our top places to park your beach towel.

Hā'ena Beach Park (Tunnels Beach).

Even if all you do is sit on the beach, you'll leave here happy. The scenic beauty is unsurpassed, with verdant mountains serving as a backdrop to the turquoise ocean. Snorkeling here is the best on the island during the calm, summer months. When the winter's waves arrive, surfers line up on the outside break.

Hanalei Bay Beach Park

When you dream of Hawai'i, this is what comes to mind: A vast bay rimmed by a wide beach and waterfalls draping distant mountains. Everyone finds something to do here—surf, kayak, swim, sail, sunbathe, walk, and celebrity-watch. Like most North Shore beaches in Hawai'i, Hanalei switches from calm waters in summer to big waves in winter.

Word of Mouth: "Nothing compares to Hanalei in all of Hawai'i." –hgjames

Māhā'ulepū Beach

You'll have to drive through private property to reach this gem, though the beach—like all in Hawai'i—is public. The two-mile stretch is unlike anything else you'll find on Kaua'i. The land is rugged, with limestone cliffs, caves, and sand dunes. While swimming here isn't always recommended, it's a great spot to wander around; a hike along the Māhā'ulepū Heritage Trail, a beautiful coastal path.

Word of Mouth: "Instead of driving to Maha'ulepu, park at the Hyatt, and walk along the dunes and cliffs to Maha'ulepu, and then along the beach, and a bit beyond past the surprise blow hole and rugged arches). One way is just over two miles." –beth_fitz

Po'ipū Beach Park

The *keiki* (children's) swimming hole makes Po'ipū a great family beach, but it's also popular with snorkelers and moderate to experienced surfers. And while Po'ipū is considered a tourist destination, Kaua'i residents come out on the weekends, adding a local flavor. Watch for the endangered Hawaiian monk seals; they like it here, too.

Polihale State Park

If you're looking for remote, if you're looking for guaranteed sun, if you're thinking of camping on the beach, drive down the bumpy five-mile-long road to the western-most point of Kaua'i. Be sure to stay for the sunset. Unless you're an experienced water person, we advise staying out of the water due to a steep, on-shore break. You can walk for miles along this beach, the longest in Hawai'i.

Word of Mouth: "[Polihale] is a wonderful place though, and if the road is open and you don't mind a long and bumpy drive, it's worth it. Despite what you may hear, you can usually do it in a regular car, but it depends on the road." –RKprov

HAWAI'I AND THE ENVIRONMENT

Sustainability. It's a word rolling off everyone's tongues these days. In a place known as one of the most remote on Earth (check your globe), Hawai'i is relies heavily on the outside world for food and material goods—estimates put the percentage of food arriving on container ships as high as 90. Like many places, though, efforts are afoot to change that. And you can help.

Shop Local Farms and Markets

From Hilo to Hanalei, farmers' markets are cropping up, providing a place for growers to sell fresh fruits and vegetables. There is no reason to buy imported mangoes, papayas, avocadoes, and bananas at grocery stores, when the ones you'll find at farmers' markets are not only fresher and bigger but tastier, too. Some markets allow the sale of fresh-packaged foods—salsa, say, or smoothies—and the on-site preparation of food—like pork laulau or roasted corn on the cob—so you can make your run to the market a dining experience.

Not only is the locavore movement vibrantly alive at farmers markets, but Hawai'i's top chefs are sourcing more of their produce—and fish, beef, chicken, and cheese—from local providers as well. You'll notice this movement on restaurant menus, featuring Ki'lauea greens or Hamakua tomatoes or locally caught mahimahi.

And while most people are familiar with Kona coffee farm tours on Big Island, if you're interested in the growing slow-food movement in Hawai'i, you'll be heartened to know many farmers are opening up their operations for tours—as well as sumptuous meals.

Support Hawai'i's Merchants

Food isn't the only sustainable effort in Hawai'i. Buying local goods like art and jewelry, Hawaiian heritage products, crafts, music, and apparel is another way to "green up" the local economy. The County of Kaua'i helps make it easy with their Kaua'i Made program (⊕ *www.kauaimade.net*), which showcases products made on Kaua'i, by Kaua'i people, using Kaua'i materials. The Maui Chamber of Commerce does something similar with its Made in Maui program (⊕ *www.madeinmaui.com*). Think of both as the Good Housekeeping Seal of Approval for locally made goods.

Then there the crafty entrepreneurs who are diverting items from the trash heap by repurposing garbage. Take Muumuu Heaven (⊕ *www.muumuuheaven.com*) on O'ahu. They got their start by reincarnating vintage aloha apparel into hip new fashions. Kini Beach (⊕ *www.Kinibeach.com*) collects discarded grass mats and plastic inflatables from Waikīkī hotels and uses them to make pricey bags and totes.

Choose Green Tour Operators

Conscious decisions when it comes to island activities go a long way to protecting Hawai'i's natural world. The Hawai'i Ecotourism Association (⊕ *www.hawaiiecotourism.org*) recognizes tour operators for, among other things, their environmental stewardship. The Hawai'i Tourism Authority (⊕ *www.hawaiitourismauthority.org*) recognizes outfitters for their cultural sensitivity. Winners of these awards are good choices when it comes to guided tours and activities.

TOP 5 KAUA'I SCENIC SPOTS

Verdant valleys, epic cliffs, plunging water-falls, and majestic canyons are just a few of the features that you'll find on Kaua'i. You might almost get used to the stunning green mountains that jut out of the land as you drive from place to place—almost. There are countless places to stop and take in the view; here are some of our favorites. Just don't forget a camera.

Hanalei Valley Overlook

On the way to Hanalei (about 1,000 meters west of the Princeville Shopping Center), this pull-off provides views of Hanalei River winding its way through wet *lo'i* (taro patches) framed by jagged green mountains. If you're staying on the North Shore, don't just stop here once. The colors will change over the course of a day, or with the weather.

Kē'ē Beach

At the end of the road on the North Shore, Kē'ē Beach is as close as you can get to the fabled cliffs of Bali Hai. Surrounded by palm and almond trees, this stretch of white sand beach is a great spot for view-ing sunsets. The Kalalau Trail begins here; if you're up for an uphill hike, the first quarter-mile or so of the trail takes you to a perch with views of both Kē'ē and the misty cliffs of Nāpali.

Kīlauea Lighthouse

Albatross, great frigate birds, and nēnē are just a few of the thousands of sea-birds that nest along the cliffs surround-ing the Kīlauea Lighthouse. This is the northernmost point on Kaua'i—in fact, it's the northernmost point in the Hawai-ian Islands. You'll get sweeping views of the North Shore here. If you hang around for a little while in winter, you're almost sure to see a whale pass by.

Word of Mouth: "We went to the lighthouse and enjoyed the views of Moku'ae'ae

Island, the mountains, and the ocean hit-ting the rocks at the base of the cliff. We also saw a pair of nēnē, and I believe they were looking for a place to build a nest in one of the bushes." –annabellefreddie

Waimea Canyon

The oft used term "breathtaking" does not do justice to your first glimpse of Waimea Canyon (otherwise known as the Grand Canyon of the Pacific). Narrow waterfalls tumble thousands of feet to streams which cut through the rust colored volcanic soil. There are plenty of spots along Route 550 to stop and stare at the canyon's awesome beauty—we recommend using the desig-nated lookouts; they have parking and restrooms. Impressive vistas don't stop at the rim of the canyon. Continue on to the end of the road to Kalalau Lookout for a view through the clouds of other worldly Kalalau Valley.

'Ōpaeka'a Falls

It would be tough to visit Kaua'i without seeing a waterfall; after rain it seems like every mountain is laced with white streaks of water. 'Ōpaeka'a is one of our favorites because it's always running, rain or shine. Water from the mighty Wailua River falls over 100 feet in a lush green setting. The lookout to the left before you reach the parking lot for the waterfall overlook has takes in the scenic Wailua River Valley.

Word of Mouth: "Reading our guidebooks we knew that Kaua'i has many beautiful waterfalls and each has its own unique-ness so that's exactly what we set out to see. We drove to see the 'Ōpaeka'a Falls and on the same road we visited the Hindu Monastery." –gss517

WEDDINGS AND HONEYMOONS

There's no question that Hawai'i is one of the country's foremost honeymoon destinations. Romance is in the air here, and the white, sandy beaches, turquoise water, swaying palm trees, balmy tropical breezes, and perpetual summer sunshine put people in the mood for love. It's easy to understand why Hawai'i is fast becoming a popular wedding destination as well, especially as the cost of airfare has gone down, and new resorts and hotels entice visitors. A destination wedding is no longer exclusive to celebrities and the superrich. You can plan a traditional ceremony in a place of worship followed by a reception at an elegant resort, or you can go barefoot on the beach and celebrate at a lū'au. There are almost as many wedding planners in the Islands as real estate agents, which makes it oh-so-easy to wed in paradise, and then, once the knot is tied, to stay and honeymoon as well.

The Big Day

Choosing the Perfect Place. When choosing a location, remember that you really have two choices to make: the ceremony location and where to have the reception, if you're having one. For the former, there are beaches, bluffs overlooking beaches, gardens, private residences, resort lawns, and, of course, places of worship. As for the reception, there are these same choices, as well as restaurants and even lū'au. If you decide to go outdoors, remember the seasons—yes, Hawai'i has seasons. If you're planning a winter wedding outdoors, be sure you have a backup plan (such as a tent), in case it rains. Also, if you're planning an outdoor wedding at sunset—which is very popular—be sure you match the time of your ceremony to the time the sun sets at that time of year. If you choose indoors, ask for pictures of the environs when you're planning. You

don't want to plan a pink wedding, say, and wind up in a room that's predominantly red. Or maybe you do. The point is, it should be your choice.

Finding a Wedding Planner. If you're planning to invite more than a minister and your loved one to your wedding ceremony, seriously consider an on-island wedding planner who can help select a location, help design the floral scheme and recommend a florist as well as a photographer, help plan the menu and choose a restaurant, caterer, or resort, and suggest any Hawaiian traditions to incorporate into your ceremony. And more: Will you need tents, a cake, music? Maybe transportation and lodging? Many planners have relationships with vendors, providing packages—which mean savings.

If you're planning a resort wedding, most have on-site wedding coordinators; however, there are many independents around the island and even those who specialize in certain types of ceremonies—by locale, size, religious affiliation, and so on. A simple "Hawai'i weddings" Google search will reveal dozens. What's important is that you feel comfortable with your coordinator. Check references. Share your budget. Get a proposal in writing. Ask how long they've been in business, how much they charge, how often you'll meet with them, and how they select vendors. Request a detailed list of the exact services they'll provide. If your idea of your wedding doesn't match their services, try someone else. If you can afford it, you might want to consider meeting the planner in person.

Getting Your License. The good news about marrying in Hawai'i is that no waiting period, no residency or citizenship requirements, and no blood tests or shots

are required. However, both the bride and groom must appear together in person before a marriage license agent to apply for a marriage license. You'll need proof of age—the legal age to marry is 18. (If you're 19 or older, a valid driver's license will suffice; if you're 18, a certified birth certificate is required.) Upon approval, a marriage license is immediately issued and costs $60, cash only. After the ceremony, your officiant will mail the marriage license to the state. Approximately 120 days later, you will receive a copy in the mail. (For $10 extra, you can expedite this process. Ask your marriage license agent when you apply for your license.) For more detailed information, visit ⊕ *www.hawaii. gov* or call ☎ 808/586-4544 (Honolulu) or 808/974-6008 (Big Island).

Also—this is important—the person performing your wedding must be licensed by the Hawai'i Department of Health, even if he or she is a licensed minister. Be sure to ask.

Wedding Attire. In Hawai'i, basically anything goes, from long, formal dresses with trains to white bikinis. Floral sundresses are fine, too. For the men, everything from tuxedos to solid-colored slacks with a nice aloha shirt can be found at island weddings. In fact, tradition in Hawai'i for the groom is a plain white aloha shirt (they do exist) with slacks or long shorts and a colored sash around the waist. If you're planning a wedding on the beach, barefoot is the way to go.

If you decide to marry in a formal dress and tuxedo, you're better off making your selections on the mainland and hand-carrying them aboard the plane. Yes, it can be a pain, but ask your wedding-gown retailer to provide a special carrying bag. After all, you don't want to chance losing your wedding dress in a wayward piece of luggage. And when it comes to fittings, again, that's something you'll want to take care of before you arrive in Hawai'i.

Local customs. When it comes to traditional Hawaiian wedding customs, the most obvious is the lei exchange in which the bride and groom take turns placing a lei around the neck of the other—with a kiss. Bridal lei are usually floral, whereas the groom's is typically made of *maile*, a green leafy garland that drapes around the neck and is open at the ends. Brides often also wear a *haku* lei—a circular floral headpiece. Other Hawaiian customs include the blowing of the conch shell, hula, chanting, and Hawaiian music.

The Honeymoon

Do you want champagne and strawberries delivered to your room each morning? A maze of a swimming pool in which to float? A five-star restaurant in which to dine? Then a resort is the way to go. If, however, you prefer the comforts of a home, try a bed-and-breakfast. A bed-and-breakfast is also good if you're on a tight budget or don't plan to spend much time in your room. On the other hand, maybe you want your own private home in which to romp naked—or just laze around recovering from the wedding planning. Maybe you want your own kitchen in which to whip up a gourmet meal for your loved one. In that case, a private vacation-rental home is the answer. Or maybe a condominium resort. That's another beautiful thing about Hawai'i: the lodging accommodations are almost as plentiful as the beaches, and there's one to match your tastes and your budget.

CRUISING THE HAWAIIAN ISLANDS

Cruising has become extremely popular in Hawai'i. For first-time visitors, it's an excellent way to get a taste of all the islands; and if you fall in love with one or even two islands, you know how to plan your next trip. It's also a comparatively inexpensive way to see Hawai'i.

The limited amount of time in each port can be an argument against cruising—there's enough to do on any island to keep you busy for a week, so some folks feel shortchanged by cruise itineraries.

Cruising to Hawai'i

Carnival Cruises. They call them "fun ships" for a reason—Carnival is all about keeping you busy and showing you a good time, both onboard and onshore. Great for families, Carnival always plans plenty of kid-friendly activities, and their children's program rates high with the little critics. Carnival offers itineraries starting in Ensenada, Vancouver, and Honolulu. Their ships stop on Maui (Kahului and Lahaina), the Big Island (Kailua-Kona and Hilo), O'ahu, and Kaua'i. ☎ 888/227–6482 ⊕ www.carnival.com.

Holland America. The grande dame of cruise lines, Holland America has a reputation for service and elegance. Holland America's Hawai'i cruises leave and return to San Diego, California, with a brief stop at Ensenada. In Hawai'i, the ship ties up at port in Maui (Lahaina), the Big Island (Kailua-Kona and Hilo), O'ahu, and for half a day on Kaua'i. Holland America also offers longer itineraries (30-plus days) that include Hawai'i, Tahiti, and the Marquesas. ☎ 877/932–4259 ⊕ www.hollandamerica.com.

Princess Cruises. Princess strives to offer affordable luxury. Their prices start out a little higher, but you get more bells and whistles (more affordable balcony rooms, nice decor, more restaurants to choose from, personalized service). They're not fantastic for kids, but they do a great job of keeping teenagers occupied. Princess's Hawaiian cruise is 14 days, round-trip from Los Angeles, with a service call in Ensenada. The *Island Princess* stops in Maui (Lahaina), the Big Island (Hilo and Kailua-Kona), O'ahu, and Kaua'i. For the cruise-goer looking for the epic voyage, Princess Cruises offers a Sydney, Australia, to Los Angeles route, which includes stops in Hawai'i and Tahiti. ☎ 800/774–6237 ⊕ www.princess.com.

Cruising within Hawai'i

Norwegian Cruise Lines. Norwegian is the only major operator to offer interisland cruises in Hawai'i. Several of their ships cruise the islands. The main one is *Pride of America* (Vintage Americana theme, very new, big family focus with lots of connecting staterooms and suites), which offers seven-day or longer itineraries within the Islands, stopping on Maui, O'ahu, the Big Island, and overnighting in Kaua'i. ☎ 800/327–7030 ⊕ www.ncl.com.

Hawai'i Nautical. Offering a completely different sort of experience, Hawai'i Nautical provides private multiple-day interisland cruises on their catamarans, yachts, and sailboats. Prices are higher, but service is completely personal, right down to the itinerary. ☎ 808/234–7245 ⊕ www.hawaiinautical.com.

Exploring Kaua'i

WORD OF MOUTH

"Nāpali, Nāpali, and Nāpali—by air, by boat, and by hikes. All are worth it. Also remember Kōke'e is actually more of seeing Nāpali. Waimea is okay but Kōke'e is exceptional."

—lifeisbeautiful

Updated
by Charles
Roessler

Even a nickname like "The Garden Island" fails to do justice to Kaua'i's beauty. Verdant trees grow canopies over the few roads, and brooding mountains are framed by long, sandy beaches, coral reefs, and sheer sea cliffs. Pristine trade winds moderate warm daily temperatures while offering comfort for deep, refreshing sleep through gentle nights.

The main road tracing Kaua'i's perimeter takes you past much more scenery than would seem possible on one small island. Chiseled mountains, thundering waterfalls, misty hillsides, dreamy beaches, lush vegetation, and small towns make up the physical landscape. Perhaps the most stunning piece of scenery is a place no road will take you—the breathtakingly beautiful Nāpali Coast, which runs along the northwest side of the island.

For adventure seekers, Kaua'i offers everything from difficult hikes to helicopter tours. The island has top-notch spas and golf courses, and its beaches are known to be some of the most beautiful in the world. Even after you've spent days lazing around drinking mai tais or kayaking your way down a river, there's still plenty to do, as well as see: Plantation villages, a historic lighthouse, wildlife refuges, a fern grotto, a colorful canyon, and deep rivers are all easily explored.

■TIP→ While exploring the island, try to take advantage of the many roadside scenic overlooks and pull over to take in the constantly changing view. Don't try to pack too much into one day. Kaua'i is small, but travel is slow. The island's sights are divided into four geographic areas, in clockwise order: the North Shore, the East Side, the South Shore, and the West Side.

GEOLOGY

Kaua'i is the oldest and northernmost of the main Hawaiian Islands. Five million years of wind and rain have worked their magic, sculpting fluted sea cliffs and whittling away at the cinder cones and caldera that prove its volcanic origin. Foremost among these is Wai'ale'ale, one of the wettest spots on earth. Its approximate 450-inch annual rainfall feeds the mighty Wailua River, the only navigable waterway in Hawai'i. The vast Alaka'i Swamp soaks up rain like a sponge, releasing it slowly into the watershed that gives Kaua'i its emerald sheen.

FLORA AND FAUNA

Kaua'i offers some of the best birding in the state, due in part to the absence of the mongoose. Many nēnē (the endangered Hawaiian state bird) reared in captivity have been successfully released here, along with an endangered forest bird called the puai'ohi. The island is also home to a large colony of migratory nesting seabirds and has two refuges protecting endangered Hawaiian waterbirds. Kaua'i's most noticeable fowl, however, is the wild chicken. A cross between jungle fowl (*moa*) brought by the Polynesians and domestic chickens and fighting cocks that escaped during the last two hurricanes, they are everywhere, and

DID YOU KNOW?

You'll find a welcome respite at gorgeous and secluded Kalalau Beach when you reach the end of the arduous 11-mile Kalalau Trail.

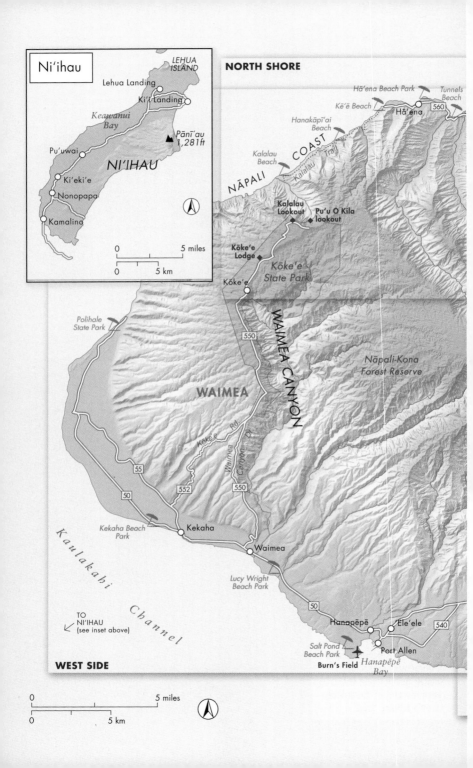

Ni'ihau

LEHUA ISLAND
Lehua Landing
Ki'i Landing
Keawanui Bay
Pānī'au 1,281ft
Pu'uwai
NI'IHAU
Ki'eki'e
Nonopapa
Kamalino

0   5 miles
0   5 km

Hā'ena Beach Park
Tunnels Beach
Kē'ē Beach
Hā'ena   560
Hanakāpī'ai Beach
Kalalau Beach
NĀPALI COAST
Kalalau Trail
Kalalau Lookout
Pu'u O Kila lookout
Kōke'e Lodge
Kōke'e State Park
Kōke'e
550
Nāpali-Kona Forest Reserve
Polihale State Park
WAIMEA
WAIMEA CANYON
Kōke'e Rd.
Waimea Canyon Dr.
55
552
550
Kekaha Beach Park
Kekaha
Waimea
50
Kaulakahi Channel
Lucy Wright Beach Park
50
Hanapēpē   'Ele'ele   540
TO NI'IHAU (see inset above)
Salt Pond Beach Park
Port Allen
Burn's Field *Hanapēpē Bay*

0   5 miles
0   5 km

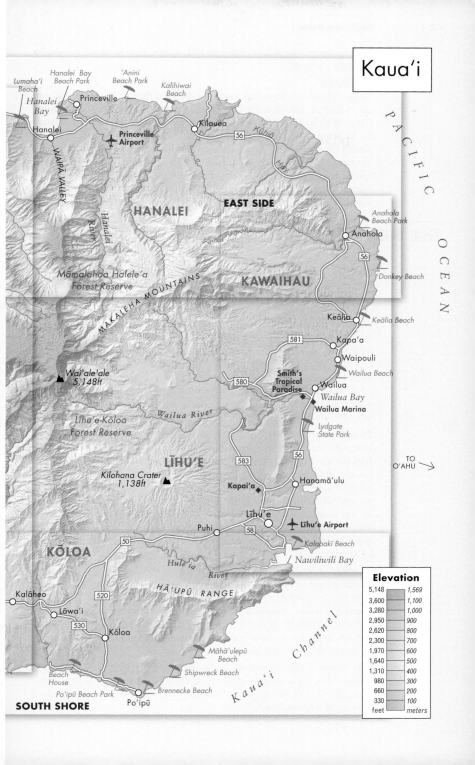

Kaua'i

Lumaha'i Beach
Hanalei Bay Beach Park
'Anini Beach Park
Kalihiwai Beach
Hanalei Bay
Hanalei
Princeville
Kīlauea
56
Kūhiō

WAIPĀ VALLEY
Princeville Airport

HANALEI
EAST SIDE

Hwy.

PACIFIC OCEAN

Anahola Beach Park
Anahola
56
Donkey Beach

Hanalei River

Māmalahoa Halele'a Forest Reserve

MAKALEHA MOUNTAINS

KAWAIHAU

Keālia
Keālia Beach

581
Kapa'a
Waipouli
Wailua Beach

Wai'ale'ale 5,148ft

Līhu'e-Kōloa Forest Reserve

580
Smith's Tropical Paradise
Wailua
Wailua Bay
Wailua Marina

Wailua River

Lydgate State Park

LĪHU'E

Kilohana Crater 1,138ft

583
56

TO O'AHU →

Kapai'a
Hanamā'ulu

Līhu'e
Līhu'e Airport

Puhi
58

KŌLOA

50

Hule'ia River

Kalapakī Beach
Nawiliwili Bay

Kalāheo

HĀ'UPŪ RANGE

520

Lāwa'i
530
Kōloa

Kaua'i Channel

Māhā'ulepū Beach

Shipwreck Beach

Beach House
Po'ipū Beach Park
Brennecke Beach
Po'ipū

SOUTH SHORE

Elevation

feet	meters
5,148	1,569
3,600	1,100
3,280	1,000
2,950	900
2,620	800
2,300	700
1,970	600
1,640	500
1,310	400
980	300
660	200
330	100
feet	meters

the roosters crow when they feel like it, not just at dawn. Consider yourself warned.

HISTORY

Kaua'i's residents have had a reputation for independence since ancient times. Called "the separate kingdom," Kaua'i alone resisted King Kamehameha's charge to unite the Hawaiian Islands. In fact, it was only by kidnapping Kaua'i's king, Kaumuali'i, and forcing him to marry Kamehameha's widow that the Garden Isle was joined to the rest of Hawai'i. That spirit lives on today as Kaua'i residents try to resist the lure of tourism dollars captivating the rest of the islands. Local building rules maintain that no structure may be taller than a coconut tree, and Kaua'i's capital city, Līhu'e, is still more small town than city.

THE NORTH SHORE

The North Shore of Kaua'i includes the environs of Kīlauea, Princeville, Hanalei, and Hā'ena. Traveling north on Route 56 from the airport, the coastal highway crosses the Wailua River and the busy towns of Wailua and Kapa'a before emerging into a decidedly rural and scenic landscape, with expansive views of the island's rugged interior mountains. As the two-lane highway turns west and narrows, it winds through spectacular scenery and passes the posh resort community of Princeville before dropping down into Hanalei Valley. Here it narrows further and becomes a federally recognized scenic roadway, replete with one-lane bridges (the local etiquette is for six or seven cars to cross at a time, before yielding to those on the other side), hairpin turns, and heart-stopping coastal vistas. The road ends at Kē'ē, where the ethereal rain forests and fluted sea cliffs of Nāpali Coast Wilderness State Park begin.

Nāpali Coast is considered the jewel of Kaua'i, and for all its greenery, it would surely be an emerald. After seeing the coast, many are at a loss for words, because its beauty is so overwhelming. Others resort to poetry. Pulitzer Prize–winning poet W. S. Merwin wrote a book-length poem, "The Folding Cliffs," based on a true story set in Nāpali. *Nāpali* means "the cliffs," and while it sounds like a simple name, it's quite an apt description. The coastline is cut by a series of impossibly small valleys, like fault lines, running to the interior, with the resulting cliffs seeming to fold back on themselves like an accordion-folded fan made of green velvet.

In winter Kaua'i's North Shore receives more rainfall than other areas of the island. Don't let this deter you from visiting. The clouds drift over the mountains of Nāmolokama creating a mysterious mood and then, in a blink, disappear, rewarding you with mountains laced with a dozen waterfalls or more. The views of the mountain—as well as the sunsets over the ocean—from the St. Regis Bar, adjacent to the lobby of the St. Regis Princeville Resort, are fantastic.

The North Shore attracts all kinds—from celebrities to surfers. In fact, Andy Irons, three-time world surfing champion, grew up riding waves along the North Shore; when he's not traversing the globe in search of waves, he lives and surfs here.

HANALEI, HĀ'ENA, AND WEST

Hā'ena is 40 mi northwest of Līhu'e; Hanalei is 5 mi southeast of Hā'ena

Crossing the historic one-lane bridge into Hanalei reveals old-world Hawai'i, including working taro farms, poi making, and evenings of throwing horseshoes at Black Pot Beach Park—found unmarked (as many places are on Kaua'i) at the east end of Hanalei Bay Beach Park. Although the current real-estate boom on Kaua'i has attracted mainland millionaires to build estate homes on the few remaining parcels of land in Hanalei, there's still plenty to see and do. It's *the* gathering place on the North Shore. Restaurants, shops, and people-watching here are among the best on the island, and you won't find a single brand name, chain, or big-box store around—unless you count surf brands like Quiksilver and Billabong.

The beach and river at Hanalei offer swimming, snorkeling, body boarding, surfing, and kayaking. Those hanging around at sunset often congregate at the Hanalei Pavilion, where a husband-and-wife-slack-key-guitar-playing combo make impromptu appearances. There's an old rumor, since quashed by the local newspaper, *The Garden Island*, that says Hanalei was the inspiration for the song "*Puff the Magic Dragon*," performed by the 1960s singing sensation Peter, Paul & Mary. Even with the newspaper's exposé, Hawai'i Movie Tours caps off its daylong visit of famous Kaua'i movie sites on the Hanalei Pier with a guide pointing out the shape of the dragon carved into the mountains encircling the town.

Once you pass through Hanalei town, the road shrinks even more as you skirt the coast and pass through Hā'ena. Blind corners, quick turns, and one-lane bridges force slow driving along this scenic stretch across the Lumaha'i and Wainiha valleys.

GETTING HERE AND AROUND

There is only one road leading beyond Princeville to Kē'ē Beach at the western end of the North Shore: Route 560. Hanalei's commercial stretch fronts this route, and you'll find parking at the shopping compounds on each side of the road. After Hanalei, parking is restricted to two main areas, Hā'ena Beach Park and a new lot at Hā'ena State Park, and there are very few pullover areas along Route 560. Traffic is usually light, though the route can become congested right after sunset.

EXPLORING

TOP ATTRACTIONS

Hanalei Valley Overlook. Dramatic mountains and a patchwork of neat taro farms bisected by the wide Hanalei River make this one of Hawai'i's loveliest sights. The fertile Hanalei Valley has been planted in taro since perhaps AD 700, save for a century-long foray into rice that ended in the early1960s. (The historic Haraguchi Rice Mill is all that remains of the era.) Many taro farmers lease land within the 900-acre Hanalei National Wildlife Refuge, helping to provide wetland habitat for four species of endangered Hawaiian waterbirds. ⊠ *Rte. 56, across from Foodland, Princeville*

★ **Kē'ē Beach State Park.** This stunning, and often overcrowded, beach marks the start of majestic Nāpali Coast. The 11-mi **Kalalau Trail** begins near the parking lot, drawing day hikers and backpackers. Another path leads from the sand to a stone hula platform dedicated to **Laka,** the goddess of hula, which has been in use since ancient times. This is a sacred site that should be approached with respect; it's inappropriate for visitors to leave offerings at the altar, which is tended by students in a local hula *hālau* (school). Local etiquette suggests observing from a distance. Most folks head straight for the sandy beach and its dreamy lagoon, which is great for snorkeling when the sea is calm. ⊠ *Drive to western end of Rte. 560.*

WORTH NOTING

Hanalei Pier. Built in 1892, the historic Hanalei Pier is a landmark seen from miles across the bay. It came to fame when it was featured in the award-winning 1957 movie *South Pacific.* Kids use it as a diving board, fishers fish, picnickers picnic. It's a great spot for a leisurely stroll. ⊠ *In Hanalei, turn makai at Aku Rd. and drive 1 block to Weli Weli Rd. Turn right. Drive to end of road, park, and walk left to beach*

Ho'opulapula Haraguchi Rice Mill. Rice grew in the taro fields of Hanalei valley for almost 80 years—beginning in the 1880s and ending in the early 1960s. Today, this history is embodied in the Haraguchi family, whose ancestors threshed, hulled, polished, separated, graded, and bagged rice in their 3,500-square-foot rice mill, which was demolished once by fire and twice by hurricanes. Rebuilt to the exacting standards of the National Register of Historic Places, the mill—and neighboring taro fields—is now open for tours on a very limited schedule. The family still farms taro on the onetime rice paddies and also operates the Hanalei Taro & Juice kiosk in Hanalei town. Reservations are required for the tour. ⊠ *Located next to Kayak Kauai right as you enter Hanalei town, 5-5070 Kūhiō Hwy.* ☎ *808/651–3399* ⊕ *www.haraguchiricemill. org* ⊠ *$65* ⊗ *Wed. for tours only; kiosk Mon.–Sat. 11–3.*

Limahuli Garden. Narrow Limahuli Valley, with its fluted mountain peaks and ancient stone taro terraces, creates an unparalleled setting for this botanical garden and nature preserve. Dedicated to protecting native plants and unusual varieties of taro, it represents the principles of conservation and stewardship held by its founder, Charles "Chipper" Wichman. Limahuli's primordial beauty and strong mana (spiritual power) eclipse the extensive botanical collection. It's one of the most gorgeous spots on Kaua'i and the crown jewel of the National Tropical Botanical Garden, which Wichman now heads. Call ahead to reserve a guided tour, or tour on your own. Be sure to check out the quality gift shop and revolutionary compost toilet, and be prepared for walking a somewhat steep hillside. ⊠ *Rte. 560, Hā'ena* ☎ *808/826–1053* ⊕ *www.ntbg.*

North Shore

PACIFIC OCEAN

Waikapala'e and Waikanaloa Wet Caves

Hā'ena Beach Park

Tunnels Beach

Maniniholo Dry Cave

Hā'ena

Kē'ē Beach State Park

Limahuli Garden

Hanakāpī'ai Beach

NĀPALI COAST

Kalalau Beach

Kalalau Trail

Wilderness State Park

Kalalau Lookout

Pu'u O Kila lookout

Kōke'e Lodge

Kōke'e State Park

Kōke'e

550

Lumaha'i Beach

Hanalei Bay Beach Park

Queen's Bath

Princeville

Hanalei Bay

Hanalei Pier

Hanalei

'Anini Beach Park

Kalihiwai Beach

Hanalei Valley Overlook

Princeville Airport

Hanalei National Wildlife Refuge

Ho'opulapula Haraguchi Rice Mill

Wai'oli Hui'ia Church and Wai'oli Mission House

WATPĀ VALLEY

HANALEI

Hanalei River

Mālaehāoa Halele'a Forest Reserve

MAKALEHA MOUNTAINS

560

Kīlauea

Kīlauea Point National Wildlife Refuge and Kīlauea Lighthouse

Nā 'Āina Kai

Moloa'a Sunrise Fruit Stand

Kīhiō

56

Anahola Beach Park

Anahola

Donkey Beach

Kēālia Beach

Kēālia

56

2 mi

2 km

0

org ✉ *Self-guided tour $15, guided tour $30 (reservations required)* ◷ *Tues.–Sat. 9:30–4.*

Maniniholo Dry Cave. According to legend, Maniniholo was the head fisherman of the Menehune—the possibly real, possibly mythical first inhabitants of the island. As they were preparing to leave Kaua'i and return home (wherever that was), Maniniholo called some of his workers to Hā'ena to collect food from the reef. They gathered so much that they couldn't carry it all and left some near the ocean cliffs, with plans to retrieve it the following day. It all disappeared during the night, however, and Maniniholo realized that imps living in the rock fissures were the culprits. He and his men dug into the cliff to find and destroy the imps, leaving behind the cave that now bears his name. Across the road from Maniniholo Dry Cave is **Hā'ena State Park.** ✉ *Rte. 560, Hā'ena.*

Waikapala'e and Waikanaloa Wet Caves. Said to have been dug by Pele, goddess of fire, these watering holes used to be clear, clean, and great for swimming. Now stagnant, they are nevertheless a photogenic example of the many haunting natural landmarks of Kaua'i's North Shore. Waikanaloa is visible right beside the highway, near the end of the road. Waikapala'e is back a few hundred yards and is accessed by a five-minute uphill walk. ✉ *Western end of Rte. 560.*

Wai'oli Hui'ia Church. Designated a National Historic Landmark, this little church—affiliated with the United Church of Christ—doesn't go unnoticed right alongside Route 560 in downtown Hanalei, and its doors are usually wide open (from 9 to 5, give or take) inviting inquisitive visitors in for a look around. Like the Wai'oli Mission House, it is an exquisite representation of New England architecture crossed with Hawaiian thatched buildings. During Hurricane 'Iniki's visit in 1992, which brought sustained winds of 160 mph and wind gusts up to 220 mph, this little church was lifted off its foundation but, thankfully, lovingly restored. Services are held at 10 AM on Sunday with many hymns sung in Hawaiian. ✉ *Located at mile marker 3 on Rte. 560* ☎ *808/826–6253.*

Wai'oli Mission House. This 1837 home was built by missionaries William and Mary Alexander. Its tidy New England architecture and formal koa-wood furnishings epitomize the prim and proper missionary influence, while the informative guided tours offer a fascinating peek into the private lives of Kaua'i's early white residents. Half-hour guided tours are available at no charge on Tuesday, Thursday, and Saturday from 9 to 3. ■ TIP➜ If no one is there when you arrive, don't despair; just ring the bell. ✉ *Kūhiō Hwy., Hanalei* ☎ *808/245–3202* ✉ *Donations accepted* ◷ *Tues., Thurs., and Sat. 9–3.*

Continued on page 56

NĀPALI COAST: EMERALD QUEEN OF KAUA'I

If you're coming to Kaua'i, Nāpali ("cliffs" in Hawaiian) is a major must-see. More than 5 million years old, these sea cliffs rise thousands of feet above the Pacific, and every shade of green is represented in the vegetation that blankets their lush peaks and folds. At their base, there are caves, secluded beaches, and waterfalls to explore.

The big question is how to explore this gorgeous stretch of coastline. You can't drive to it, through it, or around it. You can't see Nāpali from a scenic lookout. You can't even take a mule ride to it. The only way to experience its magic is from the sky, the ocean, or the trail.

FROM THE SKY

If you've booked a helicopter tour of Nāpali, you might start wondering what you've gotten yourself into on the way to the airport. Will it feel like being on a small airplane? Will there be turbulence? Will it be worth all the money you just plunked down?

Your concerns will be assuaged on the helipad, once you see the faces of those who have just returned from their journey: Everyone looks totally blissed out. And now it's your turn.

Climb on board, strap on your headphones, and the next thing you know the helicopter gently lifts up, hovers for a moment, and floats away like a spider on the wind—no roaring engines, no rumbling down a runway. If you've chosen a flight with music, you'll feel as if you're inside your very own IMAX movie.

Pinch yourself if you must, because this is the real thing. Your pilot shares history, legend, and lore. If you miss something, speak up: pilots love to show off their island knowledge. You may snap a few pictures (not too many or you'll miss the eyes-on experience!), nudge a friend or spouse, and point at a whale breeching in the ocean, but mostly you stare, mouth agape. There is simply no other way to take in the immensity and greatness of Nāpali but from the air.

See Chapter 5 for helicopter-tour information.

Helicopter flight over Nāpali Coast

GOOD TO KNOW

Helicopter companies depart from the north, east, and west shores. Our advice? Choose your departure location based on its proximity to where you're staying.

If you want more adventure—and air—choose one of the helicopter companies that flies with the doors off.

Some companies offer flights without music. Know the experience you want ahead of time. Some even sell a DVD of your flight, so you don't have to worry about taking pictures.

Wintertime rain grounds some flights; plan your trip early in your stay in case the flight gets rescheduled.

IS THIS FOR ME?

Taking a helicopter trip is the most expensive way to see Nāpali—as much as $280 for an hour-long tour.

Claustrophobic? Choose a boat tour or hike. It's a tight squeeze in the helicopter, especially in one of the middle seats.

Short on time? Taking a helicopter tour is a great way to see the island.

WHAT YOU MIGHT SEE

■ Nu'alolo Kai (an ancient Hawaiian fishing village) with its fringed reef

■ The 300-foot Hanakāpī'ai Falls

■ A massive sea arch formed in the rock by erosion

■ The 11-mile Kalalau Trail threading its way along the coast

■ The amazing striations of a'a and pāhoehoe lava flows that helped push Kaua'i above the sea

FROM THE OCEAN

Nāpali from the ocean is two treats in one: spend a good part of the day on (or in) the water, and gaze up at majestic green sea cliffs rising thousands of feet above your head.

There are three ways to see it: a mellow pleasure-cruise catamaran allows you to kick back and sip a mai tai; an adventurous raft (Zodiac) tour will take you inside sea caves under waterfalls, and give you the option of snorkeling; and a daylong outing in a kayak is a real workout, but then you can say you paddled 16 miles of coastline.

Any way you travel, you'll breathe ocean air, feel spray on your face, and see pods of spinner dolphins, green sea turtles, flying fish, and, if you're lucky, a rare Hawaiian monk seal.

Nāpali stretches from Ke'e Beach in the north to Polihale beach on the West Side. If your departure point is Ke'e, your journey will start in the lush Hanakāpī'ai Valley. Within a few minutes, you'll see caves and waterfalls galore. About halfway down the coast just after the Kalalau Trail ends, you'll come to an immense arch—formed where the sea eroded the less dense basaltic rock—and a thundering 50-foot waterfall. And as the island curves near Nu'alolo State Park, you'll begin to notice less vegetation and more rocky outcroppings.

See Chapter 4 for more boat-tour information.

(left and top right) Kayaking on Nāpali Coast
(bottom right) Dolphin on Nāpali Coast

GOOD TO KNOW

If you want to snorkel, choose a morning rather than an afternoon tour—preferably during a summer visit—when seas are calmer.

If you're on a budget, choose a non-snorkeling tour.

If you want to see whales, take any tour, but be sure to plan your vacation for December through March.

If you're staying on the North Shore or East Side, embark from the North Shore. If you're staying on the South Shore, it might not be worth your time to drive to the north, so head to the West Side.

IS THIS FOR ME?

Boat tours are several hours long, so if you have only a short time on Kaua'i, a helicopter tour is a better alternative.

Even on a small boat, you won't get the individual attention and exclusivity of a helicopter tour.

Prone to seasickness? A large boat can be surprisingly rocky, so be prepared.

WHAT YOU MIGHT SEE

■ Hawai'i's state fish—the humuhumunukunukuapuaa—otherwise known as the Christmas wrasse

■ Waiahuakua Sea Cave, with a waterfall coming through its roof

■ Tons of marine life, including dolphins, green sea turtles, flying fish, and humpback whales, especially in February and March

■ Waterfalls—especially if your trip is after a heavy rain

FROM THE TRAIL

If you want to be one with Nāpali—feeling the soft red earth beneath your feet, picnicking on the beaches, and touching the lush vegetation—hiking the Kalalau Trail is the way to do it.

Most people hike only the first 2 miles of the 11-mile trail and turn around on Hanakāpīʻai Trail. This 4-mile round-trip hike takes three to four hours. It starts at sea level and doesn't waste any time gaining elevation. (Take heart—the uphill lasts only a mile and tops out at 400 feet; then it's downhill all the way.) At the half-mile point, the trail curves west and the folds of Nāpali Coast unfurl.

Along the way you might share the trail with feral goats and wild pigs. Some of the vegetation is native; much is introduced.

After the 1-mile mark the trail begins its drop into Hanakāpīʻai. You'll pass

a couple of streams of water trickling across the trail, and maybe some banana, ginger, the native uluhe fern, and the Hawaiian ti plant. Finally the trail swings around the eastern ridge of Hanakāpīʻai for your first glimpse of the valley and then switchbacks down the mountain. You'll have to boulder-hop across the stream to reach the beach. If you like, you can take a 4-mile, round-trip fairly strenuous side trip from this point to the gorgeous Hanakāpīʻai Falls.

⇨ *See Chapter 5 for more Kalalau Trail hiking information.*

(left) Awaawapuhi mountain biker on razor-edge ridge
(top right) Feral goats in Kalalau Valley
(bottom right) Nāpali Coast

GOOD TO KNOW

Wear comfortable, amphibious shoes. Unless your feet require extra support, wear a self-bailing sort of shoe (for stream crossings) that doesn't mind mud. Don't wear heavy, waterproof hiking boots.

During winter the trail is often muddy, so be extra careful; sometimes it's completely inaccessible.

Don't hike after heavy rain—flash floods are common.

If you plan to hike the entire 11-mile trail (most people do the shorter hike described at left) you'll need a permit to go past Hanakāpī'ai.

IS THIS FOR ME?

Of all the ways to see Nāpali (with the exception of kayaking the coast), this is the most active. You need to be in decent shape to hit the trail.

If you're vacationing in winter, this hike might not be an option due to flooding—whereas you can take a helicopter or boat trip year-round.

WHAT YOU MIGHT SEE

- Big dramatic surf right below your feet
- Amazing vistas of the cool blue Pacific
- The spectacular Hanakāpī'ai Falls; if you have a permit don't miss Hanakoa Falls, less than ½ mile off the trail
- Wildlife, including goats and pigs
- Zany-looking ōhi'a trees, with aerial roots and long, skinny serrated leaves known as hala. Early Hawaiians used them to make mats, baskets, and canoe sails.

PRINCEVILLE, KĪLAUEA, AND AROUND

Princeville is 4 mi northeast of Hanalei; Kīlauea is 5 mi southeast of Princeville.

Built on a bluff offering gorgeous sea and mountain vistas, including Hanalei Bay, Princeville is the creation of a 1970s resort development. The area is anchored by a few large hotels, world-class golf courses, and lots of condos and timeshares.

Five miles down Route 56, a former plantation town, Kīlauea town itself maintains its rural flavor in the midst of unrelenting gentrification encroaching all around it.

Especially noteworthy are its historic lava-rock buildings, including **Christ Memorial Episcopal Church** on Kolo Road and, on Keneke and Kīlauea Road (commonly known as Lighthouse Road), the Kong Lung Company now an expensive shop.

GETTING HERE AND AROUND

There is only one main road through the Princeville resort area, so maneuvering a car here can be a nightmare. If you're trying to find a smaller lodging unit, be sure to get specific driving directions. Ample parking is available at the Princeville Shopping Center at the entrance to the resort. Kīlauea is about 5 mi east on Rte. 56. There's a public parking lot in the town center as well as parking at the end of Kīlauea Road for access to the lighthouse.

EXPLORING

Fodor's Choice ★

Kīlauea Point National Wildlife Refuge and Kīlauea Lighthouse. A beacon for sea traffic since it was built in 1913, this National Historic Landmark has the largest clamshell lens of any lighthouse in the world. It's within a national wildlife refuge, where thousands of seabirds soar on the trade winds and nest on the steep ocean cliffs. Endangered nēnē geese, red-footed boobies, Laysan albatross, wedge-tailed shearwaters, white- and red-tailed tropic birds, great frigate birds, Pacific golden plovers (all identifiable by educational signboards) along with native plants, dolphins, humpback whales, huge winter surf, and gorgeous views of the North Shore add to the drama of this special place, making it well worth the modest entry fee. The gift shop has a great selection of books about the island's natural history and an array of unique merchandise, with all proceeds benefiting education and preservation efforts. ⊠ *Kīlauea Lighthouse Rd., Kīlauea* ☎ *808/828–0168* ⊕ *www.kilaualighthouse. org* ☞ *$5* ☉ *Daily 10–4.*

Moloa'a Sunrise Fruit Stand. Don't let the name fool you; they don't open at sunrise (more like 7:30 AM, so come here after you watch the sun rise elsewhere). And it's not just a fruit stand. Breakfast is light and includes bagels, granola, smoothies, coffee, espresso, cappuccino, latte, and, of

course, tropical-style fresh juices (pineapple, carrot, watermelon, guava, even sugarcane, in season). This is also a great spot to get out and stretch, take in the mountain view, and pick up sandwiches to go. Select local produce is always available, although the variety is not as good as at the island's farmers' markets. What makes this fruit stand different is the fresh, natural ingredients like multigrain breads and *nori* (seaweed) wraps as a wheat-free bread alternative. ⊠ *Just past mile marker 16 mauka on Rte. 56,* ☎ 808/822–1441 ⊙ *Mon.–Sat. 7:30–5, Sun. 10–5.*

🕐 **Na 'Āina Kai.** One small sign along the highway is all that promotes this
★ once-private garden gone big time. Joyce Doty's love for plants and art now spans 240 acres and includes 13 different gardens, a hardwood plantation, a canyon, lagoons, a Japanese teahouse, a Poinciana maze, a waterfall, and a sandy beach. Throughout are more than 100 bronze sculptures, reputedly one of the nation's largest collections. The latest project is a children's garden with a 16-foot-tall Jack and the Beanstalk bronze sculpture, gecko maze, tree house, kid-size train and, of course, a tropical jungle. Located in a residential neighborhood and hoping to maintain good neighborly relations, the garden, which is now a non-profit organization, limits tours (guided only). Tour lengths vary widely, from 1½ to 5 hours. Reservations are strongly recommended. ⊠ *Rte. 56 north of mile marker 21, turn makai on Wailapa Rd. and follow signs,* ☎ 808/828–0525 ⊕ *www.naainakai.org* ⊠ *$25 for 1½-hr stroll to $70 for 5-hr hiking tour* ⊙ *Tues.–Fri., call ahead for hours.*

THE EAST SIDE

The East Side encompasses Līhu'e, Wailua, and Kapa'a. It's also known as the Coconut Coast, as there was once a coconut plantation where today's aptly named Coconut Marketplace is located. A small grove still exists on both sides of the highway. *Mauka*, a fenced herd of goats keeps the grass tended; on the *makai* side, you can walk through the grove, although it's best not to walk directly under the trees—falling coconuts can be dangerous. Līhu'e is the county seat, and the whole

Lei. Tropical flowers. Corn. Rambutan. Avocados. Huli huli chicken. Kalua pig. It's not uncommon to run across individuals selling flowers, produce, and food on the side of the road. Some are local farmers trying to make a living; others are people fund-raising for the local canoe club. Don't be afraid to stop and buy. Most are friendly and enjoy chatting.

East Side is the island's center of commerce, so early-morning and late-afternoon drive times (or rush hour) can get congested. (Because there's only one main road, if there's a serious traffic accident the entire roadway may be closed, with no way around. Not to worry; it's a rarity.)

KAPA'A AND WAILUA

Kapa'a is 16 mi southeast of Kīlauea; Wailua is 3 mi southwest of Kapa'a.

Old Town Kapa'a was once a plantation town, which is no surprise—most of the larger towns on Kaua'i once were. Old Town Kapa'a is made up of a collection of wooden-front shops, some built by plantation workers and still run by their progeny today. Kapa'a houses the two biggest grocery stores on the island, side by side: Foodland and Safeway. It also offers plenty of dining options for breakfast, lunch, and dinner, and gift shopping. To the south, Wailua comprises a few restaurants and shops, a few mid-range resorts along the coastline, and a housing community *mauka*.

GETTING HERE AND AROUND

Turn to the right out of the airport at Līhu'e for the road to Wailua. A bridge—under which the very culturally significant Wailua River gently flows—marks the beginning of town. It quickly blends into Kapa'a; there's no real demarcation. Careful, though—the zone between Līhu'e and Wailua has been the site of many car accidents. Pay attention and drive carefully, always knowing where you are going and when to turn off.

EXPLORING

TOP ATTRACTIONS

Lydgate State Park. The park, named for the Reverend J. M. Lydgate, founder of the Līhu'e English Union Church, has a large children-designed and community-built playground, pavilion, and picnic area. It also houses the remains of an ancient site where commoners who broke a royal taboo could seek refuge from punishment. It's part of an extensive complex of sacred archaeological sites that runs from Wai'ale'ale

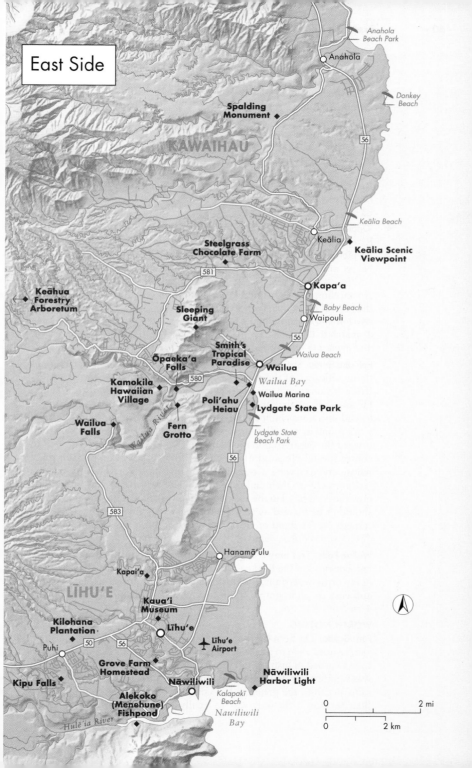

East Side

Spalding Monument

KAWAIHAU

Anahola
Anahola Beach Park

Donkey Beach

56

Keālia Beach

Steelgrass Chocolate Farm

581

Keālia

Keālia Scenic Viewpoint

Keāhua Forestry Arboretum

Kapa'a

Sleeping Giant

Baby Beach

Waipouli

56

Smith's Tropical Paradise

Ōpaeka'a Falls

Wailua

580

Wailua Beach

Wailua Bay

Kamokila Hawaiian Village

Wailua Marina

Poli'ahu Heiau

Lydgate State Park

Wailua Falls

Fern Grotto

Lydgate State Beach Park

56

Wailua River

583

Hanamā'ulu

LĪHU'E

Kapai'a

Kaua'i Museum

Kilohana Plantation

Līhu'e

Puhi

50   56

Līhu'e Airport

Grove Farm Homestead

Nāwiliwili Harbor Light

Kipu Falls

Nāwiliwili

Kalapakī Beach

Alekoko (Menehune) Fishpond

Nawiliwili Bay

Hule'ia River

0   2 mi

0   2 km

to the sea, underscoring the significance of this region to the ancient Hawaiians. In recent years the community expanded the playground to include a bridge of mazes, tunnels, and slides, as well as access to the new bike/walking path that hugs the ocean. It's located a short walk or drive south of the main park, off Nehe Drive. ⊠ *South of Wailua River turn makai off Rte. 56 onto Leho Dr. and makai onto Nalu Rd.* ☏ *Free* ☉ *Daily dawn–dusk.*

★ **'Ōpaeka'a Falls.** The mighty Wailua River produces many dramatic waterfalls, and 'Ōpaeka'a (pronounced oh-pie-kah-ah) is one of the best. It plunges hundreds of feet to the pool below and can be easily viewed from a scenic overlook with ample parking. 'Ōpaeka'a means "rolling shrimp," which refers to tasty native crustaceans that were once so abundant they could be seen tumbling in the falls. ■TIP→ Just before reaching the parking area for the waterfalls, turn left into a scenic pullout for great views of the Wailua River valley and its march to the sea. ⊠ *From Rte. 580, turn mauka onto Kuamo'o Rd. and drive 1½ mi, Wailua*

Poli'ahu Heiau. Storyboards near this ancient *heiau* (sacred site) recount the significance of the many sacred structures found along the Wailua River. It's unknown exactly how the ancient Hawaiians used Poli'ahu Heiau—one of the largest pre-Christian temples on the island—but legend says it was built by the Menehune because of the unusual stonework found in its walled enclosures. From this site, drive back downhill toward the ocean to **pōhaku hānau**, a two-piece birthing stone said to confer special blessings on all children born there, and **pōhaku piko**, whose crevices were a repository for umbilical cords left by parents seeking a clue to their child's destiny, which reportedly was foretold by how the cord fared in the rock. Some Hawaiians feel these sacred stones shouldn't be viewed as tourist attractions, so always treat them with respect. Never stand or sit on the rocks or leave any offerings. ⊠ *Rte. 580, Kuamo'o Rd., Wailua.*

Wailua Falls. You may recognize this impressive cascade from the opening sequences of the *Fantasy Island* television series. Kaua'i has plenty of noteworthy waterfalls, but this one is especially gorgeous, easy to find, and easy to photograph. ⊠ *End of Rte. 583, Ma'alo Rd., in Kapai'a 4 mi from Rte. 56.*

WORTH NOTING

Fern Grotto. The Fern Grotto has a long history on Kaua'i. For some reason, visitors seem to like it. It's really nothing more than a yawning lava tube swathed in lush fishtail ferns 3 mi up the Wailua River. Though it was significantly damaged after Hurricane 'Iniki and again after heavy rains in 2006, the greenery has completely recovered. Smith's Motor Boat Services is the only way to legally see the grotto. You can access

Taking a riverboat tour to Fern Grotto to see a fishtail fern-covered lava tube is a popular family activity.

the entrance with a kayak, but if boats are there, you may not be allowed to land. ⊠ *Depart from Wailua Marina on mauka side of Rte. 56, just south of Wailua River* ⇱ *$20* ⊙ *Departures daily 9:30–3:30* ☎ *808/821–6892.*

Kamokila Hawai'ian Village. The village is dramatically ensconced at the base of a steep, long, winding road right beside the Wailua River. Of course, in the days of King Kaumuali'i, there wasn't a road, just access by boat, and so it made the perfect hideout for his war canoes tucked away in this crook of the Wailua River. Today, there's a replica Hawaiian village in place of war canoes—numerous thatched-roof structures and abundant plant life. Yet, the lack of human activity here makes it seem abandoned, which may be why Hollywood found it an appealing location for the movie *Outbreak.* Kayaking is available on the river. ⊠ *Turn mauka on Kuamoo Rd. in Wailua, drive 1½ mi, turn left across from 'Ōpaeka'a Falls* ☎ *808/823–0559* ⇱ *$5* ⊙ *Daily 9–5.*

Keāhua Forestry Arboretum. Tree-lined and grassy, this is a perfect spot for a picnic—there are lots of picnic tables scattered throughout the parklike setting. A shallow, cascading stream makes for a fun spot for kids to splash, although the water's a bit chilly. A 1-mi walking trail meanders through mango, monkeypod, and eucalyptus trees. This is an exceptionally peaceful place—good for yoga and meditation—that is, unless the resident roosters decide to crow. ■TIP➜ If it looks like rain, don't follow the road across the stream; it often floods, leaving you stranded on the wrong side. ⊠ *In Wailua, take Kuamoo Rd. mauka 6½ mi* ⊙ *Daily dawn–dusk.*

Keālia Scenic Viewpoint. Between mile markers 9 and 10 on Highway 56 is this ocean overlook, perfect for spotting whales during their winter migration. In fact, on three Saturdays in winter, the Hawaiian Islands Humpback Whale National Marine Sanctuary conducts its annual whale count from this spot, one of several around the island. The lookout was rebuilt and doubled in size a few years ago, and it's now easy to hop on the cement bike/walking path just below for a coastal stroll or ride. Most days you can see clear to Līhu'e and beyond. If you packed them, bring your binoculars.

Sleeping Giant. Although its true name is Nounou, this landmark mountain ridge is better known as the Sleeping Giant because of its resemblance to a very large man sleeping on his back. Legends differ on whether the giant is Puni, who was accidentally killed by rocks launched at invading canoes by the Menehune, or Nunui, a gentle creature who has not yet awakened from the nap he took centuries ago after building a massive temple and enjoying a big feast. ⊠ *Mauka Rte. 56, about 1 mi north of Wailua River, backing Kapa'a.*

☺ **Smith's Tropical Paradise.** Nestled next to Wailua Marina along the mighty Wailua River, this 30-acre botanical and cultural garden offers a glimpse of exotic foliage, including fruit orchards, a bamboo rain forest, and tropical lagoons. Take the tram and enjoy a narrated tour or stroll along the mile-long pathways. It's a popular spot for wedding receptions and other large events, and its three-times-weekly lū'au is one of the island's oldest and best. ⊠ *Just south of Wailua River, mauka, on Rte. 56, Kapa'a* ☎ *808/821–6895* ⊕ *www.smithskauai.com* ☜ *$6* ⊙ *Daily 8:30–4.*

Spalding Monument. The area just north of Kapa'a known as Keālia was once planted in sugarcane. Turn onto Keālia Road just after mile marker 10 for an off-the-beaten-track 4½-mi scenic detour. Immediately on your right are a small post office and a snack shop and, on your left, rodeo grounds often in use on summer weekends. The road ascends, and 2½ mi later you'll reach a grassy area with the concrete remains of a onetime monument that bedecked the former estate of Colonel Zephaniah Spalding. It's a nice spot to picnic or to simply gaze at the nearby grazing horses. If you're an early riser, this is a great spot to watch the sun rise; if not, check the local newspaper for the next full moon and bring a bottle of wine. Continue on another bumpy 2 mi, and you'll reconnect with Highway 56 near the town of Anahola.

Steelgrass Chocolate Farm. Hawai'i is the only state in the country where *theobroma cacao* grows. As every chocolate connoisseur knows, the

COASTAL PATH

Ke Ala Hele Makalae, a bike-and-pedestrian path, hugs a good portion of the East Side coastline in the Kapa'a area. It's being built in sections, and the completed version is expected to run all the way from Līhu'e to Anahola. For now, the most accessible portion begins at Lydgate Park and loops south toward the golf course for 2½ mi. The most scenic section currently runs from north Kapa'a town past Keālia Beach and north toward Anahola. A walk or ride lets you feel the cool sea air, and it's a great way to meet local folks, who love using the path.

One of the best places for a lū'au is here at Smith's Tropical Paradise.

tree that grows the precious seed that becomes chocolate is the cacao tree. The Lydgates are on a mission to grow cacao on family farms all over the island with the hopes of one day starting a co-op that will produce Kauai Homegrown Chocolate. For now, you can tour this organic farm (in addition to cacao, they grow vanilla, timber, bamboo, and many tropical fruits) and learn how chocolate is made,"from branch to bar," as they put it. The three-hour tour includes, of course, plenty of chocolate tastings. Reservations are required for the morning tour, which begins Monday, Wednesday, and Friday at 9 AM. Children 12 and under are free. ⊠ *Located above the town of Kapaʻa (directions provided at time of reservation)* ☎ *808/821–1857* ⊕ *www.steelgrass. org* ⊇ *$6* ⊙ *Mon., Wed., Fri. for tours only.*

LĪHUʻE

7 mi southwest of Wailua

The commercial and political center of Kauaʻi County, which includes the islands of Kauaʻi and Niʻihau, Līhuʻe is home to the island's major airport, harbor, and hospital. This is where you can find the state and county offices that issue camping and hiking permits and the same fast-food eateries and big-box stores that blight the mainland. The county is seeking help in reviving the downtown; for now, once your business is done, there's little reason to linger in lackluster Līhuʻe.

GETTING HERE AND AROUND

Route 56 leads into Līhu'e from the north and Route 50 comes here from the south and west. The road from the airport (where Kaua'i's car rental agencies are) leads to the middle of Līhu'e. Many of the area's stores and restaurants are on and around Rice Street, which also leads to Kalapakī Bay and Nawiliwili Harbor.

EXPLORING

TOP ATTRACTIONS

Kaua'i Museum. Maintaining a stately presence on Rice Street, the historic museum building is easy to find. It features a permanent display, "The Story of Kaua'i," which provides a competent overview of the Garden Island and Ni'ihau, tracing the islands' geology, mythology, and cultural history. Local artists are represented in changing exhibits in the second-floor Mezzanine Gallery. The gift shop alone is worth a visit, with a fine collection of authentic Ni'ihau shell lei, feather hatband lei, hand-turned wooden bowls, reference books, and other quality arts, crafts, and gifts, many of them locally made. ⊠ *4428 Rice St., Līhu'e* 🕾 *808/245–6931* 🖃 *$7* 🕙 *Weekdays 9–4, Sat. 10–4.*

Kipu Falls. For the truly adventurous, or perhaps voyeuristic, there's Kipu Falls, located on the private property of amazingly tolerant owners. It's rare to find these falls deserted; however, the throngs lining up to jump add to the excitement. Depending upon whom you ask, the falls are 25 feet high, but if it's you standing up there, you might say higher. In addition to jumpers, there are swingers—those who opt for the rope swing. Both produce squealers and, of course, stallers. ■TIP➔ **After jumping, make your climb back up the aluminum ladder less painful by wearing water footwear.** A word of caution: Head injuries and drownings have occurred here, and rental cars have been broken into. A dirt trail approximately 1½ mi long leads to the falls. ⊠ *From Hwy. 50, at mile marker 3, turn makai onto Kipu Rd. Take the first right to stay on Kipu Rd. and drive ½ mi; park on side of road and follow dirt trail to falls.*

WORTH NOTING

Alekoko (Menehune) Fishpond. No one knows just who built this intricate aquaculture structure in the Hule'ia River. Legend attributes it to the Menehune, a possibly real, possibly mythical ancient race of people known for their small stature, industrious nature, and superb stoneworking skills. Volcanic rock was cut and fit together into massive walls 4 feet thick and 5 feet high, forming an enclosure for raising mullet and other freshwater fish that has endured for centuries. ⊠ *Hulemalu Rd., Niumalu.*

Grove Farm Homestead. Guided tours of this carefully restored 80-acre country estate offer a fascinating and authentic look at how upper-class Caucasians experienced plantation life in the mid-19th century. The tour focuses on the original home, built by the Wilcox family in 1860 and filled with a quirky collection of classic Hawaiiana. You can also see the workers' quarters, farm animals, orchards, and gardens that reflect the practical, self-sufficient lifestyle of the island's earliest Western inhabitants. Tours of the homestead are conducted twice a day, three

THE BEST SIGHTSEEING TOURS

Aloha Kaua'i Tours. You get *way* off the beaten track on these four-wheel-drive van excursions. Choose from several options, including the half-day Backroads Tour covering mostly haul-cane roads behind the locked gates of Grove Farm Plantation, and the half-day Rainforest Tour, which follows the Wailua River to its source, Mt. Wai'ale'ale. The expert guides are some of the best on the island. Rates are $75 and $80, respectively. ⊠ *Check in at Kilohana Plantation on Rte. 50 in Puhi, Līhu'e* ☏ *808/245–6400 or 800/452–1113* ⊕ *www.alohakauaitours.com.*

Hawai'i Movie Tours. Hawai'i Movie Tours' minibuses with in-van TV monitors let you see the actual scenes of films while visiting the real locations used for the filming of *Jurassic Park, Raiders of the Lost Ark, South Pacific, Blue Hawaii, Gilligan's Island,* and other Hollywood hits. The standard coastal tour is $89. We recommend this tour primarily for serious movie buffs. The four-wheel-drive Off Road Tour is $95 and takes you to film locations on private lands and rugged backcountry areas that are otherwise not easily visited. This tour is more suited for children, as many of the sites are recognizable from the multiple *Jurassic Park* filmings on the island. ⊠ *4-1596 Kūhiō Hwy., Kapa'a* ☏ *808/822–1192 or 800/628–8432* ⊕ *www.hawaiimovietour.com.*

Roberts Hawai'i Tours. The Round-the-Island Tour, sometimes called the Wailua River–Waimea Canyon Tour, gives a good overview of half the island, including Fort Elisabeth and 'Ōpaeka'a Falls. Guests are transported in air-conditioned, 25-passenger minibuses. The $79.50 trip includes a boat ride up the Wailua River to the Fern Grotto and a visit to the lookouts above Waimea Canyon. ☏ *808/245–9101 or 800/ 831–5541* ⊕ *www.robertshawaii.com.*

Waimea Historic Walking Tour. Led by a *kupuna*, a lifetime elder, this 2½- to 3-hour tour begins promptly at 9:30 AM, every Monday at the West Kaua'i Visitor Center. While sharing her personal remembrances, Aletha Kaohi leads an easy walk that explains Waimea's distinction as a recipient of the 2006 National Trust for Historic Preservation Award. The tour is free, but a reservation is required. ☏ *808/338–1332.*

days a week. To protect the historic building and its furnishings, tours may be canceled on very wet days. ■TIP→ With a six-person limit per tour, reservations are essential; the tour is not suitable for young children. ⊠ *Rte. 58, Nāwiliwili Rd., Līhu'e* ☏ *808/245–3202* ⊡ *$10* ⊙ *Tours Mon., Wed., and Thurs. at 10 and 1.*

☼ **Kilohana Plantation.** This estate dates back to 1896, when plantation manager Albert Spencer Wilcox first developed it as a working cattle ranch. His nephew, Gaylord Parke Wilcox, took over in 1936, building Kaua'i's first mansion. Today the 16,000-square-foot Tudor-style home houses specialty shops, art galleries, and Gaylord's, a pretty restaurant with courtyard seating. Nearly half the original furnishings remain, and the gardens and orchards were replanted according to the original plans. You can tour the grounds for free; children enjoy visiting the farm animals. A train runs 2½ mi through 104 acres of land representing the agricultural

SUNSHINE MARKETS

If you want to rub elbows with the locals and purchase fresh produce and flowers at very reasonable prices, head for **Sunshine Markets** (☎ 808/241–6303 ⊕ www.kauai.gov), also known as Kaua'i's farmers' markets. These busy markets are held weekly, usually in the afternoon, at locations all around the island. They're good fun, and they support small, neighborhood farmers. Arrive a little early, bring dollar bills to speed up transactions and plastic shopping bags to carry your produce, and be prepared for some pushy shoppers. Farmers are usually happy to educate visitors about unfamiliar fruits and veggies, especially when the crowd thins.

North Shore Sunshine Markets. ⊠ Waipa, mauka of Rte. 560 north of Hanalei after mile marker 3, ⊙ Tues.

2 PM ⊠ Kīlauea Neighborhood Center, on Keneke St. in Kīlauea ⊙ Thurs. 4:30 PM ⊠ Hanalei Community Center ⊙ Sat. 9:30 AM.

East Side Sunshine Markets. ⊠ Vidinha Stadium, Līhu'e, ½ mi south of airport on Rte. 51, ⊙ Fri. 3 PM ⊠ Kapa'a, turn mauka on Rte. 581/ Olohena Rd. for 1 block ⊙ Wed. 3 PM.

South Shore Sunshine Markets. ⊠ Ballpark, Kōloa, north of intersection of Kōloa Road and Rte. 520, ⊙ Mon. noon.

West Side Sunshine Markets. ⊠ Kalāheo Community Center, Kalāheo, on Papalina Rd. just off Kaumuali'i Hwy. ⊙ Tues. 3 PM ⊠ Hanapēpē Park ⊙ Thurs. 3 PM ⊠ Kekaha Neighborhood Center, Kekaha, 'Elepaio Rd. ⊙ Sat. 9 AM.

story of Kaua'i—then and now. ⊠ 3-2087 *Kaumuali'i Hwy., Rte. 50, Līhu'e* ☎ 808/245–5608 ⊙ *Mon.–Sat. 9:30–9:30, Sun. 9:30–5:30.*

Nāwiliwili. The commercial harbor at Nāwiliwili is a major port of call for container ships, U.S. Navy vessels, and passenger cruise lines. Anglers and recreational boaters use the nearby small-boat harbor. This is the main departure point for deep-sea fishing charters. There's protected swimming at Kalapakī Bay, fronting the Marriott resort, although the water quality is questionable at times. Anchor Cove Shopping Center and Harbor Mall have been refurbished and offer a good selection of shops and restaurants. ⊠ *Makai end of Wa'apā Rd., Līhu'e.*

Nāwiliwili Harbor Light. On March 1, 1917, the U.S. government purchased 3.2 acres from the Līhu'e Plantation Company—for all of $8—in order to build this lighthouse. When it comes to real estate, this could be the bargain of the century. As expected of any lighthouse, this one is perched on a peninsula with views spanning from the Nāwiliwili Harbor, down the rocky eastern coast, and out to the open ocean. The 2½-mi drive takes you through a delightfully hilly golf course. Just follow the signs promising public access to the shore on the newly paved road. Sunrises, moon rises, whale-watching, stargazing, boatwatching: you can't beat it. ⊠ *From airport entrance, go south on Rte. 51 for ½ mi. Turn left at stone wall entrance, past the (empty) guard shack. Drive 2½ mi to lighthouse.*

Stop by the farmer's market in Kapa'a to pick up locally grown mangoes and other fruits.

THE SOUTH SHORE

As you follow the main road south from Līhu'e, the landscape becomes lush and densely vegetated before giving way to drier conditions that characterize Po'ipū, the South Side's major resort area. Po'ipū owes much of its popularity to a steady supply of sunshine and a string of sandy beaches, although the beaches are smaller and more covelike than those on the West Side. With its extensive selection of accommodations, services, and activities, the South Shore attracts more visitors than any other area of Kaua'i. It's also attracting developers with big plans for the onetime sugarcane fields that are nestled in this region and enveloped by mountains. There are few roads in and out, and local residents are concerned about increased traffic as well as noise and dust pollution as a result of chronic construction. If you're planning to stay on the South Side, be sure to ask if your hotel, condo, or vacation rental will be impacted by the ongoing development during your visit.

Both Po'ipū and nearby Kōloa (site of Kaua'i's first sugar mill) can be reached via Route 520 (Maluhia Road) from the Līhu'e area. Route 520 is known locally as Tree Tunnel Road, due to the stand of eucalyptus trees lining the road that were planted at the turn of the 20th century by Walter Duncan McBryde, a Scotsman who began cattle ranching on Kaua'i's South Shore. The canopy of trees was ripped to literal shreds twice—in 1982 during Hurricane 'Iwa and again in 1992 during Hurricane 'Iniki. And, true to Kaua'i, both times the trees grew back into an impressive tunnel. It's a distinctive way to announce, "You are now on vacation," for there's a definite feel of leisure in the air here. There's still plenty to do—snorkel, bike, walk, horseback ride, take an ATV tour,

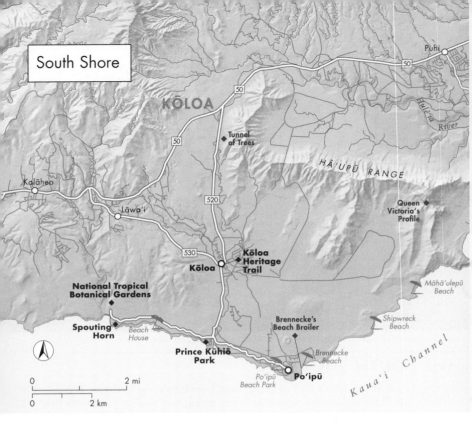

South Shore

KŌLOA

50

Tunnel
of Trees

50

HĀ'UPŪ RANGE

Fulfira River

Puhi

50

Kalāheo

Lāwa'i

520

Queen
Victoria's
Profile

530

Kōloa
Heritage
Trail

Kōloa

Māhā'ulepū
Beach

National Tropical
Botanical Gardens

Spouting
Horn

Beach
House

Brennecke's
Beach Broiler

Shipwreck
Beach

Prince Kūhiō
Park

Brennecke
Beach

Kaua'i Channel

Po'ipū
Beach Park

Po'ipū

0   2 mi

0   2 km

surf, scuba dive, shop, and dine—everything you'd want on a tropical vacation. From the west, Route 530 (Kōloa Road) slips into downtown Kōloa, a string of fun shops and restaurants, at an intersection with the only gas station on the South Shore.

KŌLOA

11 mi southwest of Līhu'e

Hawai'i's lucrative foray into sugar was born in this sleepy town, where the first sugar was milled back in 1830. You can still see the mill's old stone smokestack. Little else remains, save for the charming plantation-style buildings that have kept Kōloa from becoming a tacky tourist trap for Poipu-bound visitors. The original small-town character has been preserved by converting historic structures along the main street into boutiques, restaurants, and shops. Placards describe the original tenants and life in the old mill town. Look for Kōloa Fish Market, which offers poke and sashimi takeout, and Progressive Expressions, a popular local surf shop.

EXPLORING

Kōloa Heritage Trail. Throughout the South Shore, you'll find brass plaques and all the details of 14 historical stops along a 10-mi route—bike it, hike it, or drive it, your choice. You'll learn about Kōloa's whaling history, sugar industry, ancient Hawaiian cultural sites, the island's volcanic formation, and more. Pick up a free self-guided trail map at most any shop in Kōloa town.

PO'IPŪ

2 mi southeast of Kōloa

Thanks to its generally sunny weather and a string of golden-sand beaches dotted with oceanfront lodgings, Po'ipū is a top choice for many visitors. Beaches are user-friendly, with protected waters for *keiki* (children) and novice snorkelers, lifeguards, clean restrooms, covered pavilions, and a sweet coastal promenade ideal for leisurely strolls. Some experts have even ranked Po'ipū Beach Park number one in the nation. It depends on your preferences, of course, though it certainly does warrant high accolades.

GETTING HERE AND AROUND

Po'ipū is the one area on Kaua'i where you could get by without a car, though that could mean an expensive taxi ride from the airport and limited access to other parts of the island. To reach Po'ipū by car, follow Po'ipū Road south from Kōloa. After the traffic circle, the road curves to follow the coast, leading to some of the popular South Shore beaches.

EXPLORING

National Tropical Botanical Gardens *(NTBG)*. Tucked away in Lāwa'i Valley, these gardens include lands and a cottage once used by Hawai'i's Queen Emma for a summer retreat. Visitors can take a self-guided tour of the rambling 252-acre working **McBryde Gardens** to see and learn about plants collected throughout the tropics. It is known as a garden of "research and conservation." The 100-acre **Allerton Gardens,** which can be visited only on a guided tour, artfully display statues and water features that were originally developed as part of a private estate. Reservations are required for tours of Allerton Gardens but not for the self-guided tours of McBryde Gardens. The visitor center has a high-quality gift shop with botany-theme merchandise.

Besides harboring and propagating rare and endangered plants from Hawai'i and elsewhere, NTBG functions as a science and education center. The organization also operates gardens in Limahuli, on Kaua'i's North Shore, and in Hāna, on Maui's east shore. ⊠ *Lāwa'i Rd., across from Spouting Horn parking lot, Po'ipū* ☎ *808/742-2623* ⊕ *www.ntbg.org* ✉ *McBryde self-guided tour $20, Allerton guided tour $45* ☉ *McBryde Gardens Mon.–Sat. 9:30–2:30, hourly; Sun. 11:30–2:30, hourly. Allerton Gardens tours (by reservation) Mon.–Sat. at 9, 10, 1, and 2; Sun. at 10 and 1.*

QUICK
BITES
Stop in at Brennecke's Beach Broiler (⊠ *2100 Ho'ōne Rd., Po'ipū*
☎ *808/742-7588*). After a day at the beach, chill out with a mango margarita or a "world famous" mai tai and a pūpū platter from this longtime fixture on the beach in Po'ipū.

Prince Kūhiō Park. A triangle of grass behind the Prince Kūhiō condominiums honors the birthplace of Kaua'i's beloved Prince Jonah Kūhiō Kalaniana'ole. Known for his kind nature and good deeds, he lost his chance at the throne when Americans staged an illegal overthrow of Queen Lili'uokalani in 1893 and toppled Hawai'i's constitutional monarchy. This is a great place to view wave riders surfing a popular break known as PKs and to watch the sun sink into the Pacific. ⊠ *Lāwa'i Rd., Po'ipū.*

Spouting Horn. If the conditions are right, you can see a natural blowhole in the reef behaving like Old Faithful, shooting salt water high into the air and making a cool, echoing sound. It's most dramatic during big summer swells, which jam large quantities of water through an ancient lava tube with great force. Vendors hawk inexpensive souvenirs and collectibles in the parking lot. You may find good deals on shell jewelry, but ask for a certificate of authenticity to ensure it's a genuine Ni'ihau shell lei before paying the higher price that these intricate creations command. ⊠ *At end of Lāwa'i Rd., Po'ipū.*

THE WEST SIDE

Exploring the West Side is akin to visiting an entirely different world. The landscape is dramatic and colorful: a patchwork of green, blue, black, and orange. The weather is hot and dry, the beaches are long, the sand is dark. Ni'ihau, a private island and the last remaining place in Hawai'i where Hawaiian is spoken exclusively, can be glimpsed offshore. This is rural Kaua'i, where sugar is making its last stand and taro is still cultivated in the fertile river valleys. The lifestyle is slow, easy, and traditional, with many folks fishing and hunting to supplement their diets. Here and there modern industry has intruded into this pastoral scene: huge generators turn oil into electricity at Port Allen; scientists cultivate experimental crops of genetically engineered plants in Kekaha; the navy launches rockets at Mānā to test the "Star Wars" missile defense system; and NASA mans a tracking station in the wilds of Koke'e. It's a region of contrasts that simply shouldn't be missed.

Heading west from Līhu'e or Po'ipū, you pass through a string of tiny towns, plantation camps, and historic sites, each with a story to tell of centuries past. There's Hanapēpē, whose coastal salt ponds have been harvested since ancient times; Kaumakani, where the sugar industry still clings to life; Fort Elisabeth, from which an enterprising Russian tried to take over the island in the early 1800s; and Waimea, where Captain Cook made his first landing in the Islands, forever changing the face of Hawai'i.

From Waimea town you can head up into the mountains, skirting the rim of magnificent Waimea Canyon and climbing higher still until you reach the cool, often-misty forests of Kōke'e State Park. From the vantage point at the top of this gemlike island, 3,200 to 4,200 feet above sea level, you can gaze into the deep, verdant valleys of the North Shore and Nāpali Coast. This is where the "real" Kaua'i can still be found: the native plants, insects, and birds that are found nowhere else on arth.

HANAPĒPĒ

15 mi northwest of Po'ipū

In the 1980s Hanapēpē was fast becoming a ghost town, its farm-based economy mirroring the decline of agriculture. Today it's a burgeoning art colony, with galleries, crafts studios, and a lively art-theme street fair on Friday nights. The main street has a new vibrancy enhanced by the restoration of several historic buildings. The emergence of Kaua'i Coffee as a major West Side crop and expanded activities at Port Allen, now the main departure point for tour boats, also gave the town's economy a boost.

GETTING HERE AND AROUND

Hanapēpē, locally known as Kaua'i's "biggest little town," is just past the 'Ele'ele Shopping Center on the main highway (Route 50). A sign leads you to the town center, where street parking is easy and there's an enjoyable walking tour.

EXPLORING

TOP ATTRACTIONS

Kaua'i Coffee Visitor Center and Museum. Two restored camp houses, dating from the days when sugar was the main agricultural crop on the Islands, have been converted into a museum, visitor center, and gift shop. About 3,400 acres of McBryde sugar land have become Hawai'i's largest coffee plantation. You can walk among the trees, view old grinders and roasters, watch a video to learn how coffee is processed, sample various estate roasts, and check out the gift store. New to the grounds is a self-guided tour through a small coffee grove with informative signage; allow approximately 15 minutes to complete it. From 'Ele'ele, take Highway 50 in the direction of Waimea Canyon and veer right onto Highway 540, west of Kalāheo. The center is 2½ mi from the Highway 50 turnoff. ⊠ *870 Halawili Rd., Kalāheo* ☎ *808/335–0813* ⊕ *www.kauaicoffee.com* ☕ *Free* ⊙ *Daily 9–5.*

QUICK
BITES

It's not ice cream on Kaua'i if it's not **Lappert's Ice Cream** (⊠ *On Hwy. 50 mauka, Hanapēpē* ☎ *808/335–6121*). Guava, mac nut, pineapple, mango, coconut, banana—Lappert's is the ice cream capital of Kaua'i. Warning: Even at the factory store in Hanapēpē, the prices are no bargain. But, hey, you gotta try it.

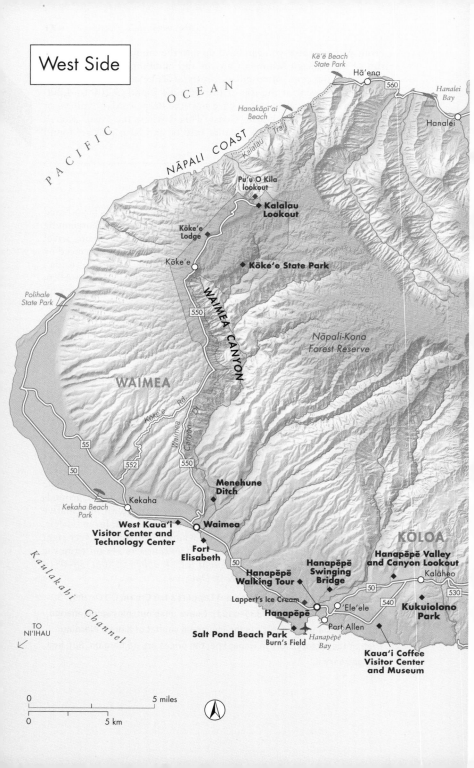

West Side

PACIFIC OCEAN

NĀPALI COAST

Kē'ē Beach
State Park

Hā'ena

560

Hanalei
Bay

Hanalei

Hanakāpī'ai
Beach

Kalalau Trail

Pu'u O Kila
lookout

Kalalau
Lookout

Kōke'e
Lodge

Kōke'e

Kōke'e State Park

Nāpali-Kona
Forest Reserve

Polihale
State Park

550

WAIMEA CANYON

WAIMEA

Kōke'e Rd.

550

Waimea Canyon Rd.

55

552

50

Menehune
Ditch

KŌLOA

Kekaha Beach
Park

Kekaha

West Kaua'i
Visitor Center
and Technology Center

Waimea

Fort
Elisabeth

50

Hanapēpē
Walking Tour

Hanapēpē
Swinging
Bridge

Hanapēpē Valley
and Canyon Lookout

Kalāheo

530

50

540

Kukuiolono
Park

Lappert's Ice Cream

Hanapēpē

Ele'ele

Port Allen

Salt Pond Beach Park

Burn's Field

Hanapēpē
Bay

Kaua'i Coffee
Visitor Center
and Museum

Kaulakahi Channel

TO
NI'IHAU

0   5 miles

0   5 km

2

WORTH NOTING

Hanapēpē Swinging Bridge. This bridge may not be the biggest adventure on Kaua'i, but it's enough to make your heart hop just a bit. It's considered a historic suspension bridge even though it was rebuilt in 1996 after the original was destroyed—like so much of the island—by Hurricane 'Iniki. What is interesting about this bridge is that it's not just for show; it actually provides the only access to taro fields across the Waimea River. If you're in the neighborhood, it's worth a stroll. ⊠ *Located mauka in downtown Hanapēpē next to Banana Patch Studios' parking lot.*

Hanapēpē Valley and Canyon Lookout. This dramatic divide and fertile river valley once housed a thriving Hawaiian community of taro farmers, with some of the ancient fields still in cultivation today. From the lookout, you can take in the farms on the valley floor with the majestic mountains as a backdrop. ⊠ *Rte. 50.*

Hanapēpē Walking Tour. This self-guided walking tour is about 1½ mi in length and takes you to 14 different plaques with historic photos and stories mounted on buildings throughout Hanapēpē town. Businesses and shops in town sell a map of the tour for $2; however, you can often pick one up for free in many of the area's promotional-brochure rack stands. ⊠ *Hanapēpē town.*

Kukuiolono Park. Translated as "Light of the God Lono," Kukuiolono has serene Japanese gardens, a display of significant Hawaiian stones, and spectacular panoramic views. This quiet hilltop park is one of Kaua'i's most scenic areas and an ideal picnic spot. There's also a small golf course. ⊠ *Pāpālina Rd., Kalāheo* ☎ *808/332–9151* 🎫 *Free* ☉ *Daily 6:30–6:30.*

Salt Pond Beach Park. This popular park lies just west of some privately owned salt ponds where Hawaiians continue the traditional practice of harvesting salt (valued for its culinary and medicinal properties). They let the sun evaporate the seawater in mud-lined drying beds, then gather the salt left behind. You can't visit the ponds, but the beach park's protected swimming cove and campgrounds are worth a stop. ⊠ *Lele Rd., Hanapēpē.*

WAIMEA, WAIMEA CANYON, AND AROUND

Waimea is 7 mi northwest of Hanapēpē; Waimea Canyon is approximately 10 mi north of Waimea.

Waimea is a serene, pretty town that has the look of the Old West and the feel of Old Hawai'i, with a lifestyle that's decidedly laid-back. It's an ideal place for a refreshment break while sightseeing on the West Side. The town played a major role in Hawaiian history since 1778, when Captain James Cook became the first European to set foot on the Hawaiian Islands. Waimea was also the place where Kaua'i's King Kaumuali'i acquiesced to King Kamehameha's unification drive in 1810, averting a bloody war. The town hosted the first Christian missionaries, who hauled in massive timbers and limestone blocks to build the sturdy Waimea Christian Hawaiian and Foreign Church in 1846. It's one of many lovely historic buildings preserved by residents who take great pride in their heritage and history.

KAUA'I'S OWN GRAND CANYON

Fodor's Choice ★ **Waimea Canyon.** Carved over countless centuries by the Waimea River and the forces of wind and rain, Waimea Canyon is a dramatic gorge nicknamed the "Grand Canyon of the Pacific"—and not by Mark Twain, as many people mistakenly think.

Hiking and hunting trails wind through the canyon, which is 3,600 feet deep, 2 mi wide, and 10 mi long. The cliff sides have been sharply eroded, exposing swatches of colorful soil. The deep red, brown, and green hues are constantly changing in the sun, and frequent rainbows and waterfalls enhance the natural beauty.

This is one of Kaua'i's prettiest spots, and it's worth stopping at both the **Pu'u ka Pele** and **Pu'u hinahina** lookouts. Clean public restrooms and parking are at both lookouts.

North of Waimea town, via Route 550, you'll find the vast and gorgeous Waimea Canyon, also known as the Grand Canyon of the Pacific. The spectacular vistas from the lookouts along the road culminate with an overview of Kalalau Valley. There are various hiking trails leading to the inner heart of Kaua'i. A camera is a necessity in this region.

GETTING HERE AND AROUND

Route 50 continues northwest to Waimea and Kekaha from Hanapēpē. You can reach Waimea Canyon and Kōke'e State Park from either town—the way is clearly marked. Some pulloff areas on Route 550 are fine for a quick view of the canyon, but the designated lookouts have bathrooms and parking.

EXPLORING

TOP ATTRACTIONS

★ **Kalalau Lookout.** At the end of the road, high above Waimea Canyon, Kalalau Lookout marks the start of a 1-mi (one-way) hike to **Pu'u o Kila Lookout.** On a clear day at either spot, you can look down at a dreamy landscape of gaping valleys, sawtooth ridges, waterfalls, and turquoise seas, where whales can be seen spouting and breaching during the winter months. If clouds obscure the spectacle, don't despair. They tend to blow through fast, giving you time to snap that photo of a lifetime before the next cloud bank drifts in. You may spot wild goats clambering on the sheer, rocky cliffs, and white tropic birds soaring gracefully on the thermals, their long tails streaming behind them. If it's very clear to the northwest, look for the shining sands of Kalalau Beach, gleaming like golden threads against the deep blue of the Pacific. ⌷ *Waimea Canyon Dr., 4 mi north of Kōke'e State Park.*

★ **Kōke'e State Park.** This 4,345-acre wilderness park is 4,000 feet above sea level, an elevation that affords you breathtaking views in all directions. You can gain a deeper appreciation of the island's rugged terrain and dramatic beauty from this vantage point. Large tracts of native ōhi'a and koa forest cover much of the land, along with many varieties of exotic plants. Hikers can follow a 45-mi network of trails through diverse landscapes that feel wonderfully remote—until the tour helicopters pass

overhead. The state recently introduced a 20-year master plan for the park that included significant development (think a 40- to 60-room lodge in a sacred meadow), but after community input meetings, the plan was scaled back. When you arrive at the park, **Kōke'e Natural History Museum** is a great place to start your visit. The friendly staff is knowledgeable about trail conditions and weather, while informative displays and a good selection of reference books can teach you more about the unique attributes of the native flora and fauna. You may also find that special memento or gift you've been looking for. ⊠ *Rte. 550* ☎ *808/335–9975* ⬛ *Donations accepted* ⊗ *Daily 10–4.*

There's only one place to buy food and hot drinks in Kōke'e State Park, and that's the dining room of rustic **Kōke'e Lodge** (⊠ *Kōke'e State Park, 3600 Kōke'e Rd., mile marker 15* ☎ *808/335–6061* ⊗ *No dinner*). It's known for its corn bread, of all things. Peruse the gift shop for T-shirts, postcards, or campy Kōke'e memorabilia.

Fort Elisabeth. The ruins of this stone fort, built in 1816 by an agent of the imperial Russian government named Anton Scheffer, are reminders of the days when Scheffer tried to conquer the island for his homeland, or so one story goes. Another claims that Scheffer's allegiance lay with King Kaumuali'I, who was attempting to regain leadership of his island nation from the grasp of Kamehameha the Great. The crumbling walls of the fort are not particularly interesting, but the informative placards are. ⊠ *Rte. 50, Waimea.*

WORTH NOTING

Menehune Ditch. Archaeologists claim that this aqueduct was built before the first Hawaiians lived on Kaua'i, and it is therefore attributed to the industrious hands of the legendary, tiny Menehune. The way the flanged and fitted cut-stone bricks are stacked and assembled indicates a knowledge of construction that is foreign to Hawai'i, and the ditch is inscribed with mysterious markings. Until someone comes up with a better explanation, the Menehune retain credit for this engineering feat. ⊠ *Menehune Rd., Waimea Valley.*

West Kaua'i Visitor and Technology Center. Local photos and informational computers with touch screens bring the island's history and attractions to life. Weekly events include lei making, a walking tour, and a crafts fair. Call for a schedule. ⊠ *9565 Kaumuali'i Hwy. (Rte. 50), Waimea* ☎ *808/338–1332* ⊕ *www.wkbpa.org* ⬛ *Free* ⊗ *Weekdays 9:30–5.*

Beaches

WORD OF MOUTH

"An early-morning walk on Kē'ē beach watching the mist rise on
the cliffs is one of my best Kaua'i memories."

—aloha

Join, Ask, Share. www.fodors.com/community/

Updated by
Kim Steuter-
mann Rogers

With more sandy beaches per mile of coastline than any other Hawaiian Island, Kaua'i could be nicknamed the Sandy Island just as easily as it's called the Garden Island. Totaling more than 50 mi, Kaua'i's beaches make up 44% of the island's shoreline—almost twice that of O'ahu, second on this list. It is, of course, because of Kaua'i's age as the eldest sibling of the inhabited Hawaiian Islands, allowing more time for water and wind erosion to break down rock and coral into sand.

But not all Kaua'i's beaches are the same. If you've seen one, you certainly haven't seen them all. Each beach is unique unto itself, for that day, that hour. Conditions, scenery, and intrigue can change throughout the day and certainly throughout the year, transforming, say, a tranquil lakelike ocean setting in summer into monstrous waves drawing internationally ranked surfers from around the world in winter.

There are sandy beaches, rocky beaches, wide beaches, narrow beaches, skinny beaches, and alcoves. Generally speaking, surf kicks up on the North Shore in winter and the South Shore in summer, although summer's southern swells aren't nearly as frequent or big as the northern winter swells that attract those surfers. Kaua'i's longest and widest beaches are found on the North Shore and West Side and are popular with beachgoers, although during winter's rains, everyone heads to the dry West Side. The East Side beaches tend to be narrower and have onshore winds less popular with sunbathers, yet fishers abound. Smaller coves are characteristic of the South Shore and attract all kinds of water lovers year-round, including monk seals.

In Hawai'i, all beaches are public, but their accessibility varies greatly. Some require an easy ½-mi stroll, some require a four-wheel-drive vehicle, others require boulder-hopping, and one takes an entire day of serious hiking. And then there are those "drive-in" beaches onto which you can literally pull up and park your car. Kaua'i is not Disneyland, so don't expect much signage to help you along the way. One of the top-ranked beaches in the whole world—Hanalei—doesn't have a single sign in town directing you to the beach. Furthermore, the majority of Kaua'i's beaches are remote, offering no facilities. ■ TIP➔ If you want the convenience of restrooms, picnic tables, and the like, stick to county beach parks.

THE NORTH SHORE

If you've ever dreamed of Hawai'i—and who hasn't—you've dreamed of Kaua'i's North Shore. *Lush, tropical,* and *abundant* are just a few words to describe this rugged and dramatic area. And the views to the

No matter what time of year you visit Kaua'i, there's a good chance you'll have a beach all to yourself.

sea aren't the only attraction—the inland views of velvety-green valley folds and carved mountain peaks will take your breath away. Rain is the reason for all the greenery on the North Shore, and winter is the rainy season. Not to worry, though; it rarely rains *everywhere* on the island at one time. ■TIP→ The rule of thumb is to head south or west when it rains in the north.

The waves on the North Shore can be big—and we mean huge—in winter, drawing crowds to witness nature's spectacle. By contrast, in summer the waters can be completely serene.

Fodor's Choice
★

Kalalau. This oft-described Garden of Eden awaits the intrepid hiker who traverses 11 arduous miles along sea cliff faces, through muddy coastal valleys, and across sometimes-raging streams—all the while schlepping food provisions and camping gear. The trek requires 6 to 10 hours of hiking, making it an adventure indeed. With serious planning and preparation, the effort is worth it. Another option is to paddle in to the beach—summer only, though; otherwise the surf is way too big. Located at the end of the trail with the same name, Kalalau is a remote, wilderness beach along the 15 mi of spectacular Nāpali Coast, itself a 6,500-acre state park. The beach is anchored by a *heiau* (a stone platform used as a place of worship) on one end and a waterfall on the other. The safest hiking to and swimming at the beach takes place during the summer months when the rains abate, so the trail can dry out, and when the North Shore's famous winter surf recedes, revealing an expansive beach cupped by low, vegetated sand dunes and a large walk-in cave on the western edge. Day hikes into the valley offer waterfalls, freshwater swimming pools, and wild, tropical fruits, as well as illegal campers

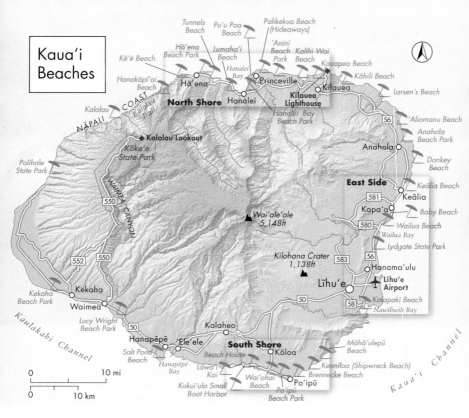

**Kaua'i
Beaches**

Tunnels
Beach
Pu'u Poa
Beach
Palikekua Beach
(Hideaways)
Hā'ena
Beach Park
Lumaha'i
Beach
'Anini
Beach
Kalihi Wai
Kalihi Wai
Park
Beach
Kauapea Beach
Kē'ē Beach
Kāhili Beach
Hanalei
Bay
Princeville
Kīlauea
Hanakāpī'ai
Beach
Hā'ena
North Shore
Hanalei
**Kīlauea
Lighthouse**
Larsen's Beach
Kalalau
Hanalei Bay
Beach Park
56
'Aliomanu Beach
Kalalau Lookout
Anahola
Beach Park
Kōke'e
State Park
Anahola
Donkey
Beach
Wai'ale'ale
5,148ft
East Side
Keālia Beach
581
Keālia
Kapa'a
Baby Beach
580
Wailua Beach
Wailua Bay
Lydgate State Park
Kilohana Crater
1,138ft
583
56
Hanama'ulu
Līhu'e
Līhu'e
Airport
50
Kekaha
Beach Park
Kekaha
Waimea
58
Kalapakī Beach
Nawiliwili Bay
Lucy Wright
Beach Park
50
Kalaheo
Hanapēpē
Ele'ele
South Shore
Māhā'ulepū
Beach
Koloa
Beach House
Salt Pond
Beach
Hanapēpē
Bay
Lawa'i
Kai
Keoniloa (Shipwreck Beach)
Brennecke Beach
Wai'ohai
Beach
Po'ipū
Kukui'ula Small
Boat Harbor
Po'ipū
Beach Park

Polihale
State Park
NĀPALI COAST
Kalalau Trail
WAIMEA CANYON
550
552
550
Kaulakahi Channel
Kaua'i Channel

0   10 mi
0   10 km

forsaking society. Don't be mistaken: Camping permits are required. ⊠ *Trailhead starts at end of Rte. 560, 7 mi west of Hanalei* ⊕ *www. hawaiistateparks.org* ☞ *No facilities.*

Hanakāpī'ai Beach. If you're not up for the 11-mi haul to Kalalau Beach, then hike 2 mi along Nāpali Coast's Kalalau Trail to Hanakāpī'ai Beach. It'll take about 1½ hours. Just don't get in the water. Ever. The water here is what locals like to call "confused." It has something to do with the radical change in water depth and sheer cliff walls creating wicked currents, rogue waves, backwash, undertow, cross waves, and rip currents. Instead, enjoy a picnic away from the ocean's edge. In the winter when the surf eats up the beach, this might mean perching on the lava-rock boulders backing the sand. To reach the beach, you'll have to boulder-hop across a stream. During heavy rains or even just after, the stream can flood, stranding hikers on the wrong side. This has resulted in helicopter rescues, so don't cross unless the boulders are visibly exposed. ⊠ *Trailhead starts at end of Rte. 560, 7 mi west of Hanalei* ⊕ *www.hawaiistateparks.org* ☞ *No facilities.*

Kē'ē Beach. Highway 560 on the North Shore literally dead-ends at this beach, which is also the trailhead for the famous Kalalau Trail and the site of an ancient *heiau* dedicated to hula. The beach is protected by a reef—except during high surf—creating a small sandy-bottom lagoon

North Shore Kaua'i

and making it a popular snorkeling destination. If there's a current, it's usually found on the western edge of the beach as the incoming tide ebbs back out to sea. Makana (a prominent peak also known as Bali Hai after the blockbuster musical *South Pacific*) is so artfully arranged, you'll definitely want to capture the memory, so don't forget your camera. The popularity of this beach makes parking difficult. ■TIP→ **Start extra early or, better yet, arrive at the end of the day, in time to witness otherworldly sunsets sidelighting Nāpali Coast.** ⊠ *End of Rte. 560, 7 mi west of Hanalei,* ☞ *Lifeguard, toilets, showers, parking lot.*

BEACHES KEY	
👫	*Restroom*
🚿	*Showers*
🏄	*Surfing*
🤿	*Snorkel/Scuba*
🧒	*Good for kids*
P	*Parking*

Fodor'sChoice
★
Hā'ena Beach Park *(Tunnels Beach).* This is a drive-up beach park popular with campers year-round. The wide bay here—named Mākua and commonly known as Tunnels—is bordered by two large reef systems creating favorable waves for surfing during peak winter conditions. In July and August, waters at this same beach are as calm as a lake, usually, and snorkelers enjoy the variety of fish life found in a hook-shape reef made up of underwater lava tubes, on the east end of the bay. ■TIP→ **During the summer months only, this is the premier snorkeling site on Kaua'i.** It's not unusual to find a food vendor parked here selling sandwiches and drinks out of a converted bread van. ⊠ *Near end of Rte. 560, across from lava-tube sea caves, after stream crossing* ☞ *Lifeguard, toilets, showers, food concession, picnic tables, grills/firepits, parking lot, camping.*

Lumaha'i Beach. Famous because it's the beach where Nurse Nellie washes that man out of her hair in *South Pacific,* Lumaha'i Beach's setting is all you've ever dreamed Hawai'i to be. That's the drawing card, and if you're adventurous and safety-conscious, a visit here is definitely worth it. The challenges are that it's hard to find, there's little parking, and there's a steep hike in; also, too many people misjudge the waves, even those never intending to set foot in the water. There's a year-round surge of onshore waves, massive sand movements (especially around the river mouth), and a steep foreshore assaulted by strong currents. Like the mythical creature from the deep, rogue waves have actually washed up on lava-rock outcroppings and pulled sightseers out to sea. Our advice: Look from the safety of the scenic overlook or walk on *dry* sand only; play in the water at another beach. ⊠ *On winding section of Rte. 560 west of Hanalei, east of mile marker 5. Park on makai side of road and walk down steep path to beach,* ☞ *No facilities.*

DID YOU KNOW?

Hanakāpī'ai Beach, 2 mi along the Kalalau Trail, is a good place to stop and have a picnic. But don't hop in for a swim—unpredictable tides and high surf make the water here very dangerous.

♻ **Hanalei Bay Beach Park**. This 2-mi,

Fodor's Choice crescent-shape beach surrounds a

★ spacious bay that is quintessential
Hawai'i. After gazing out to sea and
realizing you have truly arrived in
paradise, look landward. The sight
of the mountains, ribboned with
waterfalls, will take your breath
away. All this beauty accounts for

why coastal expert "Dr. Beach" named Hanalei the number one in the
U.S. in 2009. In winter Hanalei Bay boasts some of the biggest onshore
surf breaks in the state, attracting world-class surfers. Luckily, the beach
is wide enough to have safe real estate for your beach towel even in
winter. In summer the bay is transformed—calm waters lap the beach,
sailboats moor in the bay, and outrigger-canoe paddlers ply the sea.
Hanalei Bay is worth scheduling for an entire day, maybe two. ⊠ *In
Hanalei, turn makai at Aku Rd. and drive 1 block to Weli Weli Rd.
Parking areas are on makai side of Weli Weli Rd.* ☞ *Lifeguard, toilets,
showers, picnic tables, grills/firepits, parking lot, camping.*

Pu'u Poa Beach. The coastline along the community of Princeville is
primarily made up of sea cliffs with a couple of pockets of beaches.
The sea cliffs end with a long, narrow stretch of beach just east of the
Hanalei River and at the foot of the St. Regis Princeville Resort. Public
access is via 100-plus steps around the back of the hotel; hotel guests
can simply take the elevator down to sea level. The beach itself is subject
to the hazards of winter's surf, narrowing and widening with the surf
height. On calm days, snorkeling is good thanks to a shallow reef system pocked with sand. Sometimes a shallow sandbar extends across the
river to Black Pot Beach Park, part of the Hanalei Beach system, making
it easy to cross the river. On high-surf days, the outer edge of the reef
near the river draws internationally ranked surfers. The resort's pool is
off-limits to nonguests, but the restaurants and bars are not. ⊠ *Follow
Ka Haku Rd. to end; park in public parking on right just before hotel's
entrance; cross street for beach access* ☞ *Parking lot.*

Pali Ke Kua Beach *(Hideaways Beach)*. This is actually two very small
pocket beaches separated by a narrow rocky point. The beach area
itself is narrow and can all but disappear in wintertime. However, in
summer, the steep, rocky trail (don't trust the rusty handrails and rot-
ting ropes) that provides access reduces the number of beachgoers,
helping to create a deserted beach feel. With patches of reef and a
combination sandy/rocky bottom, the swimming and snorkeling can
be good, although winter's high surf can create dangerous conditions.
■ TIP→ Don't attempt the trail after a heavy rain—it turns into a mudslide.
⊠ *Follow Ka Haku Rd. to end; park in public parking on right just
before hotel's entrance; follow dirt trail between parking lot and condominium complex* ☞ *Parking lot.*

♻ **'Anini Beach Park**. A great family park, 'Anini is unique in that it features
one of the longest and widest fringing reefs in all Hawai'i, creating a shallow lagoon that's good for snorkeling and quite safe in all but the highest
of winter surf. The reef follows the shoreline for some 2 mi and extends

BEACH SAFETY ON KAUA'I

Hawai'i's world-renowned, beautiful beaches can be extremely dangerous at times due to large waves and strong currents—so much so that the state rates wave hazards using three signs: a yellow square (caution), a red stop sign (high hazard), and a black diamond (extreme hazard). Signs are posted and updated three times daily or as conditions change.

Visiting beaches with lifeguards is strongly recommended, and you should swim only when there's a normal caution rating. Never swim alone or dive into unknown water or shallow breaking waves. If you're unable to swim out of a rip current, tread water and wave your arms in the air to signal for help.

Even in calm conditions, there are other dangerous things in the water to be aware of, including razor-sharp coral, jellyfish, eels, and sharks, to name a few.

Jellyfish cause the most ocean injuries, and signs are posted along beaches when they're present. Reactions to a sting are usually mild (burning sensation, redness, welts); however, in some cases they can be severe (breathing difficulties). If you're stung, pick off the tentacles, rinse the affected area with water, and apply ice.

The chances of getting bitten by a shark in Hawaiian waters are very low; sharks attack swimmers or surfers three or four times per year. Of the 40 species of sharks found near Hawai'i, tiger sharks are considered the most dangerous because of their size and indiscriminate feeding behavior. They're easily recognized by their blunt snouts and vertical bars on their sides.

Here are a few tips to reduce your shark-attack risk:

- Swim, surf, or dive with others at beaches patrolled by lifeguards.

- Avoid swimming at dawn, dusk, and night, when some shark species may move inshore to feed.

- Don't enter the water if you have open wounds or are bleeding.

- Avoid murky waters, harbor entrances, areas near stream mouths (especially after heavy rains), channels, or steep drop-offs.

- Don't wear high-contrast swimwear or shiny jewelry.

- Don't swim near dolphins, which are often prey for large sharks.

- If you spot a shark, leave the water quickly and calmly; never provoke or harass a shark, no matter how small.

The Web site ⊕ www.oceansafety. soest.hawaii.edu/index.asp provides statewide beach hazard maps as well as weather and surf advisories.

1,600 feet offshore at its widest point. During times of low tide—usually occurring around the full moon of the summer months—much of the reef is exposed. 'Anini is inarguably the windsurfing mecca of Kaua'i, even for beginners, and it also attracts participants in the growing sport of kiteboarding. ■ TIP→ Try the Sara Special at the lone food vendor here— 'Anini Beach Lunch Shak, which is really a lunch wagon. ⊠ *Turn makai off Rte. 56 onto Kalihiwai Rd., on Hanalei side of Kalihiwai Bridge; follow road left at "Y" to reach 'Anini Rd. and beach* ⌒ *Toilets, showers,*

food concession, picnic tables, grills/ firepits, parking lot, camping.

Kalihiwai Beach. A winding road leads down a cliff face to this picture-perfect beach. A jewel of the North Shore, Kalihiwai Beach is on par with Hanalei, just without the waterfall-ribbon backdrop. It's another one of those drive-up beaches, so it's very accessible. Most people park on the sand under the grove of ironwood trees. Families set up camp for the day at the west end of the beach, near the stream, where young kids like to splash and older kids like to body board. This is also a good spot to disembark for a kayaking adventure up the stream. It's not a long paddle, but it's calm,

so it's perfect for beginning paddlers. On the eastern edge of the beach, from which the road descends, there's a locals' favorite surf spot during winter's high surf. The onshore break can be dangerous during this time. During the calmer months of summer, Kalihiwai Beach is a good choice for beginning board riders and swimmers. The toilets here are the portable kind. ⊠ *Turn makai off Rte. 56 onto Kalihiwai Rd., on Kīlauea side of Kalihiwai Bridge* ☞ *Toilets, parking lot.*

Kauapea Beach (*Secret Beach*). This beach went relatively unknown—except by some intrepid fishermen, of course—for a long time, hence the common reference to it as "Secret Beach." You'll understand why once you stand on the shore of Kauapea and see the solid wall of rock 100 feet high, maybe more, that cups the length of the beach, making it fairly inaccessible. For the hardy, there is a steep hike down the western end. From there, if you make the long trek across the beach—toward Kīlauea Point National Wildlife Refuge—and if you arrive just after sunrise, you may witness a school of dolphins just offshore. You may also run across a gathering of another kind on the beach—nudists. Because of its remote location, Kauapea is popular with nude sunbathers, although the county is trying to curtail the shedding of clothes here. A consistent on-shore break makes swimming here questionable. ⊠ *Turn makai on Kalihiwai Rd. just past the turnoff for Kīlauea; take second dirt road to its end; park and follow dirt trail* ☞ *Parking lot.*

★ **Kāhili Beach** (*Rock Quarry*). You wouldn't know it today, but this beach on Kīlauea Bay was once an interisland steamer landing and a rock quarry. Today, it's a fairly quiet beach, although when the surf closes out many other North Shore surf spots, the break directly offshore from Kīlauea Stream near the abandoned quarry is still rideable. For the regular oceangoer, summer's your best bet, although the quickly sloping ocean bottom doesn't make for great swimming or snorkeling. The stream estuary is quite beautiful, and the ironwood trees and false kamani growing in the generous sand dunes at the rear of the beach provide protection from the sun. Kids like to play here, as do soaring great frigate birds overhead. In March 2006, the streambed emptying into the ocean here grew to immense proportions when Ka Loko Dam broke, sending a wall of water—as well as life and property—to the sea. ⊠ *Turn makai on Wailapa Rd.; drive for ½ mi and turn left on dirt road, following it to its end* ☞ *No facilities.*

Larsen's Beach. The long, wide fringing reef here is this beach's trademark. The waters near shore are often too shallow for swimming; if you go in, wear a rash guard to protect against prickly sea urchins on the bottom. High surf during the winter of 2009 blew out a section of reef, creating some tricky currents for the novice oceangoer. Like many other North Shore beaches, this one requires a hike, although it's not as steep as others. ⊠ *Turn makai at north intersection of Ko'lau Rd., drive 1¼ mi to dirt turnoff on left marked by a slender pole and a "beach access" sign in yellow lettering, and park at end of road* ☞ *Parking lot.*

THE EAST SIDE

The East Side of the island is considered the "windward" side, a term you'll often hear in weather forecasts. It simply means the side of the island receiving onshore winds. The wind helps break down rock into sand, so there are plenty of beaches here. Unfortunately, only a few of those beaches are protected, so many are not ideal for beginning ocean goers, though they are perfect for long sunrise ambles. On super-windy days, kiteboarders sail along the east shore, sometimes jumping waves and performing acrobatic maneuvers in the air.

'Aliomanu Beach. Because of the time change, most visitors to Hawai'i awake before the sun rises. Enjoy those early hours by heading to the easily accessible and lesser-known 'Aliomanu Beach for a long morning walk and witness that great, orange orb emerging over the ocean's horizon. The waters off 'Aliomanu Beach are protected by the fringing reef 100 yards or so out to sea, making snorkeling as good as at many more popular areas; however, currents can be tricky, especially near the stream tucked in the beach's elbow toward the northern end, and at the river mouth on the southern end that demarcates 'Aliomanu Beach from its neighbor Anahola Beach. A good walk is to start at the river mouth and head north, skirting a seawall midway; aqua shoes are recommended, especially for rounding the rocky point at the northern tip. ■TIP➔ With its shallow waters, this is a popular fishing and family beach, so stick to weekdays if you want quiet. ⊠ *Turn makai just north of*

BEST BEACHES

He says "to-mah-toe," and she says "to-may-toe." When it comes to beaches on Kaua'i, the meaning behind that axiom holds true: People are different. What rocks one person's world wreaks havoc for another. Here are some additional tips on how to choose a beach that's right for you.

BEST FOR FAMILIES

Lydgate State Park, East Side. The kid-designed playground, the protected swimming pools, and Kamalani Bridge guarantee you will not hear these words from your child: "Mom, I'm bored."

Po'ipū Beach Park, Po'ipū, South Shore. The *keiki* (children's) pool and lifeguards make this a safe spot for kids. The near-perpetual sun isn't so bad, either.

BEST STAND-UP PADDLING

'Anini Beach Park, North Shore. The reef and long stretch of beach give beginners to stand-up paddling a calm place to give this new sport a try. You won't get pummeled by waves here.

Wailua Beach, East Side. On the East Side, the Wailua River bisects the beach and heads inland 2 mi, providing stand-up paddlers with a long and scenic stretch of water before they have to figure out how to turn around.

BEST SURFING

Hanalei Bay Beach Park, North Shore. In the winter, Hanalei Bay offers a range of breaks, from beginner to advanced. You may even see the Irons Brothers—international surf champions—paddling out here. They grew up surfing these waters.

Wai'ohai Beach, South Shore. Surf instructors flock to this spot with their students for its gentle, near-shore break. Then, as students advance, they can paddle out a little farther to an intermediate break—if they dare.

BEST SUNSETS

Kē'ē Beach, North Shore. Even in the winter, when the sun sets in the south and out of view, you won't be disappointed here, because the "magic hour," as photographers call the time around sunset, paints Nāpali Coast with a warm gold light.

Polihale State Park, West Side. This due-west-facing beach may be tricky to get to, but it does offer the most unobstructed sunset views on the island. The fact that it's so remote means you won't have strangers in your photos, but you will want to depart right after sunset or risk getting lost in the dark.

BEST FOR SEEING AND BEING SEEN

Hā'ena Beach Park, North Shore. Behind those gated driveways and heavily foliaged yards that line this beach live—at least, part-time—some of the world's most celebrated music and movie moguls. Need we say more?

Hanalei Bay Beach Park, North Shore. We know we tout this beach often, but it deserves the praise. It's a mecca for everyone—regular joes, surfers, fishers, young, old, locals, visitors, and, especially, the famous. Could you recognize Jennifer Aniston and Courteney Cox? How about Pierce Brosnan and Ben Stiller? They—and more—have frequented this beach.

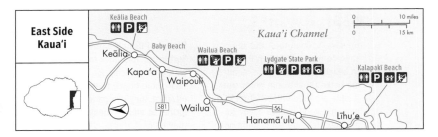

mile marker 14 on 'Aliomanu Rd.; park in dirt parking lot where road bends 90 degrees to the left ☞ Parking lot.

Anahola Beach Park. Anahola is known as the most Hawaiian of all communities on Kaua'i, so Anahola Beach Park is definitely a locals' hangout, especially for families with small children. A child's first birthday is considered a big bash (including rented tents, picnic tables, and catered lū'au food) for family and friends in Hawai'i, and this is a popular location for the celebration. The shallow and calm water at the beach road's end is tucked behind a curving finger of land and perfect for young ones. As the beach winds closer to the river mouth, there's less protection and a shore break favorable for body boarders if the trades are light or kona winds are present. Children like to frolic in the river, and pole fishermen often set up at the river mouth. On Tuesday and Thursday at 5 PM, Puna Dawson's hula *hālau* (school) meets and welcomes visitors to watch and participate. If you come at sunrise, the view of Kalalea Mountains with the Anahola River trailing in front of it makes for a good photographic opportunity. ✉ *Turn makai just south of mile marker 14 on Anahola Rd. and drive 1 mi ☞ Lifeguard, toilets, showers, picnic tables, grills/firepits, parking lot, camping.*

Donkey Beach. This beach has one of the most unusual names of all on Kaua'i and is rarely known by its proper Hawaiian name, Palikū. Līh'ue Plantation Company once kept a herd of mules and donkeys in the pasture adjacent to the beach, hence the nickname. It's a popular spot for au naturel sunbathers, and if the waves are right, body boarders and surfers might be spotted offshore. However, the waters here are rough and not recommended for swimming and snorkeling. Instead, we suggest a morning walk or mountain-bike trek along the easy trail that overlooks the beach. Start at the northern end of Keālia Beach (or in Kapa'a town for a longer walk or bike ride) and head north. The trail splinters just past Donkey Beach and then splinters again; however, it does go all the way to Anahola Beach. ✉ *Just north of Keālia Kai subdivision entrance on Rte. 56, turn makai into parking lot. Hike down to beach ☞ Toilets, parking lot.*

Keālia Beach. A half mile long and adjacent to the highway heading north out of Kapa'a, Keālia Beach attracts body boarders and surfers year-round (possibly because the local high school is just up the hill). Keālia is not generally a great beach for swimming or snorkeling. The waters are usually rough and the waves crumbly because of an onshore break (no protecting reef) and northeasterly trade winds. A scenic lookout

KAUA'I'S BEST SWIMMING HOLES

You don't have to head to the beach to go swimming, and we're not talking chlorinated swimming pools, either. There are so many beaches and swimming holes around Kaua'i that you should never have to set foot in chlorine. But there's a difference between swimming in the ocean at the beach and swimming in these spots. These tend to be more remote, and—as the term *swimming hole* implies—they are enclosed. That doesn't mean they're safer than swimming in the ocean, with its possible rips and currents. Never dive—hidden boulders abound. Wear protective footwear—those boulders can have sharp edges. Stay away during or just after heavy rains and high surf, and do not take a shower under waterfalls, as tempting as it may sound, because you never know when a rock will come tumbling down.

Keāhua Forestry Arboretum. Not the deepest of swimming holes, this is, however, a good choice for families. The cascading stream makes for a fun spot for kids to splash. Stay away during heavy rains, as flash flooding does occur. ✉ *In Wailua, take Kuamoo Rd. mauka 6½ mi.*

Kipu Falls. This is a swimming hole extraordinaire, because as well as swimming, the more adventurous will enjoy leaping off the 25-foot waterfall or entering the water via a swinging rope. Although it's on private property, the owners have yet to fence off access. A dirt trail approximately ½ mi in length leads to the falls. ■TIP→ A fair number of injuries occur here. If you use this swimming hole, err on the side of safety. ✉ *From Hwy. 50, at mile marker 3 turn makai onto Kipu Road. Take first right to stay on Kipu Road and drive ½ mi, park on side of road, and follow dirt trail to the falls.*

Queen's Bath. Listen to us when we tell you not to attempt this in winter. This is one of those places where rogue waves like to roam; unfortunately, so do people. Several have drowned here during North Shore swells, so always check ocean conditions. During summer, this is an experience unlike many others around Kaua'i, as the winter surf recedes, revealing a lava shelf with two good-size holes for swimming—sometimes even snorkeling. Turtles cruise in and out, too, via an underwater entry. It's said that Queen Emma once bathed here; hence, the name. The trail down is short but steep; then there's a section of lava-rock scrambling before you get to the swimming holes. Over the years, the county has periodically closed access due to safety reasons and residents' complaints. Access is in tony Princeville, amid private residences, so be sure to park only in the designated spot. If it's full, do not park on the street, and do not park on anyone's lawn or driveway. ✉ *In Princeville from Ka Haku Rd., turn makai on Punahele and right on Kapi'olani.*

Uluwehi Falls. If you paddle upriver a couple of miles and hike a mile or so inland, you'll discover the 120-foot Uluwehi Falls, more commonly known as Secret Falls, with a big swimming area. Now, you could do this on your own—if you're familiar with the river and the trail; however, we recommend hiring one of the many Wailua River kayak guides so you don't get lost.

In front of the Kaua'i Marriott, Kalapakī Beach is usually a safe bet for swimming and water sports.

on the southern end, accessed off the highway, is a superb location for saluting the morning sunrise or spotting whales during winter. A level, paved trail follows the coastline north and is one of the most scenic coastal trails on the island for walking, running, and biking. ⊠ *At mile marker 10 on Rte. 56* ☞ *Lifeguard, toilets, showers, picnic tables, parking lot.*

☺ **Baby Beach.** There aren't many swimming beaches on Kaua'i's East Side; however, this one usually ranks highly with mothers of small children because there's a narrow lagoonlike area between the beach and the near-shore reef perfect for small children. Of course, in winter, watch for east and northeast swells that would not make this such a safe option. There are no beach facilities—no lifeguards, so watch your babies. ⊠ *In Kapa'a, turn mauka at the Chevron gas station onto Keaka Rd., then left on Moa-makai Rd. Parking is off-street between Makaha and Panihi Rds.*

Wailua Beach. Some say the first Polynesians to migrate to Hawai'i landed at Wailua Beach. At the river's mouth, petroglyphs carved on boulders are sometimes visible during low surf and tide conditions. Surfers, body boarders, and bodysurfers alike enjoy this beach year-round thanks to its dependable waves (usually on the north end); however, because of Hawai'i's northeast trade winds, these waves are not the "cleanest" for surf aficionados. Many families spend the day under the Wailua Bridge at the river mouth, even hauling out their portable grills and tables to go with their beach chairs. During summer months, outrigger canoe races are often held on the river, which happens to be the largest in all Hawai'i. Numerous tour outfitters offer kayaking and hiking expeditions up the river. There are even waterskiing boats for hire and, more

The beach at Salt Pond Beach Park is worth a stop for its protected swimming cove.

popular, tour boats running to the Fern Grotto, an amphitheater-shape cave with perfect acoustics and, as the name implies, ferns growing everywhere, even from the ceiling. The great news about Wailua Beach is that it's almost impossible to miss; however, parking can be a challenge. ⊠ *The best parking for the north end of the beach is on Papaloa Rd. behind the Shell station. For the southern end of the beach, the best parking is in the Wailua River State Park (where the toilets—the portable kind—are also found); to get there, turn mauka on Kuamoʻo Rd. and left into the park, then walk along the river and under the bridge* ☞ *Toilets, showers, parking lot.*

Lydgate State Park. This is hands-down the best family beach park on Kauaʻi. The waters off the beach are protected by a hand-built break-water creating two boulder-enclosed saltwater pools for safe swimming and snorkeling just about year-round (although after heavy rains, river debris collects here, contaminating the water). The smaller of the two is perfect for *keiki* (children). Behind the beach is Kamalani Playground, designed by the children of Kauaʻi and built by the community. Children of all ages—that includes you—enjoy the swings, lava-tube slides, tree-house, and more. Picnic tables abound in the park, and a large covered pavilion is available by permit for celebrations. Kamalani Bridge is a second playground—also built by the community and based on the children's design—south of the original. (The two are united by a bike and pedestrian path that is part of the Nāwiliwili-to-Anahola path project currently under construction.) There used to be a second, smaller pavilion that was surrounded by campsites. Unfortunately, however, in early 2007 the pavilion burned, the result of a bonfire gone awry. Those perfectly built campsites are now sitting vacant while the county council irons out security concerns. ■TIP→ This park system is perennially popular; the quietest times to visit are early mornings and weekdays. If you want to witness a "baby lūʻau," Lydgate State Park attracts them year-round, especially in summers. ⊠ *Just south of Wailua River, turn makai off Rte. 56 onto Lehu Dr. and left onto Nalu Rd.* ☞ *Lifeguard, toilets, showers, picnic tables, grills/firepits, playgrounds, parking lot.*

Ⓒ ★ **Kalapakī Beach.** Five minutes south of the airport in Līhuʻe, you'll find this wide, sandy-bottom beach fronting the Kauaʻi Marriott. One of the big attractions is that this beach is almost always safe from rip currents and undertow because it's around the backside of a peninsula, in its own cove. There are tons of activities here, including all the usual water sports—beginning and intermediate surfing, stand up paddling, body boarding, bodysurfing, and swimming—plus, there are two outrigger canoe clubs paddling in the bay and the Nāwiliwili Yacht Club's boats sailing around the harbor. Kalapakī is the only place on Kauaʻi where sailboats—in this case Hobie Cats—are available for rent (at Kauaʻi Beach Boys, which fronts the beach next to Duke's Canoe Club restaurant). Visitors can also rent snorkel gear, surfboards, body boards, and kayaks from Kauaʻi Beach Boys. A volleyball court on the beach is often used by a loosely organized group of local players; visitors are always welcome. ■TIP→ Families prefer the stream end of the beach, whereas those seeking more solitude prefer the cliff side of the beach. Duke's Canoe Club restaurant is one of only a couple of restaurants on the island actually on a beach; the restaurant's lower level is casual, even welcoming beach attire and sandy feet, perfect for lunch or an afternoon cocktail. ⊠ *Off Wapaʻa Rd., which runs from Līhuʻe to Nāwiliwili* ☞ *Toilets, food concession, picnic tables, grills/firepits, parking lot.*

THE SOUTH SHORE

The South Shore's primary access road is Highway 520, a tree-lined, two-lane, windy road. As you drive along it, there's a sense of tunneling down a rabbit hole into another world, à la Alice. And the South Shore is certainly a wonderland. On average, it rains only 30 inches per year, so if you're looking for fun in the sun, this is a good place to start. The beaches with their powdery-fine sand are consistently good year-round, except during high surf, which, if it hits at all, will be in summer. If you want solitude, this isn't it; if you want excitement—well, as much excitement as quiet Kauaʻi offers—this is the place for you.

Fodorʻs Choice ★ **Māhāʻulepū Beach.** This 2-mi stretch of coast with its sand dunes, limestone hills, sinkholes, and caves is unlike any other on Kauaʻi. Remains of a large, ancient settlement, evidence of great battles, and the discovery of a now-underwater petroglyph field indicate that Hawaiians lived in this area as early as 700 AD. Māhāʻulepūʻs coastline is unprotected and rocky, which makes venturing into the ocean hazardous. There are three beach areas with bits of sandy-bottom swimming; however, we think the best way to experience Māhāʻulepū is simply to roam, especially at sunrise. ■TIP→ Access to this beach is via private property. The owner allows access during daylight hours, but be sure to depart before sunset or risk getting locked in for the night. ⊠ *Continue on Poʻipū Rd.*

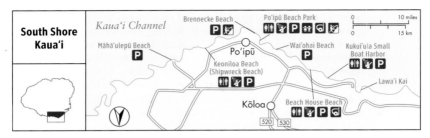

past Hyatt (it turns into dirt road) to T-intersection and turn makai; road ends at beach parking area ☞ Parking lot.

Keoniloa Beach *(Shipwreck Beach)*. Few except the public-relations specialists at the Grand Hyatt Kaua'i Resort and Spa—which backs the beach—refer to this beach by anything other than its common name: Shipwreck Beach. Its Hawaiian name means "long beach." Both make sense. It is a long stretch of crescent-shape beach punctuated by cliffs on both ends, and, yes, a ship was once wrecked here. With its onshore break, the waters off Shipwreck are best for body boarding and bodysurfing; however, the beach itself is plenty big for sunbathing, sand castle–building, Frisbee, and other beach-related fun. Fishermen pole-fish from shore and off the cliff and sometimes pick *opihi* (limpets) off the rocks lining the foot of the cliffs. The eastern edge of the beach is the start of an interpretive dune walk (complimentary) held by the hotel staff; check with the concierge for dates and times. ✉ *Continue on Po'ipū Rd. past Hyatt, turn makai on 'Āinako Rd.* ☞ *Toilets, showers, parking lot.*

Brennecke Beach. There's little beach here on the eastern end of Po'ipū Beach Park, but Brennecke Beach is synonymous on the island with surfing and bodysurfing, thanks to its shallow sandbar and reliable shore break. Because the beach is small and often congested, surfboards are prohibited near shore. The water on the rocky eastern edge of the beach is a good place to see the endangered green sea turtles noshing on plants growing on the rocks. ✉ *Turn makai off Po'ipū Rd. onto Ho'owili Rd., then left onto Ho'ōne Rd.; beach is at intersection with Kuai Rd.* ☞ *Picnic tables, parking lot.*

Ⓒ ★ **Po'ipū Beach Park.** The most popular beach on the South Side, and perhaps on all of Kaua'i, is Po'ipū Beach Park. The snorkeling's good, the body boarding's good, the surfing's good, the swimming's good, and the fact that the sun is almost always shining is good, too. The beach can be crowded at times, especially on weekends and holidays, but that just makes people-watching that much more fun. You'll see *keiki* (children) experiencing the ocean for the first time, snorkelers trying to walk with their flippers on, 'ukulele players, birthday-party revelers, young and old, visitors and locals. Even the endangered Hawaiian monk seal often makes an appearance. ✉ *From Po'ipū Rd., turn right on Ho'ōne Rd.* ☞ *Lifeguard, toilets, showers, food concession, picnic tables, grills/firepits, playground, parking lot.*

Wai'ohai Beach. The first hotel built in Po'ipū in 1962 overlooked this beach, adjacent to Po'ipū Beach Park. Actually, there's little to distinguish where one starts and the other begins other than a crescent-shape

CLOSE UP

Seal-Spotting on the South Shore

When strolling on one of Kaua'i's lovely beaches, don't be surprised if you find yourself in the rare company of Hawaiian monk seals. These are among the most endangered of all marine mammals, with perhaps fewer than 1,200 remaining. They primarily inhabit the northwestern Hawaiian Islands, although more are showing their sweet faces on the main Hawaiian Islands, especially on Kaua'i. They're fond of hauling out on the beach for a long snooze in the sun, particularly after a night of gorging on fish. They need this time to rest and digest, safe from predators.

During the past several summers, female seals have birthed young on the beaches around Kaua'i, where they stay to nurse their pups for upward of six weeks. It seems the seals enjoy particular beaches for the same reasons we do: the shallow, protected waters.

If you're lucky enough to see a monk seal, keep your distance and let it be. Although they may haul out near people, they still want and need their space. Stay several hundred feet away, and forget photos unless you've got a zoom lens. It's illegal to do anything that causes a monk seal to change its behavior, with penalties that include big fines and even jail time. In the water, seals may appear to want to play. It's their curious nature. Don't try to play with them. They are wild animals—mammals, in fact, with teeth. If you have concerns about the health or safety of a seal, or just want more information, contact the **Hawaiian Monk Seal Conservation Hui** (☎ *808/651–7668* ⊕ *www.kauaiseals.com*).

---

reef at the eastern end of Wai'ohai Beach. That crescent, however, is important. It creates a small, protected bay—good for snorkeling and beginning surfers. If you're a beginner, this is the spot. However, when a summer swell kicks up, the near-shore conditions become dangerous; offshore, there's a splendid surf break for experienced surfers. The beach itself is narrow and, like its neighbor, gets very crowded in summer. ⊠ *From Po'ipū Rd., turn right on Ho'ōne Rd.* ☞ *Parking lot.*

Beach House Beach. Don't pack the beach umbrella, beach mats, and cooler for this one—just your snorkel gear. The beach, nicknamed after the neighboring Beach House restaurant and on the road to Spouting Horn, is a small slip of sand during low tide and a rocky shoreline when it's high; however, it is conveniently located by the road's edge, and its rocky coastline and somewhat rocky bottom make it great for snorkeling. (As a rule, sandy-bottom beaches are not great for snorkeling. The rocks create safe hiding places and grow the food that fish and other marine life like to eat.) A sidewalk along the coastline on the restaurant side of the beach makes a great vantage point from which to peer into the water and look for the Hawaiian green sea turtle. It's also a gathering spot to watch the sun set. ■ TIP→ Make reservations for dinner at the Beach House days in advance and time it around sunset. ⊠ *From Po'ipū Rd., turn onto Lāwa'i Rd.; park on street near restaurant or in public parking lot across from beach* ☞ *Toilets, showers, parking lot.*

SUN SAFETY ON KAUA'I

Hawai'i's weather—seemingly never-ending warm, sunny days with gentle trade winds—can be enjoyed year-round with good sun sense. Because of Hawai'i's subtropical location, the length of daylight here changes little throughout the year. The sun is particularly strong, with a daily UV average of 14. Visitors should take extra precaution to avoid sunburns and long-term cancer risks due to sun exposure.

The Hawai'i Dermatological Society recommends these sun safety tips:

■ Plan your beach, golf, hiking, and other outdoor activities for the early morning or late afternoon, avoiding the sun between 10 am and 4 pm, when it's the strongest.

■ Apply a broad-spectrum sunscreen with a sun protection factor (SPF) of at least 15. Hawai'i lifeguards use sunscreens with an SPF of 30. Cover areas that are most prone to burning like your nose, shoulders, tops of feet, and ears. And don't forget to use sun-protection products on your lips.

■ Apply sunscreen at least 30 minutes before you plan to be outdoors and reapply every two hours, even on cloudy days. Clouds scatter sunlight, so you can still burn on an overcast day.

■ Wear light, protective clothing, such as a long-sleeve shirt and pants, broad-brimmed hat, and sunglasses.

■ Stay in the shade whenever possible—especially on the beach—by using an umbrella. Remember that sand and water can reflect up to 85% of the sun's damaging rays.

■ Children need extra protection from the sun. Apply sunscreen frequently and liberally on children over six months of age and minimize their time in the sun. Sunscreen is not recommended for children under six months.

◷ **Kukui'ula Small Boat Harbor.** This is a great beach to sit and people-watch as diving and fishing boats, kayakers, and canoe paddlers head out to sea. Shore and throw-net fishermen frequent this harbor as well. It's not a particularly large harbor, so it retains a quaint sense of charm, unlike Nāwiliwili Harbor or Port Allen. The bay is a nice, protected area for swimming, but with all the boat traffic kicking up sand and clouding the water, it's probably not good for snorkeling. Outside the breakwater, there is a decent surf spot. ✉ *From Po'ipū Rd., turn onto Lāwa'i Rd.; watch for small green sign* ☞ *Toilets, showers, picnic tables, grills/firepits, parking lot.*

Fodor's Choice   **Lawa'i Kai.** One of the most spectacular beaches on the South Shore is
★   inaccessible by land unless you tour the National Tropical Botanical Garden's Allerton Garden, which we highly recommend, or trespass behind locked fences, which we don't recommend. On the tour, you'll see the beach, but you won't lounge on it or frolic in the calm water behind the promontory on the eastern point of the beach. One way to legally access the beach on your own is by paddling a kayak 1 mi from Kukui'ula Harbor. However, you have to rent the kayaks elsewhere and haul them on top of your car to the harbor. Also, the wind and waves

The sunny South Shore beaches have some good surf breaks. Head to Poʻipū Beach for board rentals or lessons.

usually run westward, making the in-trip a breeze but the return trip a workout against Mother Nature. Another way is to boulder-hop along the coast from Spouting Horn—a long trek over sharp lava rock that we do not recommend. ■TIP→ Do not attempt this beach in any manner during a south swell. ⊠ *For kayakers, from Poʻipū Rd., turn onto Lāwaʻi Rd. and park at Kukuiʻula small boat harbor* ☞ *No services.*

THE WEST SIDE

The West Side of the island receives hardly enough rainfall year-round to water a cactus, and because it's also the leeward side, there are few tropical breezes. That translates to sunny and hot with long, languorous, and practically deserted beaches. You'd think the leeward waters—untouched by wind—would be calm, but there's no reef system, so the waters are not as inviting as one would like. ■TIP→ The best place to gear up for the beaches on the West Side is on the South Shore or East Side. Although there's some catering to visitors here, it's not much.

☺ **Salt Pond Beach Park**. A great family spot, Salt Pond Beach Park features a naturally made, shallow swimming pond behind a curling finger of rock where *keiki* (children) splash and snorkel. This pool is generally safe except during a large south swell, which usually occurs in summer, if at all. The center and western edge of the beach are popular with body boarders and bodysurfers. On a cultural note, the flat stretch of land to the east of the beach is the last spot in Hawaiʻi where ponds are used to harvest salt in the dry heat of summer. The beach park is popular with locals and can get crowded on weekends and holidays. ⊠ *From Rte. 50* *in Hanapēpē, turn makai onto Lele Rd., Rte. 543* ☞ *Lifeguard, toilets, showers, picnic tables, grills/firepits, parking lot, camping.*

Lucy Wright Beach Park. Named in honor of the first native Hawaiian schoolteacher, this beach is on the western banks of the Waimea River. It is also where Captain James Cook first came ashore in the Hawaiian Islands in 1778. If that's not interesting enough, the sand here is not the white, powdery kind you see along the South Shore. It's a combination of pulverized, black lava rock and lighter-colored reef. In a way, it looks a bit like a mix of salt and pepper. Unfortunately, the intrigue of the beach doesn't extend to the waters, which are murky (thanks to river runoff) and choppy (thanks to an onshore break). Instead, check out the Waimea Landing State Recreation Pier, from which fishers drop their lines. It's located about 100 yards west of the river mouth. ✉ *From Rte. 50 in Waimea, turn makai on Pokile Rd.* ☞ *Toilets, picnic tables, parking lot.*

Kekaha Beach Park. This is one of the premier spots on Kaua'i for sunset walks and the start of the state's longest beach. We don't recommend much water activity here without first talking to a lifeguard: The beach is exposed to open ocean and has an onshore break that can be hazardous any time of year. Or, if you would like to run on a beach, this is the one—the hard-packed sand goes on for miles, all the way to Nāpali Coast, but you won't get past the Pacific Missile Range Facility and its post-9/11 restrictions. Another bonus for this beach is its relatively dry weather year-round. If it's raining where you are, try Kekaha Beach Park. Toilets here are the portable kind. ✉ *From Rte. 50, drive to the west side of Kekaha and park across from mile marker 27* ☞ *Lifeguard, toilets, showers, picnic tables, grills/firepits, parking lot.*

Polihale State Park. The longest stretch of beach in Hawai'i starts in Kekaha and ends about 15 mi away at the start of Nāpali Coast. At the Nāpali end of the beach is the 5-mi-long, 140-acre Polihale State Park. In addition to being long, this beach is 300 feet wide in places and backed by sand dunes 50 to 100 feet tall. Polihale is a remote beach accessed via a 5-mi cane-haul road (four-wheel drive preferred but not required) at the end of Route 50 in Kekaha. Many locals wheel their four-wheel-drive vehicles up and over the sand dunes right onto the beach, but don't try this in a rental car. You're sure to get stuck and found in violation of your rental-car agreement.

On weekends and holidays Polihale is a popular locals' camping location, but even on "busy" days this beach is never crowded. On days of high surf, only experts surf the waves. In general, the water here is extremely rough and not recommended for recreation; however, there's one small fringing reef, called Queen's Pond, where swimming is usually safe. Neighboring Polihale Beach is the Pacific Missile Range Facility (PMRF), operated by the U.S. Navy. Since September 11, 2001, access to the beaches fronting PMRF has been restricted. ✉ *Drive to end of Rte. 50 and continue on dirt road; several access points along the way* ☞ *Toilets, showers, picnic tables, grills/firepits, parking lot, camping.*

Water Sports and Tours

WORD OF MOUTH

"My personal advice is to not do the Zodiac if this will be your first tour of the Nāpali Coast. The slower boats allow you to just enjoy the scenery and take pictures without having to hold on so you don't fly off the boat!"

—nobigdeal

Updated by
Kim Steuter-
mann Rogers

So, you've decided to vacation on an island. That means you're going to run into a little water at some time. Ancient Hawaiians are notorious water sports fanatics—they invented surfing, after all—and that proclivity hasn't strayed far from today's mindset. Even if you're not into water sports or sports in general, there's a slim chance that you'll leave this island without getting out on the ocean, as Kaua'i's top attraction—Nāpali Coast—is something not to be missed.

For those who can't pack enough time snorkeling, fishing, Boogie boarding, or surfing into a vacation, Kaua'i has it all—everything except parasailing, that is, as it's illegal to do it here (though not on Maui, the Big Island, or Oahu). If you need to rent gear for any of these activities, you'll find plenty of places with large selections at reasonable prices. And no matter what part of the island you're staying on, you'll have several options for choice spots to enjoy playing in the water.

One thing to note, and we can't say this enough—the waters off the coast of Kaua'i have strong currents and can be unpredictable, so always err on the side of caution and know your limits.

BOAT TOURS

Deciding to see Nāpali Coast by boat is an easy decision. Choosing the outfitter to go with is not. There are numerous boat-tour operators to choose from, and, quite frankly, they all do a good job. Before you even start thinking about whom to go out with, answer these three questions: What kind of boat do I prefer? Where am I staying? Do I want to go in the morning or afternoon? Once you settle on these three, you can easily zero in on the tour outfitter.

First, the boat. The most important thing is to match your personality and that of your group with the personality of the boat. If you like thrills and adventure, the rubber, inflatable rafts—often called Zodiacs, which Jacques Cousteau made famous and which the U.S. Coast Guard uses—will entice you. They're fast, sure to leave you drenched, and quite bouncy. If you prefer a smoother, more leisurely ride, then the large catamarans are the way to go. The next boat choice is size. Both the rafts and catamarans come in small and large. Again—think smaller, more adventurous; larger, more leisurely. ■TIP➡ Do not choose a smaller boat because you think there will be fewer people. There might be fewer people, but you'll be jammed together sitting atop strangers. If you prefer privacy over socializing, go with a larger boat, so you'll have more room to spread out. One advantage to smaller boats, however, is that—depending on ocean conditions—some may slip into a sea cave or two. If that sounds interesting to you, call the outfitter and ask their policy on entering sea caves. Some won't, no matter the conditions, because they consider the caves sacred or because they don't want to cause any environmental damage.

There are three points boats leave from around the island (Hanalei, Port Allen, and Waimea), and all head to the same spot: Nāpali Coast. Here's the inside skinny on which is the best: If you're staying on the North Shore, choose to depart out of the North Shore. If you're staying anywhere else, depart out of the West Side. It's that easy. Sure, the North Shore is closer to Nāpali Coast; however, you'll pay more for less overall time. The West Side boat operators may spend more time getting to Nāpali Coast; however, they'll spend about the same amount of time along Nāpali, plus you'll pay less. Finally, you'll also have to decide whether you want to go on a morning tour, which includes a deli lunch and a stop for snorkeling, or an afternoon tour, which does not stop to snorkel but does include a sunset over the ocean. The morning tours with snorkeling are more popular with families and those who love dolphins. You don't have to be an expert snorkeler or even have any prior experience, but if it is your first time, note that although there will be some snorkeling instruction, there might not be much. Hawaiian spinner dolphins are so plentiful in the mornings that some tour companies guarantee you'll see them, though you won't get in the water and swim with them. The afternoon tours are more popular with nonsnorkelers—obviously—and photographers interested in capturing the setting sunlight on the coast.

CATAMARAN TOURS

Fodor's Choice
★
Blue Dolphin Charters. This company operates 63-foot and 65-foot sailing (rarely raised and always motoring) catamarans designed with three decks of spacious seating with great visibility. ■TIP→ The lower deck is best for shade seekers. Upgrades from snorkeling to scuba diving—no need for certification—are available and run $35, but the diving is really best for beginners or people who need a refresher course. On Tuesday and Friday a tour of Nāpali Coast includes a detour across the channel to Ni'ihau for snorkeling and diving. Blue Dolphin likes to say they have the best mai tais "off the island," and the truth is, they probably do. Morning snorkel tours of Nāpali include a deli lunch, and afternoon sunset sightseeing tours include a meal of kalua pork, teriyaki chicken, Caesar salad, and chocolate-chip cookies. Prices range from $109 to $175. Two-hour whale watching/sunset tours, offered during winter, run $69. ⊠ *In Port Allen Marina Center. Turn makai onto Rte. 541 off Rte. 50, at 'Ele'ele* ☎ *808/335–5553 or 877/511–1311* ⊕ *www. kauaiboats.com.*

Capt. Andy's Sailing Adventures. Departing from Port Allen and running two 55-foot sailing catamarans, Capt. Andy's runs the same five-hour snorkeling and four-hour sunset tours along Nāpali Coast as everyone else, though we're not crazy about the boat's layout, which has most of the seating inside the cabin. They also embark out of Kukui'ula Harbor in Po'ipū for a two-hour sunset sail along the South Shore—with live Hawaiian music—every Wednesday, Friday, and Sunday evening during winter, and on Sunday during summer. ■TIP→ If the winds and swells are up on the North Shore, this is usually a good choice—especially if you're prone to seasickness. This is the only tour boat operator that allows infants on board—but only on the two-hour trip. Note, if you have reservations for the shorter tour, you'll check in at their Kukuiʻula Harbor office. Prices range from $69 to $139. ✉ *In Port Allen Marina Center. Turn makai onto Rte. 541 off Rte. 50 at ʻEleʻele* ☎ *808/335–6833 or 800/535–0830* ⊕ *www.napali.com.*

FodorsChoice ★ **Captain Sundown**. If you're staying on the North Shore, it's really pretty simple. Captain Sundown is the choice. Get this: Captain Bob has been cruising Nāpali Coast for 35 years—six days a week, sometimes twice a day. (And right alongside Captain Bob is his son Captain Larry.) To say he knows the area is a bit of an understatement. Here's

> ### BEST BOAT TOURS
>
> **Best for snorkeling:** Z-Tourz
>
> **Best for romance:** Capt. Andy's Poʻipū Sail
>
> **Best for thrill seekers:** Nāpali Explorer (Zodiac 1)
>
> **Best for mai tais:** Blue Dolphin Charters
>
> **Best for pregnant women:** Capt. Andy's
>
> **Best for charters:** Captain Sundown
>
> **Best for price:** Nāpali Riders

the other good thing about this tour: they take only 15 passengers. Now, you'll definitely pay more, but it's worth it. You don't check in too early—around 8 AM—and there's no rushing down the coastline. The morning snorkeling cruise is a leisurely six hours. The breathtaking views of the waterfall-laced mountains behind Hanalei and Hāʻena start immediately, but then it's around Kēʻē Beach and the magic of Nāpali Coast unfolds before you. All the while, the captains are trolling for fish, and if they catch any, guests get to reel 'em in. Afternoon sunset sails (seasonal) run three hours and check in around 3 PM—these are BYOB. Prices range from $125 to $162. During the winter months, Captain Bob moves his operation to Nāwiliwili Harbor, where he runs four- to five-hour whale watching tours. ✉ *Meet in Hanalei at Tahiti Nui parking lot* ☎ *808/826–5585* ⊕ *www.captainsundown.com and www.whale-watching-kauai.com.*

Catamaran Kahanu. This Hawaiian-owned-and-operated company has been in business since 1985 and runs a 40-foot power catamaran with 18-passenger seating. The five-hour morning tour includes snorkeling at Nuʻalolo Kai. The four-hour afternoon tour includes a hot dinner and sunset. The boat is smaller than most and may feel a tad crowded, but the tour feels more personal, with a laid-back ʻohana style. Salt water runs through the veins of Captain Lani. Guests can learn the ancient cultural practice of weaving onboard. There's no alcohol allowed. Seasonal whale watching tours are also available. Prices range from $95 to $135. ✉ *From Rte. 50, turn left on Rte. 541 at ʻEleʻele, proceed just past Port Allen Marina Center, turn right at sign; check-in booth on left* ☎ *808/645–6176 or 888/213–7711* ⊕ *www.catamarankahanu.com.*

HoloHolo Charters. Choose between a 50-foot sailing catamaran trip to Nāpali Coast and a 65-foot powered catamaran trip to the island of Niʻihau. Both boats have large cabins and little outside seating. Originators of the Niʻihau tour, HoloHolo Charters built their 65-foot powered catamaran with a wide beam to reduce side-to-side motion, and twin 425 HP turbo diesel engines specifically for the 17-mi channel crossing

Get out on the water and see the Nāpali Coast in style on a luxe cruising yacht.

to Ni'ihau. ■ TIP→ It's the only outfitter running daily Ni'ihau tours. Prices range from $99 to $179. ⊠ *Check in at Port Allen Marina Center. Turn makai onto Rte. 541 off Rte. 50, at 'Ele'ele* ☎ *808/335–0815 or 800/848–6130* ⊕ *www.holoholocharters.com.*

★ **Kaua'i Sea Tours.** This company operates a 61-foot sailing catamaran designed almost identically to that of Blue Dolphin Charters—hence with all the same benefits, like great views and spacious seating. Snorkeling tours anchor at Makole (a good snorkeling spot), and in summer, guests can choose the "combo" tour, which includes a shuttle ride to shore on an inflatable raft and a tour of an ancient fishing village— a unique cultural experience. If snorkeling isn't your thing, try the four-hour sunset tour, with mai tais and a hot buffet dinner. Prices range from $99 to $170. ⊠ *Check in at Port Allen Marina Center. Turn makai onto Rte. 541 off Rte. 50, at 'Ele'ele* ☎ *808/826–7254 or 800/733–7997* ⊕ *www.kauaiseatours.com.*

Liko Kaua'i Cruises. There are many things to like about Liko Kaua'i Cruises. The 49-foot powered cat will enter sea caves, ocean conditions permitting. Sometimes, even Captain Liko himself—a born-and-bred West Side boy—still takes the captain's helm. We particularly like the layout of his boat—most of the seating is in the bow, so there's good visibility. There's just one problem: Even though it departs out of Kīkīaola Harbor in Waimea, at four hours in length the snorkeling tour is altogether too short. The rate is $140. ⊠ *Mauka off Rte. 50 in Waimea just before Shell gas station* ☎ *808/338–0333 or 800/732–5456* ⊕ *www.liko-kauai.com.*

DOES RAIN MEAN CANCELLATION?

If it's raining where you're staying, that doesn't mean it's raining over the water, so don't shy away from a boat tour. Besides, it's not the rain that should concern you—it's the wind. Especially from due north and south, wind creates surface chop and makes for rough riding. Larger craft are designed to handle winter's ocean swells, however, so unless monster waves are out there, your tour should depart without a hitch. If the water is too rough, your boat captain may reroute to calmer waters. It's a tough call to make, but your comfort and safety are always the foremost factor. ■ TIP→ In winter months, North Shore departures are canceled much more often than those departing the West Side. This is because the boats are smaller and the waves are bigger on this side of the island. If you want the closest thing to a guarantee of seeing Nāpali Coast in winter, choose a West Side outfitter. Oh, and even if your tour boat says it cruises the "entire Nāpali," keep in mind that "ocean conditions permitting" is always implied.

Nāpali Catamaran. One of the few tour groups departing Hanalei, this company has been around for a long time. Once you're on board, it takes only five minutes before you're witnessing the magnificence of Nāpali Coast. Its 34-foot, powered catamaran is small enough—and with no mast, short enough—to dip into sea caves. In summer, they run two four-hour snorkeling tours per day, stopping at the best snorkeling site along Nāpali—Nu'alolo Kai. In winter, business slows as the surf picks up, and they run whale watching tours, ocean conditions permitting. If it weren't for the bench seating bisecting the boat—meaning one group of passengers enjoys unobstructed views of the open ocean instead of Nāpali either on the way out or back—we'd really be happy. Rate is $150, on the high side for a four-hour tour. ⊠ *In Ching Young Village in Hanalei* ☎ *808/826–6853 or 800/255–6853* ⊕ *www.napalicatamaran.com.*

RAFT TOURS

Capt. Andy's Rafting Expeditions. This company used to be known as Captain Zodiac; however, the outfit has changed hands over the years. It first started running Nāpali in 1974, and currently, Capt. Andy's (as in the sailing catamaran Capt. Andy's) is operating the business. Departing out of Port Allen, this tour is much like the other raft tours, offering both snorkeling and beach-landing excursions. The rafts are on the smaller side—24 feet with a maximum of 15 passengers—and all seating is on the rubber hulls, so hang on. They operate three different rafts, so there's a good chance of availability. Price is $159 in summer; $139 in winter, including snorkeling at Nu'alolo Kai (ocean conditions permitting), sightseeing along Nāpali Coast, a hiking tour through an ancient Hawaiian fishing village, and a hot buffet lunch on the beach. In 2010, Capt. Andy's introduced a three-hour morning whale watch raft tour (winter only). You're closer to the water on the Zodiacs, so you'll have great views of humpbacks, spinner dolphins, sea turtles, and other wildlife. ⊠ *In Port Allen Marina Center. Turn makai*

onto Rte. 541 off Rte. 50 at 'Ele'ele
☎ *808/335–6833 or 800/535–0830*
⊕ *www.napali.com.*

Kauai Sea Tours. This company holds a special permit from the state to land at Nu'alolo Kai along Nāpali Coast, ocean conditions permitting. Here, you'll enjoy a picnic lunch, as well as an archaeological tour of an ancient Hawaiian fishing village, ocean conditions permitting. Kauai Sea Tours operates four 24-foot inflatable rafts—maximum occupancy 14. These are small enough for checking out the insides of sea caves and the undersides of waterfalls. Three different tours are available, depending on the season. Prices range from $99 to $129. ✉ *Check in at Port Allen Marina Center. Turn makai onto Rte. 541 off Rte. 50, at 'Ele'ele* ☎ *808/826–7254 or 800/733–7997* ⊕ *www.kauaiseatours.com.*

Fodor's Choice ★

Nāpali Explorer. Owned by a couple of women, these tours operate out of two locations: Waimea, a tad closer to Nāpali Coast than most of the other West Side catamaran tours, and Hanalei. Departing out of the West Side, the company runs two different sizes of inflatable rubber raft: a 48-foot, 35-passenger craft with an onboard toilet, freshwater shower, shade canopy, and seating in the stern (which is surprisingly smooth and comfortable) and bow (which is where the fun is); and a 26-foot, 16-passenger craft for the all-out fun and thrills of a white-knuckle ride in the bow. Departing out of Hanalei, the *Ocean Adventurer* is a 38-foot, 25-passenger rigid-hull inflatable. The smaller vessel stops at Nu'alolo Kai in the summer and ties up onshore for a tour of the ancient fishing village. Rates are $95 to $139, including snorkeling. Charters are available. ✉ *Follow Rte. 50 west to Waimea; office is mauka across from the Shimp Station, Waimea* ✉ *In Hanalei, meet at the river mouth, at the end of Weke Rd. Hanalei* ☎ *808/338–9999 or 877/335–9909* ⊕ *www.napaliexplorer.com.*

Nāpali Riders. This tour-boat outfitter distinguishes itself in two ways. First, it cruises the entire Nāpali Coast, clear to Kē'ē Beach and back. Second, it has an unbeatable price, because it's a no-frills tour—no lunch provided, just beverages and snacks. The company runs four-hour snorkeling trips out of Kīkīaola Harbor in Waimea on a 30-foot inflatable raft with a 32-passenger maximum—if it's full, you'll definitely feel like a sardine. The cost is $109 for the morning tour and $89 for the afternoon tour. ✉ *In Waimea, makai, approximately 1 mi after crossing Waimea River, across from Rte. 550* ☎ *808/742–6331* ⊕ *www.napaliriders.com.*

★ **Z-Tourz.** What we like about Z-Tourz is that it is the only boat company to make snorkeling its priority. As such, it focuses on the South Shore's abundant reefs, stopping at two locations. If you want to see Nāpali, this boat is not for you; if you want to snorkel with Hawai'i's

4

myriad tropical reef fish and turtles (pretty much guaranteed), this is your boat. Z-Tourz runs daily three-hour tours on a 26-foot rigid-hull inflatable (think Zodiac) with a maximum of 16 passengers. These snorkel tours are guided, so someone actually identifies what you're seeing. Rate is $94. Check in at Kukui'ula Harbor in Po'ipū. ⊠ *From Po'ipū Rd., turn onto Lawai Rd., drive 1 mi, turn left on Amio Rd. to harbor* ☎ *808/742–7422 or 888/998–6879* ⊕ *www.ztourz.com.*

RIVERBOAT TOURS TO FERN GROTTO

This 2-mi, upriver trip culminates at a yawning lava tube that is covered with enormous fishtail ferns. During the boat ride, guitar and 'ukulele players regale you with Hawaiian melodies and tell the history of the river. It's a kitschy bit of Hawaiiana, worth the little money ($20) and short time required. Flat-bottom, 150-passenger riverboats (that rarely fill up) depart from Wailua Marina at the mouth of the Wailua River. ∎TIP→ It's extremely rare, but occasionally after heavy rains the tour doesn't leave from the grotto. If you're traveling in winter, ask beforehand. Round-trip excursions take 1½ hours, including time to walk around the grotto and environs. Tours run at 9:30, 10, 11:30, 1:30, 2, and 3:30 daily. Reservations are not required. Contact **Smith's Motor Boat Services** (☎ *808/821–6892* ⊕ *www.smithskauai.com*) for more information on getting to Fern Grotto.

BODY BOARDING AND BODYSURFING

The most natural form of wave riding is bodysurfing, a popular sport on Kaua'i because there are many shore breaks around the island. Wave riders of this style stand waist-deep in the water, facing shore, and swim madly as a wave picks them up and breaks. It's great fun and requires no special skills and absolutely no equipment other than a swimsuit. The next step up is body boarding, also called Boogie boarding. In this case, wave riders lie with their upper body on a foam board about half the length of a traditional surfboard and kick as the wave propels them toward shore. Again, this is easy to pick up, and there are many places around Kaua'i to practice. The locals wear short-finned flippers to help them catch waves, although they are not necessary for and even hamper beginners. It's worth spending a few minutes watching these experts as they spin, twirl, and flip—that's right—while they slip down the face of the wave. Of course, all beach safety precautions apply, and just because you see wave riders of any kind in the water doesn't mean the water is safe for everyone. Any snorkeling-gear outfitter also rents body boards.

Some of our favorite bodysurfing and body-boarding beaches are **Brennecke, Wailua, Keālia, Kalihiwai,** and **Hanalei.**

DEEP-SEA FISHING

Simply step aboard and cast your line for mahimahi, 'ahi, ono, and marlin. That's about how quickly the fishing—mostly trolling with lures—begins on Kaua'i. The water gets deep quickly here, so there's less cruising time to fishing grounds. Of course, your captain may elect to cruise to a hot location where he's had good luck lately.

There are oodles of charter fishermen around; most depart from Nāwiliwili Harbor in Līhu'e, and most use lures instead of live bait. Inquire about each boat's "fish policy," that is, what happens to the fish if any are caught. Some boats keep all; others will give you enough for a meal or two. On shared charters, ask about the maximum passenger count and about the fishing rotation; you'll want to make sure everyone gets a fair shot at reeling in the big one. Another option is to book a private charter. Shared and private charters run four, six, and eight hours in length.

BOATS AND CHARTERS

Explore Kaua'i Sportfishing. If you're staying on the West Side, you'll be glad to know that Nāpali Explorer (of the longtime rafting tour business) is now running fishing trips out of Port Allen under the name Explore Kaua'i Sportfishing. It offers shared and exclusive charters of four, six, and eight hours in a 41-foot Concord called *Happy Times*. The shared tours max out at six fishers, and a portion of the catch is shared with all. The boat is also used for specialty charters—that is, film crews, surveys, burials, and even Ni'ihau fishing. Rates start at $145 per person. ⊠ *Check in at Port Allen Small Boat Harbor* ☎ *808/338–9999 or 877/335–9909* ⊕ *www.napali-explorer.com.*

Captain Don's Sport Fishing & Ocean Adventure. Captain Don is very flexible and treats everyone like family—he'll stop to snorkel or whale watch if that's what the group (four to six) wants. Saltwater fly-fishermen (bring your own gear) are welcome. He'll even fish for bait and let you keep part of whatever you catch. The *June Louise* is a 34-foot twin diesel. Rates start at $135 for shared, $575 for private charters. ⊠ *Nāwiliwili Small Boat Harbor* ☎ *808/639–3012* ⊕ *www. captaindonsfishing.com.*

Hana Pa'a. The advantage with Hana Pa'a is that it takes fewer people (minimum two, maximum four), but you pay for it. Rates start at $310 for shared, $600 for private charters. The company's fish policy is flexible, and the boat is roomy. The *Maka Hou II* is a 38-foot Bertram. ⊠ *Nāwiliwili Harbor* ☎ *808/823–6031 or 866/776–3474* ⊕ *www. fishkauai.com.*

Kai Bear. The father of this father-and-son duo has it figured out: He lets the son run the business and do all the work. Or so he says. Fish policy: Share the catch. Rates start at $159 for a four-hour, shared charter (six fishermen max) and run all the way to $2,000 for an eight-hour, keep-all-the-fish-you-want exclusive charter. What's particularly nice about this company are the boats: the 38-foot Bertram *Kai Bear* and the 42-foot Bertram *Grander*. Very roomy. ⊠ *Nāwiliwili Small Boat Harbor* ☎ *808/652–4556* ⊕ *www.kaibear.com.*

DID YOU KNOW?

There are plenty of choice spots for surfers of all levels on Kaua'i—we recommend Po'ipū Beach or Hanalei Bay for beginners and Wailua and Keālia beaches if you're more advanced.

The Forbidden Isle

Seventeen miles from Kaua'i, across the Kaulakahi Channel, sits the privately owned island of Ni'ihau. It's known as the Forbidden Isle, because access is limited to the Robinson family, who owns it, and the 200 or so native Hawaiians who were born there.

Ni'ihau was bought from King Kamehameha in 1864 by a Scottish widow, Eliza Sinclair. Sinclair was introduced to the island after an unusually wet winter; she saw nothing but green pastures and thought it would be an ideal place to raise cattle. The cost was $10,000. It was a real deal, or so Sinclair thought.

Unfortunately, Ni'ihau's usual rainfall is about 12 inches a year, and the land soon returned to its normal, desert-like state. Regardless, Sinclair did not

abandon her venture, and today the island and ranching operation are owned by Bruce Robinson, Eliza Sinclair's great-great-grandson.

Visits to the island are restricted to custom hunting expeditions and flight-seeing tours through Ni'ihau Helicopter. Tours depart from Kaumakani and avoid the western coastline, especially the village of Pu'uwai. There's a four-passenger minimum for each flight, and reservations are essential. A picnic lunch on a secluded Ni'ihau beach is included, with time for swimming, beachcombing, and snorkeling. The half-day tour is $325 per person.

For more information contact **Ni'ihau Tours** (🖃 *Box 690370, Makaweli 96769* ☎ *808/335–3500 or 877/441–3500* ⊕ *www.niihau.us*).

KAYAKING

Kaua'i is the only Hawaiian island with navigable rivers. As the oldest inhabited island in the chain, Kaua'i has had more time for wind and water erosion to deepen and widen cracks into streams and streams into rivers. Because this is a small island, the rivers aren't long, and there are no rapids; that makes them perfectly safe for kayakers of all levels, even beginners.

For more advanced paddlers, there aren't many places in the world more beautiful for sea kayaking than Nāpali Coast. If this is your draw to Kaua'i, plan your vacation for the summer months, when the seas are at their calmest. ■TIP→ **Tour and kayak-rental reservations are recommended at least two weeks in advance during peak summer and holiday seasons.** In general, tours and rentals are available year-round, Monday through Saturday. Pack a swimsuit, sunscreen, a hat, bug repellent, water shoes (sport sandals, aqua socks, old tennis shoes), and motion sickness medication if you're planning on sea kayaking.

RIVER KAYAKING

Tour outfitters operate on the Hulē'ia, Wailua, and Hanalei rivers with guided tours that combine hiking to waterfalls, as in the case of the first two, and snorkeling, as in the case of the third. Another option is renting kayaks and heading out on your own. Each has its advantages and disadvantages, but it boils down as follows:

If you want to swim at the base of a remote 100-foot waterfall, sign up for a five-hour kayak (4-mi round-trip) and hiking (2-mi round-trip) tour of the **Wailua River.** It includes a dramatic waterfall that is best accessed with the aid of a guide, so you don't get lost. ■TIP→ Remember—it's dangerous to swim under waterfalls no matter how good a water massage may sound. Rocks and logs are known to plunge down, especially after heavy rains.

If you want to kayak on your own, choose the **Hanalei River.** It's most scenic from the kayak itself—there are no trails to hike to hidden waterfalls. And better yet, a rental company is right on the river—no hauling kayaks on top of your car.

If you're not sure of your kayaking abilities, head to the **Hulē'ia River;** 3½-hour tours include easy paddling upriver, a nature walk through a rain forest with a cascading waterfall, a rope swing for playing Tarzan and Jane, and a ride back downriver—into the wind—on a motorized, double-hull canoe.

As for the kayaks themselves, most companies use the two-person sit-on-top style that is quite buoyant—no Eskimo rolls required. The only possible danger comes in the form of communication. The kayaks seat two people, which means you'll share the work (good) with a guide, or your spouse, child, parent, or friend (the potential danger part). On the river, the two-person kayaks are known as "divorce boats." Counseling is not included in the tour price.

SEA KAYAKING

In its second year and second issue, *National Geographic Adventure* ranked kayaking Nāpali Coast second on its list of America's Best 100 Adventures, right behind rafting the Colorado River through the Grand Canyon. That pretty much says it all. It's the adventure of a lifetime in one day, involving eight hours of paddling. Although it's good to have some kayaking experience, feel comfortable on the water, and be reasonably fit, it doesn't require the preparation, stamina, or fortitude of, say, climbing Mt. Everest. Tours run May through September, ocean conditions permitting. In the winter months sea-kayaking tours operate on the South Shore—beautiful, but not Nāpali.

EQUIPMENT AND TOURS

Kayak Kaua'i. Based in Hanalei, this company offers guided tours on the Hanalei and Wailua rivers, and along Nāpali Coast. It has a great shop right on the Hanalei River for kayak rentals and camping gear. The guided Hanalei River Kayak and Snorkel Tour starts at the shop and heads downriver, so there's not much to see of the scenic river valley. (For that, rent a kayak on your own.) Instead, this three-hour tour paddles down to the river mouth, where the river meets the sea. Then, it's a short paddle around a point to snorkel at either Pu'u Poa Beach or, ocean conditions permitting, a bit farther at Hideaways Beach. This is a great choice if you want to try your paddle at a bit of ocean kayaking.

A second location in Kapaʻa is the base for Wailua River guided tours and kayak rentals. It's not right on the river, however, so shuttling is involved. For rentals, the company provides the hauling gear necessary for your rental car. Guided tours range from $85 to $214. Kayak rentals range from $28 to $75, depending on the river, depending on kayak size (single or double). ⊠ *Hanalei: 1 mi past Hanalei bridge, on makai side* ⊠ *Kapaʻa: south end of Coconut Marketplace near movie theaters* ☎ *808/826–9844 or 800/437–3507* ⊕ *www.kayakkauai.com.*

HAWAIʻI STATE SPORT: CANOE PADDLING

During summer, it's not unusual to see Hawaiʻi's state sport in action: outrigger canoe racing. These are the same styles of canoes ancient Hawaiians paddled in races that pitted one chief's warriors against another's. Summer is regatta season, and the half dozen or more canoe clubs around the island gather to race in ¼-mi, ½-mi, and longer races. You can catch the hundreds of paddlers lining the beaches and cheering on their clubs, oftentimes in Hanalei, Kalapaki, and Waimea Bay, as well as the Wailua River.

Kayak Wailua. We can't quite figure out how this family-run business offers pretty much the same Wailua River kayaking tour as everyone else—except for lunch and beverages, which are BYO—for half the price, but it does. They say it's because there are no discounts and no commission to activities and concierge desks. The 4½-hour kayak, hike, and waterfall swim costs $39.95, and the less popular, 3-hour kayak-to-a-swimming-hole costs $34.95. We say fork over the extra $5 for the longer tour and hike to the beautiful 150-foot Secret Falls. ⊠ *In Wailua next to the Wailua Shell Food Mart* ☎ *808/822–3388* ⊕ *www.kayakwailua.com.*

Fodorʻs Choice ★ **Nāpali Kayak.** A couple of longtime guides ventured out on their own a few years back to create this company, which focuses solely on sea kayaking—Nāpali Coast in summer, as the name implies, and the South Shore in winter (during peak times only). These guys are highly experienced and still highly enthusiastic about their livelihood, so much so, that REI Adventures hires them to run their multiday, multisport tours. Now, that's a feather in their cap, we'd say. Prices start at $200. You can also rent kayaks; prices range from $25 to $75. If you want to try camping on your own at Kalalau (you'll need permits), Nāpali Kayak will provide outfitted kayaks and transportation drop-off and pick-up. ⊠ *5-575 Kūhiō Hwy., next to Postcards Café* ☎ *808/826–6900 or 866/977–6900* ⊕ *www.napalikayak.com.*

↻ **Outfitters Kauaʻi.** This well-established tour outfitter operates year-round river-kayak tours on the Hulēʻia and Wailua rivers, as well as sea-kayaking tours along Nāpali Coast in summer and the South Shore in winter. Outfitters Kauaʻi's specialty, however, is the **Kipu Safari.** This all-day adventure starts with kayaking up the Hulēʻia River and includes

KAUAI'I'S TOP THREE WATER ACTIVITIES

Tour company/ Outfitter	Length	AM/PM	Departure Point	Adult/Kid Price	Kids' Ages	Snack or Meal	Alcoholic Beverages Included	Boat Type	Capacity	Worth Noting
Snorkel Cruise										
Captain Sundown	6 hrs.	AM	North Shore	$162/$142	7–12	Meal	No	Cat	15	Departs out of Hanalei Bay; exquisite scenery at very start
Nāpali Explorer	4–5 hrs.	AM	West Side	$139/$99	5–12	Meal	No	Inflatable	35	Departs out of West Side, so it's closer to the Nāpali Coast
Z-Tourz	3 hrs.	AM	South Shore	$94/$84	5–12	Meal	No	Inflatable	16	Provides all snorkel gear, including wetsuits
Ni'ihau Cruise										
Blue Dolphin Charters	7 hrs.	AM	West Side	$175/$139	5–11	Meal	Yes	Cat	49	Offers upgrade to scuba
HoloHolo Charters	7 hrs.	AM	West Side	$179/$129	6–12	Meal	Yes	Cat	49	Fast, smooth boat built for open ocean; runs 7 days a week
Kayak										
Ocean										
Nāpali Kayak	9 hrs.	AM	North Shore	$200	15+	Meal	NA	NA	NA	Owners are long-term Nāpali guides
Wailua River										
Outfitters Kaua'i	5 hrs.	AM/PM	East Side	$98/$78	5–14	Meal	NA	NS	NA	Top kayak equipment
Hanalei River										
Kayak Kaua'i	3 hrs.	AM/PM	North Shore	$85/$65	4–11	Water	NA	NA	NA	Only guides on Hanalei River

a rope swing over a swimming hole, a wagon ride through a working cattle ranch, a picnic lunch by a private waterfall, hiking, and two "zips" across the rain-forest canopy (strap on a harness, clip into a cable, and zip over a quarter of a mile). It ends with a ride on a motorized double-hull canoe. It's a great tour for the family, because no one ever gets bored. The Kipu Safari costs $178; other guided tours range from $98 to $225. ✉ *2827-A Po'ipū Rd., Po'ipū* ☎ *808/742–9667 or 888/742–9886* ⊕ *www.outfitterskauai.com.*

Wailua Kayak & Canoe. This is the only purveyor of kayak rentals on the Wailua River, which means no hauling your kayak on top of your car (a definite plus). Rates are $45 for a single, $75 for a double, for either a morning or afternoon. Guided tours are also available with rates ranging from $55 to $90. This outfitter promotes itself as "Native Hawaiian owned and operated." ✉ *Across from Wailua Beach, turn mauka at Kuamo'o Rd. and take first left, 169 Wailua Rd., Kapa'a* ☎ *808/821–1188* ⊕ *www.wailuakayakandcanoe.net.*

KITEBOARDING

Several years ago, the latest wave-riding craze to hit the islands was kiteboarding, and the sport is still going strong. As the name implies, there's a kite and a board involved. The board you strap on your feet; the kite is attached to a harness around your waist. Steering is accomplished with a rod that's attached to the harness and the kite. Depending on conditions and the desires of the kiteboarder, the kite is played out some 30 to 100 feet in the air. The result is a cross between waterskiing—without the boat—and windsurfing. Speeds are fast and aerobatic maneuvers are involved. Unfortunately, neither lessons nor rental gear is available for the sport on Kaua'i (Maui is a better bet), so if you aren't a seasoned kiteboarder already, you'll have to be content with watching the pros—who can put on a pretty spectacular show. The most popular year-round spots for kiteboarding are **Kapa'a Beach Park, 'Anini Beach Park,** and **Māhā'ulepū Beach.**

SCUBA DIVING

The majority of scuba diving on Kaua'i occurs on the South Shore. Boat and shore dives are available, although boat sites surpass the shore sites for a couple of reasons. First, they're deeper and exhibit the complete symbiotic relationship of a reef system, and second, the visibility is better a little farther offshore.

The dive operators on Kaua'i offer a full range of services, including certification dives, referral dives, boat dives, shore dives, night dives, and drift dives. ■TIP→ As for certification, we recommend completing your confined-water training and classroom testing before arriving on the island. That way, you'll spend less time training and more time diving.

BEST SPOTS

The best and safest scuba-diving sites are accessed by boat on the South Shore of the island, right off the shores of Poʻipū. The captain selects the actual site based on ocean conditions of the day. Beginners may prefer shore dives, which are best at **Kōloa Landing** on the South Shore year-round and **Mākua (Tunnels) Beach** on the North Shore in the calm summer months. Keep in mind, though, that you'll have to haul your gear a ways down the beach.

For the advanced diver, the island of Niʻihau—across an open ocean channel in deep and crystal-clear waters—beckons and rewards, usually with some big fish. Seasport Divers, Fathom Five, and Bubbles Below venture the 17 mi across the channel in summer when the crossing is smoothest. Divers can expect deep dives, walls, and strong currents at Niʻihau, where conditions can change rapidly. To make the long journey worthwhile, three dives and Nitrox are included.

EQUIPMENT, LESSONS, AND TOURS

Bubbles Below. Marine ecology is the emphasis here aboard the 36-foot Kai Manu custom-built Radon. This company discovered some pristine dive sites on the West Side of the island where white-tip reef sharks are common—and other divers are not. Thanks to the addition of a 32-foot powered catamaran—the six-passenger *Dive Rocket*—the group also runs Niʻihau, Nāpali, and North Shore dives year-round (depending on ocean conditions, of course). A bonus on these tours is the Grinds pizza served between dives. Open-water certification dives, check-out dives, and intro shore dives are available upon request. There's a charge of $120 for a standard two-tank boat dive and up to $25 extra for rental gear, though different tours can be up to $295. ✉ *Port Allen Small Boat Harbor; turn makai onto Rte. 541 from Rte. 50 in ʻEleʻele* ☎ *808/332–7333 or 866/524–6268* ⊕ *www.bubblesbelowkauai.com.*

Fodor's Choice

★   **Ocean Quest Watersports/Fathom Five**. A few years ago, Fathom Five, the South Shore boat-diving specialist, teamed up with Ocean Quest Watersports, a separate company specializing in shore dives at Tunnels on the North Shore. Today, they offer it all: boat dives, shore dives, night dives, certification dives. They're pretty much doing what everyone else is with a couple of twists. First, they offer a three-tank premium charter for those really serious about diving. Second, they operate a Nitrox continuous-flow mixing system, so you can decide the mix rate. Third, they tag on a twilight dive to the standard, one-tank night dive, making the outing worth the effort. Fourth, their shore diving isn't an afterthought. Finally, we think their dive masters are pretty darn good, too. They even dive Niʻihau in the summer aboard their 35-foot Force. Prices start at $70 for a one-tank shore dive and top out at $495 for full certification. The standard two-tank boat dive runs $120 plus $35 for gear rental, if needed. ■ TIP→ In summer, book way in advance. ✉ *Just south of Kōloa on Poʻipū Rd., 3450 Poʻipū Rd.* ☎ *808/742–6991 or 800/972–3078* ⊕ *www.fathomfive.com.*

Sacred Seas Scuba/North Shore Divers. This company specializes in shore diving only, typically at Kōloa Landing (year-round) and Tunnels (summers). They're not only geared toward beginning divers—for whom

SCUBA Q&A

Q: Do I have to be certified to go scuba diving?

A: Absolutely not. You can try Discover Scuba, which allows you to dive up to 40 feet after an introductory lesson in a pool. Most dive outfitters on Kaua'i offer this introductory program.

Q: Can I dive if I have asthma?

A: Only if your doctor signs a medical release—the original of which you must present to your dive outfitter.

Q: Can I get certified on Kaua'i?

A: Yes. Start to finish, it'll take three days. Or, you can complete your classroom and confined-water training at home and just do your checkout dives on Kau'ai.

Q: How old do you have to be to learn how to dive?

A: Most certifying agencies require that you be at least 12 years old (with PADI it's 10) when you start your scuba-diving course. You will normally receive a junior certification, which can be upgraded to a full certification when you are 15 years old.

Q: Can I wear contact lenses or glasses while diving?

A: You can either wear contact lenses with a regular mask or opt for a prescription mask—just let your dive outfitter know in advance.

Q: What if I forget my certification card?

A: Let your dive outfitter know immediately; with advance notice, they can usually dig up your certification information online.

they provide a very thorough and gentle certification program as well as the Discover Scuba program—but also offer night dives and scooter (think James Bond) dives. Their main emphasis is a detailed review of marine biology, such as pointing out rare dragon eel and harlequin shrimp tucked away in pockets of coral. ■TIP→ Hands down, we recommend Sacred Seas Scuba for beginners, certification (all levels), and refresher dives. One reason is that the instructor-to-student ratio never exceeds 1:4—that's true of all the company's dive groups. Rates range from $79 for a one-tank certified dive to $450 for certification—all dive gear included. ☎ 877/441–3483 or 808/635–7327 ⊕ www. sacredseasscuba.com.

Seasport Divers. Rated highly by readers of Rodale's *Scuba Diving* magazine, Seasport Divers' 48-foot *Anela Kai* tops the chart for dive-boat luxury. But owner Marvin Otsuji didn't stop with that. In 2006, he added a second boat—*Anuhea*, a 32-foot catamaran—that's outfitted for diving, but we like it as an all-around charter. The company does a brisk business, which means it won't cancel at the last minute because of a lack of reservations, like some other companies, although it may book up to 18 people per boat. ■TIP→ There are slightly more challenging trips in the morning; mellower dive sites are in the afternoon. The company also runs a good-size dive shop for purchase and rentals, as well as a classroom for certification. Ni'ihau trips are available in summer. All trips leave from Kukui'ula Harbor in Po'ipū. Rates start

Continued on page 124

SNORKELING IN HAWAI'I

The waters surrounding the Hawaiian Islands are filled with life—from giant manta rays cruising off the Big Island's Kona Coast to humpback whales giving birth in Maui's Mā'alaea Bay. Dip your head beneath the surface to experience a spectacularly colorful world: pairs of milletseed butterflyfish dart back and forth, red-lipped parrotfish snack on coral algae, and spotted eagle rays flap past like silent spaceships. Sea turtles bask at the surface while tiny wrasses give them the equivalent of a shave and a haircut. Remember, water quality and marine life will vary depending on time of year and location. Sandy bottom bays and river mouths generally are not great snorkel spots.

Certainly few destinations are as accommodating to every level of snorkeler as Hawai'i. Beginners can tromp in from sandy beaches while more advanced divers descend to shipwrecks, reefs, craters, and sea arches just offshore. Because of Hawai'i's extreme isolation, the island chain has fewer fish species than Fiji or the Caribbean—but many of the fish that are here exist nowhere else. The Hawaiian waters are home to the highest percentage of endemic fish in the world.

The key to enjoying the underwater world is slowing down. Look carefully. Listen. You might hear the strange crackling sound of shrimp tunneling through coral, or you may hear whales singing to one another during winter. A shy octopus may drift along the ocean's floor beneath you. If you're hooked, pick up a waterproof fishkey from Long's Drugs. You can brag later that you've looked the Hawaiian turkeyfish in the eye.

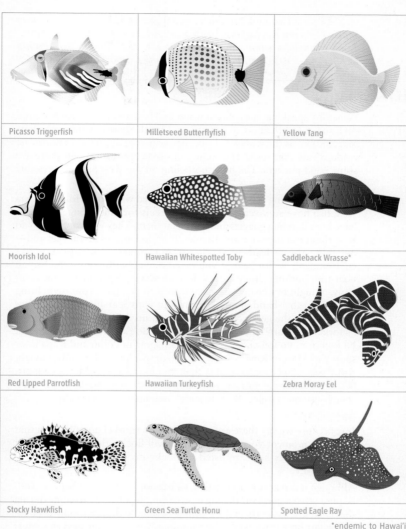

Picasso Triggerfish	Milletseed Butterflyfish	Yellow Tang
Moorish Idol	Hawaiian Whitespotted Toby	Saddleback Wrasse*
Red Lipped Parrotfish	Hawaiian Turkeyfish	Zebra Moray Eel
Stocky Hawkfish	Green Sea Turtle Honu	Spotted Eagle Ray

*endemic to Hawai'i

POLYNESIA'S FIRST CELESTIAL NAVIGATORS: HONU

Honu is the Hawaiian name for two native sea turtles, the hawksbill and the green sea turtle. Little is known about these dinosaur-age marine reptiles, though snorkelers regularly see them foraging for *limu* (seaweed) in Hawaiian waters. Most female honu nest in the uninhabited northwestern Hawaiian Islands, but more and more are nesting on the main islands. Scientists suspect that they navigate the seas via magnetism—sensing the earth's poles. Amazingly, they will journey up to 800 miles to nest—it's believed that they return to their own birth sites. After about 60 days of incubation, nestlings emerge from the sand at night and find their way back to the sea by the reflection of the stars and moon. on the water.

at $125 for a two-tank boat dive; rental gear is $25 extra. ⊠ *Check-in office on Po'ipū Rd. just north of Lāwa'i Rd. turnoff to Spouting Horn. Look for yellow submarine in parking lot, 2827 Po'ipū Rd., Po'ipū* ☎ *808/742–9303 or 800/685–5889* ⊕ *www.seasportdivers.com.*

SNORKELING

Generally speaking, the calmest water and best snorkeling can be found on Kaua'i's North Shore in summer and South Shore in winter. The East Side, known as the windward side, has year-round, prevalent northeast trade winds that make snorkeling unpredictable, although there are some good pockets. The best snorkeling on the West Side is accessible only by boat.

A word on feeding fish: Don't. As Captain Ted with HoloHolo Charters says, fish have survived and populated reefs for much longer than we have been donning goggles and staring at them. They will continue to do so without our intervention. Besides, fish food messes up the reef and—one thing always leads to another—can eliminate a once-pristine reef environment. As for gear, if you're snorkeling with one of the Nāpali boat-tour outfitters, they'll provide it. However, depending on the company, it might not be the latest or greatest. If you have your own, bring it. On the other hand, if you're going out with SeaFun or Z-Tourz *(see Boat Tours),* the gear is top-notch. If you need to rent, hit one of the "snorkel-and-surf" shops such as Snorkel Bob's in Kōloa and Kapa'a, Nukumoi in Po'ipū and Waimea, or Seasport in Pōipū and Kapa'a, or shop Wal-Mart or Kmart if you want to drag it home. Typically, though, rental gear will be better quality than that found at Wal-Mart or Kmart.
■ TIP➔ If you wear glasses, you can rent prescription masks at the rental shops—just don't expect them to match your prescription exactly.

BEST SPOTS

Just because we say these are good places to snorkel doesn't mean that the exact moment you arrive, the fish will flock—they are wild, after all. The beaches here are listed in clockwise fashion starting on the North Shore.

Although it can get quite crowded, **Kē'ē Beach** (⊠ *At the end of Rte. 560*) is quite often a good snorkeling destination. Just be sure to come during the off-hours, say early in the morning or later in the afternoon. ■ TIP➔ Snorkeling here in winter can be hazardous. Summer is the best and safest time, although you should never swim beyond the reef.

★ The search for **Tunnels (Mākua)** (⊠ *At Hā'ena Beach Park, near end of Rte. 560, across from lava-tube sea caves, after stream crossing*) is as tricky as the snorkeling. Park at Hā'ena Beach Park and walk east—away from Nāpali Coast—until you see a sand channel entrance in the water, almost at the point. Once you get here, the reward is

WORD OF MOUTH

"We've snorkeled at Kē'ē Beach on Kaua'i's North Shore, and it was great when we were there. You have to get there early to get a parking spot. There's also Tunnels Beach near there." –Samsaf

If you manage to get up close and personal with a Hawaiian Monk Seal, consider yourself lucky—it's an endangered species.

fantastic. The name of this beach comes from the many underwater lava tubes, which always attract marine life. The shore is mostly beach rock interrupted by three sand channels. You'll want to enter and exit at one of these channels (or risk stepping on a sea urchin or scraping your stomach on the reef). Follow the sand channel to a drop-off; the snorkeling along here is always full of nice surprises. Expect a current running east to west. ■TIP→ Snorkeling here in winter can be hazardous; summer is the best and safest time for snorkeling.

Lydgate Beach Park (⊠ *Just south of Wailua River, turn makai off Rte. 56 onto Lehu Dr. and left onto Nalu Rd.*) is the absolute safest place to snorkel on Kaua'i. With its lava-rock wall creating a protected swimming pool, this is the perfect spot for beginners, young and old. The fish are so tame here it's almost like swimming in a saltwater aquarium.

You'll generally find good year-round snorkeling at **Po'ipū Beach Park** (⊠ *From Po'ipū Rd., turn right on Ho'ōne Rd.*), except during summer's south swells (which are not nearly as frequent as winter's north swells). The best snorkeling fronts the Marriott Waiohai Beach Club. Stay inside the crescent shape created by the sandbar and rocky point. The current runs east to west.

Don't pack the beach umbrella, beach mats, or cooler for snorkeling at **Beach House (Lāwa'i Beach)** (⊠ *Makai side of Lāwa'i Rd.; park on road in front of Lāwa'i Beach Resort*). Just bring your snorkeling gear. The beach—named after its neighbor the Beach House restaurant (yum)—is on the road to Spouting Horn. It's a small slip of sand during low tide and a rocky shoreline during high tide. However, it's right by the road's edge, and its rocky coastline and somewhat rocky bottom make it great

Winter brings big surf to Kaua'i's North Shore. You can see some of the sport's biggest celebrities catching waves at Hā'ena and Hanalei Bay.

for snorkeling. Enter and exit in the sand channel (not over the rocky reef) that lines up with the Lāwa'i Beach Resort's center atrium. Stay within the rocky points anchoring each end of the beach. The current runs east to west.

★ **Nu'alolo Kai** was once an ancient Hawaiian fishpond and is now home to the best snorkeling along Nāpali Coast (and perhaps on all of Kaua'i). The only way to access it is by boat, and only a few Nāpali snorkeling-tour operators are permitted to do so. We recommend Nāpali Explorer and Kaua'i Sea Tours *(see Boat Tours)*.

Fodor's Choice With little river runoff and hardly any boat traffic, the waters off the
★ island of **Ni'ihau** are some of the clearest in all Hawai'i, and that's good for snorkeling. Like Nu'alolo Kai, the only way to snorkel here is to sign on with one of the two tour boats venturing across a sometimes rough open ocean channel: Blue Dolphin Charters and HoloHolo *(see Boat Tours)*. Sammy the monk seal likes to hang out behind Lehua Rock off the north end of Ni'ihau and swim with the snorkelers.

TOURS

SeaFun Kaua'i. This guided snorkeling tour, for beginners and intermediates alike, is led by a marine expert, so not only is there excellent how-to instruction, but the guide actually gets in the water with you and identifies marine life. You're guaranteed to spot tons of critters you'd never see on your own. This is a land-based operation and the only one of its kind on Kaua'i. (Don't think those snorkeling cruises are guided snorkeling tours—they rarely are. A member of the boat's crew serves as lifeguard, not a marine-life *guide*.) A half-day tour includes all your snorkeling gear—and a wet suit to keep you warm—and stops at two snorkeling locations, chosen based on ocean conditions. The cost is $80. ✉ *Check in at Kilohana Plantation in Puhi, next to Kaua'i Community College* ☎ *808/245–6400 or 800/452–1113* ⊕ *www.alohakauaitours.com.*

STAND-UP PADDLING

Unlike kiteboarding, this is a new sport that even a novice can pick up—*and* have fun doing. Technically, it's not really a new sport but a reinvigorated one from the 1950s. Beginners start with a heftier surf-board and a longer-than-normal canoe paddle. And, just as the name implies, stand-up paddlers stand on their surfboards and paddle out from the beach—no timing a wave and doing a push-up to stand. The perfect place to learn is a river (think Hanalei or Wailua) or a calm lagoon (try '**Anini** or **Kalapakī**). But this sport isn't just for beginners. Tried-and-true surfers turn to it when the waves are not quite right for their preferred sport, because it gives them another reason to be on the water. Stand-up paddlers catch waves earlier and ride them longer than long-board surfers. In the past couple years, professional stand-up pad-dling competitions have popped up.

EQUIPMENT AND LESSONS

Not all surf instructors teach stand-up paddling, but more and more are, like Blue Seas Surf School and Titus Kinimaka Hawaiian School of Surfing *(see Surfing).*

Hawaiian Surfing Adventures. This stand at Hanalei Beach Park rents stand-up paddle equipment ($20 for the first hour; $10 for each addi-tional hour). Lessons are available on the scenic Hanalei River or in Hanalei Bay, and include one hour of instruction and two hours to practice with the board (lessons start at $55). The company also offers surf board rentals and surfing lessons ✉ *Hanalei Beach Park, Hanalei* ☎ *808/482-0749* ⊕ *www.hawaiiansurfingadventures.com.*

Kaua'i Beach Boys. This outfitter is located right on the beach at Kalapakī, so there's no hauling your gear on your car. ✉ *Kalapakī Beach Līhu'e* ☎ *808/632–0071.*

SURFING

Good ol' stand-up surfing is alive and well on Kaua'i, especially in win-ter's high-surf season on the North Shore. If you're new to the sport, we highly recommend taking a lesson. Not only will this ensure you're up and riding waves in no time, but instructors will provide the right board for your experience and size, help you time a wave, and give you a push to get your momentum going. ■TIP→ You don't need to be in top physical shape to take a lesson. Because your instructor helps push you into the wave, you won't wear yourself out paddling. If you're experienced and want to hit the waves on your own, most surf shops rent boards for all levels, from beginners to advanced.

Humpback whales arrive at Kaua'i in December and stick around until early April. Head out on a boat tour for a chance to see these majestic creatures breach.

BEST SPOTS

Perennial-favorite beginning surf spots include **Po'ipū Beach** (the area fronting the Marriott Waiohai Beach Club); **Hanalei Bay** (the area next to the Hanalei Pier); and the stream end of **Kalapakī Beach**. More advanced surfers move down the beach in Hanalei to an area fronting a grove of pine trees known as **Pine Trees**. When the trade winds die, the north ends of **Wailua** and **Keālia** beaches are teeming with surfers. Breaks off **Po'ipū** and **Beach House/Lāwa'i Beach** attract intermediates year-round. During high surf, the break on the cliff side of **Kalihiwai** is for experts only.

LESSONS

Blue Seas Surf School. Surfer and instructor Charlie Smith specializes in beginners (especially children) and will go anywhere on the island to find just the right surf. His soft-top, long boards are very stable, making it easier to stand up. Rates start at $75 for a 1½-hour lesson. (Transportation provided, if needed.) ⊠ *Meet at beach; location varies depending on surf conditions* ☎ *808/634–6979* ⊕ *www. blueseassurfingschool.com.*

Margo Oberg Surfing School. Seven-time world surfing champion Margo Oberg runs a surf school that meets on the beach in front of the Sheraton Kaua'i in Po'ipū. Group lessons are $68 for two hours, though Margo herself rarely teaches anymore. ⊠ *Po'ipū Beach* ☎ *808/332–6100* ⊕ *www.surfonkauai.com.*

Nukumoi Surf Co. The parents of Kaua'i-grown and world-famous Rochelle Ballard own this surf shop. Not that the instructors who teach surfing here these days taught Rochelle, but they are die-hard surfers, even if they never made the international scene. Lessons run $75 for two hours with no more than four students per instructor. Their primary surf spot is the beach fronting the Sheraton. ⊠ *On Ho'one Rd. across from Po'ipū Beach Park* ☎ *808/742–8019* ⊕ *www.nukumoisurf.com.*

Titus Kinimaka Hawaiian School of Surfing. Famed as a pioneer of big-wave surfing, this Hawaiian believes in giving back to his sport. Beginning, intermediate, and "extreme" lessons, including tow-in, are available. If you want to learn to surf from a living legend, this is the man. ■**TIP→** He employs other instructors, so if you want Titus, be sure to ask for him. (And good luck because if the waves are going off, he'll be surfing, not teaching.) Rates are $55 for a 90-minute group lesson; $65 for a 90-minute group stand-up paddle lesson; $150 for a one-hour, tow-in lesson. ⊠ *Meets at Quicksilver shop in Hanalei* ☎ *808/652–1116.*

EQUIPMENT

Hanalei Surf Company. You can rent boards here and shop for rash guards, wetsuits, and some hip surf-inspired apparel. ⊠ *Mauka at Hanalei Center, 5-5161 Kūhiō Hwy., Hanalei* ☎ *808/826–9000.*

Nukumoi Surf Co. If you're looking for convenience, this is the spot. No toting boards on your car, because this shop is located right across from the beach. ⊠ *On Ho'one Rd. across from Po'ipū Beach Park* ☎ *808/742–8019.*

Nukumoi Surf Co. West Side. There isn't great surfing on the West Side, but this is the only surf shop west of Po'ipū. ⊠ *In Waimea, makai on Rte. 50* ☎ *808/338–1617.*

Progressive Expressions. This full-service shop has a choice of rental boards and a whole lotta shopping. ⊠ *On Kōloa Rd. in Old Kōloa Town* ☎ *808/742–6041.*

Tamba Surf Company. This is your best bet for surf rentals on the East Side. ⊠ *Mauka on north end of Hwy. 56 in Kapa'a; across from Scotty's Beachside BBQ; 4-1543 Kūhiō Hwy., Kapa'a* ☎ *808/823–6942.*

WHALE WATCHING

Every winter North Pacific humpback whales swim some 3,000 mi over 30 days, give or take a few, from Alaska to Hawai'i. Whales arrive as early as November and sometimes stay through April, though they seem to be most populous in February and March. They come to Hawai'i to breed, calve, and nurse their young.

TOURS

Of course, nothing beats seeing a whale up close. During the season, any boat on the water is looking for whales; they're hard to avoid, whether the tour is labeled "whale watching" or not. Consider the whales a lucky-strike extra to any boating event that may interest you. If whales are definitely your thing, though, you can narrow down your tour boat decision by asking a few whale-related questions like whether there's a hydrophone on board, how long the captain has been running tours in Hawaii, and if anyone on the crew is a marine biologist or trained naturalist.

Several boat operators will add two-hour, afternoon whale watching tours during the season that run on the South Shore (not Nāpali). Operators include **Blue Dolphin, Catamaran Kahanu, HoloHolo,** and **Nāpali Explorer** *(see Boat Tours)*. Capt. Andy's now has a three-hour morning whale watch tour along the West Side. Trying one of these excursions is a good option for those who have no interest in snorkeling or sightseeing along Nāpali Coast, although keep in mind, the longer you're on the water, the more likely you'll be to see the humpbacks.

One of the more unique ways to, *possibly,* see some whales is atop a kayak. For such an encounter, try **Outfitters Kaua'i**'s South Shore kayak trip *(see Kayaking Tours)*. There are a few lookout spots around the island with good land-based viewing: Kīlauea Lighthouse on the North Shore, the Kapa'a Scenic Overlook just north of Kapa'a town on the East Side, and the cliffs to the east of Keoniloa (Shipwreck) Beach on the South Shore.

WINDSURFING

Windsurfing on Kaua'i isn't nearly as popular as it is on Maui, but 'Anini Beach Park is the place if you're going to windsurf or play the spectator. Rentals and lessons are available from **Windsurf Kaua'i** (☎ *808/828–6838*). Lessons run $100 for three hours; rentals run $25 per hour. The instructor will meet you on 'Anini Beach.

Golf, Hiking, and Outdoor Activities

WORD OF MOUTH

"Of all the helicopter rides, the ones on Kaua'i offer the most jaw-dropping, awe-inspiring scenery of any island. Also, on Kaua'i, don't miss Waimea Canyon. There is nothing like it on any other island. For spectacular, "up in the heavens" hiking, you can't beat Kōke'e State Park."

—montereybob

Updated by
Kim Steuter-
mann Rogers

For those of you who love ocean sports but need a little break from all that sun, sand, and salt, there are plenty of options on Kaua'i to keep you busy on the ground. You can hike the island's many trails, or consider taking your vacation into flight with a treetop zipline. You can have a backcountry adventure in a four-wheel drive, or relax in an inner tube floating down the cane-field irrigation canals.

Before booking tours, check with your concierge to find out what the forecast is for water and weather conditions. ■TIP→ Don't rely on The Weather Channel or your iPhone for accurate weather reports, as they're often reporting O'ahu weather. If you happen to arrive during a North Shore lull in the surf, you'll want to plan to be on the ocean in a kayak or snorkeling on the reef. If it's raining, ATV tours are the activity of choice.

For the golfer in the family, Kaua'i's spectacular courses are rated among the most scenic as well as the most technical. Princeville Golf Course has garnered accolades from three national publications, and Po'ipū Bay Golf Course hosted the prestigious season-end PGA Grand Slam of Golf for 13 years, although Tiger (he won a record five-straight tournaments) and company are, unfortunately, now heading elsewhere for this tourney.

One of the most popular Kaua'i experiences is to see the island from the air. In an hour, you can see waterfalls, craters, and other places that are inaccessible even by hiking trails (some say that 70% or more of the island is inaccessible). The majority of flights depart from the Līhu'e airport and follow a clockwise pattern around the island. ■TIP→ If you plan to take an aerial tour, it's a good idea to fly when you first arrive, rather than saving it for the end of your trip. It will help you visualize what's where on the island, and it may help you decide what you want to see from a closer vantage point during your stay. Many companies advertise a low-price 30- or 40-minute tour, which they rarely fly, so don't expect to book a flight at the advertised rate. The most popular flight is 60 minutes long, and some companies offer DVDs for an additional charge, so there's no need to spend your time in the air snapping pictures.

AERIAL TOURS

If you only drive around Kaua'i in your rental car, you will not see *all* of Kaua'i. There is truly only one way to see it all, and that's by air. Helicopter tours are the favorite way to get a bird's-eye view of Kaua'i—they fly at lower altitudes, hover above waterfalls, and wiggle their way into areas that a fixed-wing aircraft cannot. That said, if you've already tried the helitour, how about piloting a microlight? Or flying in the open cockpit of a biplane—à la the Red Baron?

★ **Blue Hawaiian Helicopters.** This multi-island operator flies the latest in helicopter technology, the Eco-Star, costing $1.8 million. It has 23% more interior space for its six passengers, has unparalleled viewing, and offers a few extra safety features. As the name implies, the helicopter is also a bit more environmentally friendly, with a 50% noise-reduction rate. Flights run a tad shorter than others (50 to 55 minutes instead of the 55 to 65 minutes that other companies tout), but the flight feels very complete. The rate is $225 and includes taxes and fuel surcharge. A DVD of your actual tour is available for an additional $25. ⊠ *Harbor Mall in Nāwiliwili, Līhuʻe* ☎ *808/245–5800 or 800/745–2583* ⊕ *www.bluehawaiian.com.*

> **WORD OF MOUTH**
>
> "If you choose to do a helicopter/airplane ride, go early in your trip. Ours got postponed due to plane trouble, so we went our last day and found that we'd missed the best snorkeling at Tunnels, because we didn't know what the reef "looked like" until we saw if from above. We'll always regret that (unless we get back one day, of course)."– HawaiiVirgin

FodorsChoice
★ **Inter-Island Helicopters.** This company flies a four-seater Hughes 500 helicopters *with the doors off.* (Everyone gets a window seat.) It can get chilly at higher elevations, so bring a sweater and wear long pants. You can enjoy the standard flight (50 to 55 minutes) plus a spectacular tour option that includes landing by a waterfall for a picnic and swim. Tours depart from Hanapēpē's Port Allen Airport. Prices range from $260 to $355 per person and include taxes and fuel surcharge. ⊠ *From Rte. 50, turn makai onto Rte. 543 in Hanapēpē* ☎ *808/335–5009 or 800/656–5009* ⊕ *www.interislandhelicopters.com.*

Jack Harter Helicopters. Jack Harter was the first company to offer helicopter tours on Kauaʻi. The company flies the six-passenger ASTAR helicopter with floor-to-ceiling windows, and the four-person Hughes 500, which is flown with no doors. The doorless ride can get windy, but it's the best bet for taking reflection-free photos. Pilots provide information on the Garden Island's history and geography through two-way intercoms. The company flies out of Līhuʻe and has a second office at the Kauaʻi Marriott. Tours are 60 to 65 minutes and 90 to 95 minutes and cost $259 to $384, including taxes and fuel surcharge. ⊠ *4231 Ahukini Rd., Līhuʻe* ☎ *808/245–3774 or 888/245–2001* ⊕ *www.helicopters-kauai.com.*

★ **Safari Helicopters.** This company flies the "Super" ASTAR helicopter, which offers floor-to-ceiling windows on its doors, four roof windows, and Bose X-Generation headphones. Two-way microphones allow passengers to converse with the pilot. The price is $224 and includes taxes and fuel surcharge; a DVD is $40 extra. ⊠ *3225 Akahi St., Līhuʻe* ☎ *808/246–0136 or 800/326–3356* ⊕ *www.safariair.com.*

Sunshine Helicopter Tours. If the name of this company sounds familiar, it may be because its pilots fly on all the main Hawaiian Islands. On Kauaʻi, Sunshine Helicopters departs out of three different locations: Līhuʻe, Princeville, and Port Allen. They fly the six-passenger FX STAR and super roomy six-passenger WhisperSTAR birds. The standard

50-minute flight starts at $229 and includes taxes and fuel surcharge. A 30-minute North Shore–only flight is available out of Princeville for $199. ✉ 3-3222 *Kūhiō Hwy., Līhu'e* ✉ *3441 Kuiloko Rd., Port Allen Airport, Hanapēpē Princeville Airport, Princeville* ☎ *808/245–8881 or 888/245–4354* ⊕ *www.helicopters-hawaii.com.*

Tropical Biplanes. This company flies a bright-red Waco biplane, built in 2002 and based on a 1936 design. An open cockpit and staggered wing design mean there's nothing between you and the sights. The plane can carry two passengers in front and flies at an altitude of 1,500 feet, at about 85 mph. The one-hour price for two is $386 and includes taxes and fuel surcharge. ✉ *Līhu'e Airport Commuter Terminal* ☎ *808/246–9123 or 888/280-9123* ⊕ *www.tropicalbiplanes.com.*

LESSONS

★ **Birds in Paradise.** A serene cruise over the island, skimming clouds with the breeze in your hair—microlight flying is a meditative and magical way to take in the sights. Although many lessons are available, the most popular package is the 50–60-minute option for $236 (includes taxes and fuel surcharge). In 2009, the company added a fifth microlight to its fleet. ✉ *Salt Pond Beach Park/Port Allen Airport* ☎ *808/822–5309* ⊕ *birdsinparadise.com.*

ATV TOURS

Although all the beaches on the island are public, much of the interior land—once sugar and pineapple plantations—is privately owned. This is really a shame, because the valleys and mountains that make up the vast interior of the island easily rival the beaches in sheer beauty. The good news is some tour operators have agreements with landowners that make exploration possible, albeit a bit bumpy, and unless you have back troubles, that's half the fun. ■ TIP➔ If it looks like rain, book an ATV tour ASAP. That's the thing about these tours: the muddier, the better.

★ **Kaua'i ATV Tours.** This is *the* thing to do when it rains on Kaua'i. Consider it an extreme mud bath. Now with three tours, Kaua'i ATV in Kōloa is the originator of the island's all-terrain-vehicle excursions. Its $125 three-hour "Kōloa" tour takes you through a private sugar plantation and historic cane-haul tunnel. The $155 four-hour "Waterfall" tour visits secluded waterfalls and includes a picnic lunch. This popular option includes a hike through a bamboo forest and a swim in a freshwater pool at the base of the falls—to rinse off all that mud. In 2009, Kaua'i ATV added a four-hour tour that combines ATV and kayaking, for $175. You must be 16 or older to operate your own ATV, but Kaua'i ATV also offers its four-passenger "Ohana Bug" and two-passenger "Mud Bugs" to accommodate families with kids ages five and older. ✉ *3477A Weliweli Rd., Kōloa* ☎ *808/742–2734 or 877/707–7088* ⊕ *www.kauaiatv.com.*

Kipu Ranch Adventures. This 3,000-acre property extends from the Huleia River to the top of Mt. Haupu. *Jurassic Park, Indiana Jones,* and *Mighty Joe Young* were filmed here, and you'll see the locations for all of them on the $125 three-hour Ranch Tour. The $150 four-hour Waterfall

One of the most visited sites on Kaua'i is Waimea Canyon. Make sure to stop at Pu'u ka Pele and Pu'u hinahina lookouts.

Tour includes a visit to two waterfalls and a picnic lunch. Kipu Ranch was once a sugar plantation, but today it is a working cattle ranch, so you'll be in the company of bovines as well as pheasants, wild boars, and peacocks. ⌖ *Take Puhi Bypass Rd. off Hwy. 50 and turn right on Kipu Rd.* ☎ *808/246–9288* ⊕ *www.kiputours.com.*

BIKING

Kaua'i is a labyrinth of cane-haul roads, which are fun for exploring on two wheels. The challenge is finding roads where biking is allowed and then not getting lost in the maze. Maybe that explains why Kaua'i is not a hub for the sport . . . yet. Still, there are some epic rides for those who are interested—both the adrenaline-rush and the mellower beach-cruiser kind. If you want to grind out some mileage, the main highway that skirts the coastal areas is generally safe, though there are only a few designated bike lanes. It's hilly, but you'll find that keeping your eyes on the road and not the scenery is the biggest challenge. "Cruisers" should head to Kapa'a. A new section of Ke Ala Hele Makalae, a pedestrian trail that runs along the East Side of Kaua'i, was completed in the summer of 2009, totaling 6½ mi of completed path. You can rent bikes (with helmets) from the activities desks of certain hotels, but these are not the best quality. You're better off renting from Kaua'i Cycle in Kapa'a, Outfitters Kaua'i in Po'ipū, or Pedal 'n' Paddle in Hanalei.

★ **Ke Ala Hele Makalae** (*Nāwiliwili to Anahola Bike/Pedestrian Path*). For the cruiser, this path follows the coastline on Kaua'i's East Side.

Eventually, it will run some 20 mi and offer scenic views, picnic pavilions, and restroom facilities along the way—all in compliance with the Americans with Disabilities Act. For now, it runs from Lydgate Beach Park to Donkey Beach. The easiest way to access the completed sections of the path is from Keālia Beach. Park here and head north into rural lands with spectacular coastline vistas or head south into Kapa'a for a more interactive experience. ⊠ *Trailhead: 1 mi north of Kapa'a; park at north end of Keālia Beach.*

Moalepe Trail. This trail is perfect for intermediate to advanced riders. The first 2 mi of this 5-mi, double-track road winds through pastureland. The real challenge begins when you reach the steep and rutted switchbacks, which during a rainy spell can be hazardous to attempt. Moalepe dead-ends at the Kuilau Trail. If you choose to continue down the Kuilau Trail, it will end at the Keāhua Arboretum stream. ⊠ *From Kūhiō Hwy. in Kapa'a drive mauka on Kuamo'o Rd. for 3 mi and turn right on Kamalu Rd. It dead-ends at Olohenā Rd. Turn left and follow until the road veers sharply to the right. The trailhead will be right in front of you.*

Powerline Trail. Advanced riders like this trail. It's actually a service road for the electric company that splits the island. It's 13 mi in length; the first 5 mi goes from 620 feet in elevation to almost 2,000. The remaining 8 mi descends gradually over a variety of terrain, some technical. Some sections will require carrying your bike. The views will stay with you forever. Trailhead is *mauka* just past the stream crossing at Keāhua Arboretum, or at the end of the appropriately named Powerline Road in Princeville, past Princeville Ranch Stables. ■ TIP➔ When it's wet—in summer or winter—this trail is a mess. Check with a knowledgeable bike shop for trail conditions first.

Spalding Monument Loop. For the novice rider, this loop offers a good workout and a summit ocean view that is not overly strenuous to reach. If you pick up a bike at Kaua'i Cycle in Kapa'a, you can ride a mile up Ke Ala Hele Makalae path to reach the head of the loop, and even make a snack stop at the Kealia Store without a detour. From Kealia Store, ride up a gradual incline 2 mi through horse pastures to Spalding Monument, named for a former plantation owner, although there is no longer any signage. Palms circle the lava-rock wall, where you can picnic while enjoying a 180-degree ocean view. Behind you is the glorious mountain backdrop of Kalalea. Follow the paved road north toward Kalalea for 2 more mi. Turn right at the highway, and it's another 2 mi south to a parking lot for Donkey Beach on the ocean side. The lot is not far from mile marker 12 and sits on the top of a hill. Follow the path down to the beach and turn right on Ke Ala Hele Makalae, following what was once an old cane-haul road that heads right back into Kapa'a town. ⊠ *The loop begins at the Kealia Store, past mile marker 10 on the mauka side of the road.*

Continued on page 140

HAWAI'I'S PLANTS 101

Hawai'i is a bounty of rainbow-colored flowers and plants. The evening any home, travel any road, or visit any local park and you'll see a spectacular array of colored blossoms and leaves. What most visitors don't know is that most of the plants they are seeing are not native to Hawai'i; rather, they were introduced during the last two centuries as ornamental plants, or for timber, shade, or fruit.

Hawai'i boasts nearly every climate on the planet, excluding the two most extreme: arctic tundra and arid desert. The Islands have wine-growing regions, cactus-speckled ranchlands, icy mountaintops, and the rainiest forests on earth.

Plants introduced from around the world thrive here. The lush lowland valleys along the windward coasts are predominantly populated by non-native trees including yellow- and red-fruited **guava**, silvery-leafed **kukui**, and orange-flowered **tulip trees**.

The colorful **plumeria flower**, very fragrant and commonly used in lei making, and the giant multicolored **hibiscus flower** are both used by many women as hair adornments, and are two of the most common plants found around homes and hotels. The umbrella-like **monkeypod tree** from Central America provides shade in many of Hawai'i's parks including Kapiolani Park in Honolulu. Hawai'i's largest tree, found in Lahaina, Maui, is a giant **banyan tree.** Its canopy and massive support roots cover about two-thirds of an acre. The native **o'hia tree,** with its brilliant red brush-like flowers, and the **hapu'u**, a giant tree fern, are common in Hawai'i's forests and are also used ornamentally in gardens and around homes.

Bougainville	Guava	Monkeypod
Banyan	Ohia Lehua*	Tulip Tree
Plumeria	Pandanus	Hibiscus
Anthurium	Kukui	Hapu'u

*endemic to Hawai'i

5

IN FOCUS HAWAI'I'S PLANTS 101

DID YOU KNOW?

Over 2,200 plant species are found in the Hawaiian Islands, but only about 1,000 are native. Of these, 282 are so rare, they are endangered. Hawai'i's endemic plants evolved from ancestral seeds arriving on the islands over thousands of years as baggage on birds, floating on ocean currents, or drifting on winds from continents thousands of miles away. Once here, these plants evolved in isolation creating many new species known nowhere else in the world.

Wailua Forest Management Road. For the novice mountain biker, this is an easy ride, and it's also easy to find. From Route 56 in Wailua, turn *mauka* on Kuamo'o Road and continue 6 mi to the picnic area, known as Keāhua Arboretum; park here. The potholed four-wheel-drive road includes some stream crossings—■TIP➡ stay away during heavy rains, because the streams flood—and continues for 2 mi to a T-stop, where you should turn right. Stay on the road for about 3 mi until you reach a gate; this is the spot where the gates in the movie *Jurassic Park* were filmed, though it looks nothing like the movie. Go around the gate and down the road for another mile to a confluence of streams at the base of Mt. Wai'ale'ale. Be sure to bring your camera.

Waimea Canyon Road. For those wanting a road workout, climb this road, also known as Route 550. After a 3,000-foot climb, the road tops out at mile 12 adjacent to Waimea Canyon, which will pop in and out of view on your right as you ascend. From here it continues several miles (mostly level) past the Kōke'e Museum and ends at the Kalalau Lookout. It's paved the entire way, uphill, and curvy. ■TIP➡ There's not much of a shoulder—sometimes none—so be extra cautious. The road gets busier as the day wears on, so you may want to consider a sunrise ride. By the way, bikes aren't allowed on the hiking trails in and around Waimea Canyon and Koke'e State Park, but there are miles of wonderful 4WD roads perfect for mountain biking. Check at Kōke'e Lodge for a map and conditions. ✉ *Road turns mauka off Rte. 50 just after grocery store in downtown Waimea.*

EQUIPMENT AND TOURS

★ **Kaua'i Cycle.** This reliable, full-service bike shop rents, sells, and repairs bikes. Cruisers, mountain bikes (front- and full-suspension), and road bikes are available for $20 to $45 per day and $110 to $250 per week with directions to trails. The Ke Ala Hele Makalae is right out their back door. ✉ *Across from Taco Bell, 934 Kūhiō Hwy., Kapa'a* ☎ 808/821–2115 ⊕ *www.kauaicycle.com.*

Outfitters Kaua'i. Hybrid "comfort" and mountain bikes (both full suspension and hardtails), as well as road bikes, are available at this shop in Po'ipū. You can ride right out the door to tour Po'ipū or get information on how to do a self-guided tour of Kōe'e State Park and Waimea Canyon. The company also leads sunrise coasting tours (under the name **Bicycle Downhill**) from Waimea Canyon to the island's West Side beaches. Rentals cost $25 to $45 per day. Tours cost $98. ✉ *2827-A Po'ipū Rd., Po'ipū* ⊹ *Follow Po'ipū Rd. south from Kōloa town; shop is on right before turnoff to Spouting Horn* ☎ 808/742–9667 or 888/742–9887 ⊕ *www.outfitterskauai.com.*

Pedal 'n' Paddle. This company rents old-fashioned, single-speed beach cruisers and hybrid road bikes for $15 to $20 per day, $60 to $80 per week. In the heart of Hanalei, this is a great way to cruise the town; the more ambitious cyclist can head to the end of the road. Be careful, though, because there are no bike lanes on the twisting and turning road to Kē'ē. ✉ *Ching Young Village, Rte. 560, Hanalei* ☎ 808/826–9069 ⊕ *www.pedalnpaddle.com.*

Our top choice for playing golf on the East Side of Kaua'i is here, at the Kaua'i Lagoons Golf Club.

GOLF

For golfers, the Garden Isle might as well be known as the Robert Trent Jones Jr. Isle. Four of the island's nine courses, including Po'ipū Bay—onetime home of the PGA Grand Slam of Golf—are the work of Jones, who maintains a home at Princeville. Combine these four courses with those from Jack Nicklaus, Robin Nelson, and local legend Toyo Shirai, and you'll see that golf sets Kaua'i apart from the other islands as much as the Pacific Ocean does. ■ TIP→ Afternoon tee times can save you big bucks.

Kaua'i Lagoons Golf Club. With the development of the Kaua'i Lagoons Resort, the golf club is getting a face-lift, albeit a slow one due to the economy. Yes, Jack is back. When Nicklaus is done with this course, 27 championship-style holes (the links-style course is gone) will await golfers. For now, 18 holes are playable, including the course's signature #16, with a green that sits perched on a precarious point (oh, the ocean views), and #18, the island green named "The Bear" for its challenging play into the trade winds. Construction is expected to continue through 2010. ⊠ 3351 Ho'olaulea Way, Līhu'e ☎ 808/241–6000 or 800/634–6400 ⊕ www.kauailagoonsgolf.com ⚡ 18 holes. 6,977 yds. Par 72. Greens fee: $125 ☞ Facilities: Driving range, putting green, golf carts, rental clubs, lessons.

Kiahuna Golf Club. A meandering creek, lava outcrops, and thickets of trees give Kiahuna its character. Robert Trent Jones Jr. was given a smallish piece of land just inland at Po'ipū and defends par with smaller targets, awkward stances, and optical illusions. In 2003, a

group of homeowners bought the club and brought Jones back to renovate the course (it was originally built in 1983), adding tees and revamping bunkers. The pro here boasts his course has the best putting greens on the island. This is the only course on Kaua'i with a complete set of juniors' tee boxes. ⊠ *2545 Kiahuna Plantation Dr., Kōloa* ☎ *808/742–9595* ⊕ *www.kiahunagolf.com* ⅃ *18 holes. 6,214 yds. Par 70. Greens fee: $99* ☞ *Facilities: Driving range, putting green, rental clubs, lessons, pro shop, restaurant, bar.*

Kukuiolono Golf Course. Local legend Toyo Shirai designed this fun, funky 9-holer where holes play across rolling, forested hills that afford views of the distant Pacific. Though Shirai has an eye for a good golf hole, Kukuiolono is out of the way and a bit rough and so probably not for everyone. But at $9 for the day, it's a deal—bring cash, though, as they don't accept credit cards. No tee times. ⊠ *854 Pu'u Rd., Kalāheo* ☎ *808/332–9151* ⅃ *9 holes. 3,173 yds. Par 36. Greens fee: $9* ☞ *Facilities: Driving range, putting green, golf carts, pull carts, rental clubs.*

Po'ipū Bay Golf Course. Po'ipū Bay has been called the Pebble Beach of Hawai'i, and the comparison is apt. Like Pebble Beach, Po'ipū is a links course built on headlands, not true links land. And as at Monterey Bay, there's wildlife galore—except that the animals are not quite as intrusive to play. It's not unusual for golfers to see monk seals sunning on the beach below, sea turtles bobbing outside the shore break, and humpback whales leaping offshore. From 1994 to 2006, the course (designed by Robert Trent Jones Jr.) hosted the annual PGA Grand Slam of Golf. That means Tiger was a frequent visitor—and winner—here. Starting April 2010, the course will close (pro shop will remain open) in order to redo all 18 greens; it's scheduled to reopen in November 2010, but schedules are hard to keep in Hawai'i, so if your heart is set on playing here, check first. ⊠ *2250 Ainako St., Kōloa* ☎ *808/742–8711* ⊕ *www.poipubaygolf.com* ⅃ *18 holes. 6,612 yds. Par 72. Greens fee: $220* ☞ *Facilities: Driving range, putting green, rental clubs, golf carts, golf academy/lessons, restaurant, bar.*

Fodor's Choice ★ **Princeville Resort.** Robert Trent Jones Jr. built two memorable courses overlooking Hanalei Bay, the 27-hole Princeville Makai Course (1971) and the 18-hole Prince Course (1990). The Prince was ranked by *Golf Digest* as Hawai'i's number-one golf course on its 2006 list of America's Top 100 Greatest Courses. It's certifiably rated Hawai'i's second toughest (behind O'ahu's Ko'olau). This is jungle golf, with holes running through dense forest and over tangled ravines, out onto headlands for breathtaking ocean views, then back into the jungle. In mid-2009, the Makai Course closed for extensive renovations, including new turf throughout, reshaped greens and bunkers, refurbished cart paths and comfort stations, and the creation of an extensive practice facility. It's scheduled to reopen sometime in 2010; call in advance. **Makai Golf Course :** ⊠ *4080 Lei O Papa Rd., Princeville* ☎ *808/826–3580* ⊕ *www.princeville.com* ⅃ *27 holes. 6,886 yds. Par 72. Greens fee: $175* ☞ *Facilities: Driving range, putting green, rental clubs, golf carts, pro shop, golf academy/lessons, snack bar.* **Prince Golf Course :** ⊠ *5-3900 Kūhiō Hwy., Princeville* ☎ *808/826–5001* ⊕ *www.princeville.com* ⅃ *18 holes. 6,960 yds. Par 72.*

Greens fee: $200 ☞ Facilities: Driving range, putting green, rental clubs, golf carts, pro shop, golf academy/lessons, restaurant, bar.

Wailua Municipal Golf Course. Voted by *Golf Digest* as one of Hawai'i's 15 best golf courses, this seaside course was first built as a 9-hole golf course in the 1930s. The second 9 holes were added in 1961. Course designer Toyo Shirai created a course that is fun but not punishing. Not only is this an affordable game with minimal water hazards, but it is challenging enough to have been chosen to host three USGA Amateur Public Links Championships. The trade winds blow steadily on the east side of the island and make the game all the more challenging. An ocean view and affordability make this one of the most popular courses on the island. Tee times are accepted up to seven days in advance. ⊠ *5350 Kūhiō Hwy., 5 mins north of airport, Līhu'e* ☎ *808/241–6666* ⚑*. 18 holes. Par 72. Greens fee: $60 weekdays, $70 weekends. Half price after 3 PM. Cart rental: $18. Cash or traveler's checks only ☞ Facilities: Driving range, rental clubs, golf carts, pro shop, lessons, snack bar.*

HIKING

The best way to experience the *'āina*—the land—on Kaua'i is to step off the beach and hike into the remote interior. You'll find waterfalls so tall you'll strain your neck looking, pools of crystal-cool water for swimming, tropical forests teeming with plant life, and ocean vistas that will make you wish you could stay forever.

■ TIP➔ **For your safety wear sturdy shoes—preferably water-resistant ones.** All hiking trails on Kaua'i are free, so far. There's a development plan in the works that will turn the Waimea Canyon and Kōke'e state parks into admission-charging destinations. Whatever it may be, it will be worth it.

★ **Hanalei-Okolehao Trail.** *Okolehao* basically translates to "moonshine" in Hawaiian. This trail follows the Hihimanu Ridge, which was established in the days of Prohibition, when this backyard liquor was distilled from the roots of ti plants. The 2-mi hike climbs 1,200 feet and offers a 360-degree view of Hanalei Bay and Wai'oli Valley. Thanks to Kaua'i Sierra Club volunteers, this trail survived Hurricane 'Iniki. It took eight years of hauling chain saws and weed whackers up the ridge to clear the trail. Your ascent begins at the China Ditch off the Hanalei River. Follow the trail through a lightly forested grove, at the Y take the first right, and then take the next left up a steep embankment. From here the trail is well marked. Most of the climb is lined with hala, ti, wild orchid, and eucalyptus. You'll get your first of many ocean views at mile marker 1. ⊠ *Follow Ohiki Rd. (north of the Hanalei Bridge) 7 mi to the U.S. Fish and Wildlife Service parking area. Directly across the street is a small bridge that marks the trailhead.*

Ho opi'i Falls. Tucked among the winding roads and grassy pastures of Kapahi, 3 mi inland from Kapa'a town, is an easy hike to two waterfalls. A 10-minute walk will deliver you to the creek. Follow it around to see the first set of falls. The more impressive second falls

Continued on page 148

BIRTH OF THE ISLANDS

How did the volcanoes of the Hawaiian Islands evolve here, in the middle of the Pacific Ocean? The ancient Hawaiians believed that the volcano goddess Pele's hot temper was the key to the mystery; modern scientists contend that it's all about plate tectonics and one very hot spot.

Plate Tectonics & the Hawaiian Question: The theory of plate tectonics says that the Earth's surface is comprised of plates that float around slowly over the planet's molten interior. The vast majority of earthquakes and volcanic eruptions occur near plate boundaries—the San Francisco earthquakes in 1906 and 1989, for example, were the result of activity along the nearby San Andreas Fault, where the Pacific and North American plates meet. Hawai'i, more than 1,988 miles from the nearest plate boundary, is a giant exception. For years scientists struggled to explain the island chain's existence—if not a fault line, what caused the earthquakes and volcanic eruptions that formed these islands?

What's a hotspot? In 1963, J. Tuzo Wilson, a Canadian geophysicist, argued that the Hawaiian volcanoes must have been created by small concentrated areas of extreme heat beneath the plates. Wilson hypothesized that there is a hotspot beneath the present-day position of the Big Island. Its heat produced a persistent source of magma by partly melting the Pacific Plate above it. The magma, lighter than the surrounding solid rock, rose through the mantle and crust to erupt onto the sea floor, forming an active seamount. Each flow caused the seamount to grow until it finally emerged above sea level as an island volcano. Plausible so far, but why then, is there not one giant Hawaiian island?

HAWAIIAN CREATION MYTH

Holo Mai Pele, often played out in hula, is the Hawaiian creation myth. Pele sends her sister Hi'iaka on an epic quest to fetch her lover Lohi'au. Overcoming many obstacles, Hi'iaka reaches full goddess status and falls in love with Lohi'au herself. When Pele finds out, she destroys everything dear to her sister, killing Lohi'au and burning Hi'iaka's 'ohi'a groves. Each time lava flows from a volcano, 'ohi'a trees sprout shortly after, in a constant cycle of destruction and renewal.

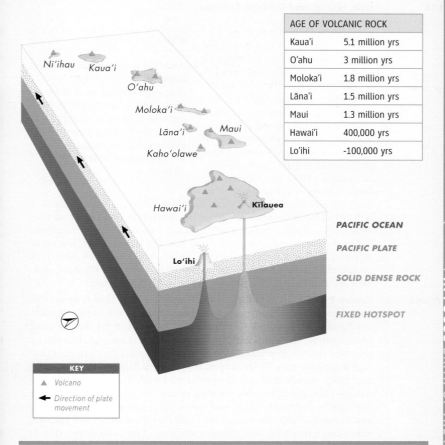

AGE OF VOLCANIC ROCK	
Kaua'i	5.1 million yrs
O'ahu	3 million yrs
Moloka'i	1.8 million yrs
Lāna'i	1.5 million yrs
Maui	1.3 million yrs
Hawai'i	400,000 yrs
Lo'ihi	-100,000 yrs

PACIFIC OCEAN

PACIFIC PLATE

SOLID DENSE ROCK

FIXED HOTSPOT

KEY
▲ *Volcano*
← *Direction of plate movement*

Volcanoes on the Move: Wilson further suggested that the movement of the Pacific Plate itself eventually carries the island volcano beyond the hotspot. Cut off from its magma source, the island volcano becomes dormant. As the plate slowly moved, one island volcano would become extinct just as another would develop over the hotspot. After several million years, there is a long volcanic trail of islands and seamounts across the ocean floor. The oldest islands are those farthest from the hotspot. The exposed rocks of Kaua'i, for example, are about 5.1 million years old, but those on the Big Island are less than .5 million years old, with new volcanic rock still being formed.

An Island on the Way: Off the coast of the Big Island, the volcano known as Lo'ihi is still submerged but erupting. Scientists long believed it to be a retired seamount volcano, but in the 1970s they discovered both old and new lava on its flanks, and in 1996 it erupted with a vengeance. It is believed that several thousand years from now, Lo'ihi will be the newest addition to the Hawaiian Islands.

are a mere 25 minutes away. The swimming hole alone is worth the journey. Just climb the rooted path next to the first falls and turn left on the trail above. Turn left on the very next trail to descend back into the canyon and follow the leafy path that zigzags along the creek. The falls and the swimming hole will lie below. Now is your chance to live that Indiana Jones fantasy of swinging from tree limb to tree limb. Okay, it's not quite that

WORD OF MOUTH

"I would also recommend hiking boots for Kaua'i. Some trails were okay with Tevas, but we wore our hiking boots on the Kalalau trail and several others, and I'm glad we did. The Kalalau is indeed very muddy and slippery in places, and very rocky in other places."
–QueenMab

exciting, but you will be grateful for all the trees on the descent that will help you brace yourself on the steep decline, and once you step into that cool, clear water, you'll be glad you made the extra effort. ⊠ *On the north end of Kapa'a, ¼ mi past the last lookout, is a small side road called Kawaihau. Follow the road up 3 mi, then turn right on Kapahi Rd. into a residential neighborhood. Kapahi Rd. dead-ends near the trailhead. Look for the yellow gate on your left.*

Fodor's Choice   **Kalalau Trail.** Of all the hikes on the island, Kalalau Trail is by far the
    ★   most famous and in many regards the most strenuous. A moderate hiker can handle the 2-mi trek to Hanakapi'ai Beach, and for the seasoned outdoorsman, the additional 2 mi up to the falls is manageable. But be prepared to rock-hop along a creek and ford waters that can get waist high during the rain. Round-trip to Hanakapi'ai Falls is 8 mi. This steep and often muddy trail is best approached with a walking stick. The narrow trail will deliver one startling ocean view after another along a path that is alternately shady and sunny. Wear hiking shoes or sandals, and bring drinking water since the creeks on the trail are not potable. Snacks are always encouraged on a strenuous hike such as this one. If your plan is to venture the full 11 mi into Kalalau, you need to acquire a camping permit. ⊠ *Drive north past Hanalei to the end of the road. Trailhead is directly across from Kē'ē Beach.*

Māhā'ulepū Heritage Trail. This trail offers the novice hiker an accessible way to appreciate the rugged southern coast of Kaua'i. A cross-country course wends its way along the water, high above the ocean, through a lava field and past a sacred *heiau* (stone structure). Walk all the way to Māhā'ulepū, 2 mi north, for a two-hour round-trip. ⊠ *Drive north on Poi'pū Rd., and turn right at the Poi'pū Bay Golf Course sign. The street name is Ainako, but the sign is hard to see. Drive down to the beach and park in the lot ⊕ www.hikemahaulepu.org.*

Sleeping Giant Trail. An easy and easily accessible trail practically in the heart of Kapa'a, the Sleeping Giant Trail—or simply Sleeping Giant—gains 1,000 feet over 2 mi. We prefer an early morning—say, sunrise—hike, with sparkling blue-water vistas, up the east-side trailhead. At the top you can see a grassy grove with a picnic table; don't stop here. Continue carefully along the narrow trail toward the Giant's nose and chin. From here there are 360-degree views of the island. ⊠ *In Wailua,* *turn mauka off Rte. 56 onto Haleilio Rd.; proceed 1 mi to small parking area on right.*

Waimea Canyon and Kōke'e State Parks. This park contains a 50-mi network of hiking trails of varying difficulty that take you through acres of native forests, across the highest-elevation swamp in the world, to the river at the base of the canyon, and onto pinnacles of land sticking their necks out over Nāpali Coast. All hikers should register at Kōke'e Natural History Museum, where you'll find trail maps, current trail information, and specific directions. All mileage mentioned below is one way.

> **LILIKO'I ALERT**
>
> If you're hiking in May and June, you'll see *liliko'i*—often referred to as passion fruit—scattered like yellow eggs among the ferns. It tastes as sweet and floral as it smells—bite the tip of the rind off and you'll see speckled jelly with tiny black seeds; then slurp it right out of the skin. If you miss liliko'i season, scout out delicious liliko'i mustards and jams sold by local grocers. Liliko'i pie is also served at a few Hawaiian eateries.

The **Kukui Trail** descends 2½ mi and 2,200 feet into Waimea Canyon to the edge of the Waimea River—it's a steep climb. The **Awa'awapuhi Trail,** with 1,600 feet of elevation gains and losses over 3¼ mi, feels more gentle than the Kukui Trail, but it offers its own huffing-and-puffing sections in its descent along a spiny ridge to a perch overlooking the ocean.

The 3½-mi **Alaka'i Swamp Trail** is accessed via the **Pihea Trail** or a four-wheel-drive road. There's one strenuous valley section, but otherwise it's a pretty level trail—once you access it. This trail is a birder's delight and includes a painterly view of Wainiha and Hanalei valleys at the trail's end. The trail traverses the purported highest-elevation swamp in the world on a boardwalk so as not to disturb the fragile plant- and wildlife.

The **Canyon Trail** offers much in its short trek: spectacular vistas of the canyon and the only dependable waterfall in Waimea Canyon. The easy, 2-mi hike can be cut in half if you have a four-wheel-drive vehicle. If you were outfitted with a headlamp, this would be a great hike at sunset as the sun's light sets the canyon walls ablaze with color. ⊠ *Kōke'e Natural History Museum: Kōke'e Rd., Rte. 550* ☎ *808/335–9975 for trail conditions.*

EQUIPMENT AND TOURS

Fodor'sChoice ★ **Kaua'i Nature Tours.** Father and son scientists started this hiking tour business. As such, their emphasis is on education and the environment. If you're interested in flora, fauna, volcanology, geology, oceanography, and the like, this is the company for you. They offer daylong hikes along coastal areas, beaches, and in the mountains. Hikes range from easy to strenuous, and rates range from $110 to $140. ⊠ *Meets at designated spots around the island. Provides transportation* ☎ *808/742–8305 or 888/233–8365* ⊕ *www.kauainaturetours.com.*

Princeville Ranch Adventures. This 4-mi hike traverses Princeville Ranch, crossing through a rain forest and to a five-tier waterfall for lunch and swimming. Moderately strenuous hiking is required. Fee is $129.

It's said to be the wettest place on Earth—Mt. Wai'ale'ale gets about 450 inches of rain per year.

✉ *West of Princeville Airport on Rte. 56, between mile markers 27 and 28, Princeville* ☎ *808/826–7669 or 888/955–7669* ⊕ *www.adventureskauai.com.*

HORSEBACK RIDING

Most of the horseback-riding tours on Kaua'i are primarily walking tours with very little trotting and no cantering or galloping, so no experience is required. Zip. Zilch. Nada. If you're interested, most of the stables offer private lessons. The most popular tours are the ones including a picnic lunch by the water. Your only dilemma may be deciding what kind of water you want—waterfalls or ocean. You may want to make your decision based on where you're staying. The "waterfall picnic" tours are on the wetter North Shore, and the "beach picnic" tours take place on the South Side.

CJM Country Stables. Just past the Hyatt in Po'ipū, CJM Stables offers a three-hour picnic ride, with noshing on the beach, as well as the more popular two-hour trail ride. The landscape here is rugged and beautiful, featuring sand dunes and limestone bluffs. CJM sponsors seasonal rodeo events that are free and open to the public. Prices range from $98 to $125. ✉ *1½ mi from Hyatt Regency Kaua'i off Po'ipū Rd., Kōloa* ☎ *808/742–6096* ⊕ *www.cjmstables.com.*

Esprit de Corps. If you ride, this is the company for you. Esprit de Corps has three- to eight-hour rides and allows some trotting and cantering based on the rider's experience and comfort with the horse. What's also nice is the maximum group size: six. Weddings on horseback can be

LEPTOSPIROSIS

Leptospirosis is a bacterial disease that is transmitted from animals to humans. It can survive for long periods of time in freshwater and mud contaminated by the urine of infected animals, such as mice, rats, and goats.

The bacteria enter the body through the eyes, ears, nose, mouth, and broken skin. To avoid infection, don't drink untreated water from the island's streams; don't wade in waters above the chest or submerge skin with cuts and abrasions in island streams or rivers.

Symptoms are often mild and resemble the flu—fever, diarrhea, chills, nausea, headache, vomiting, and body pains—and may occur 2 to 20 days after exposure. If you think you have these symptoms, see a doctor right away.

arranged (in fact, Dale, the owner, is a wedding officiant, specializing in Jewish and interfaith marriages), and custom rides for less experienced and younger riders (as young as two) are available, as well as private lessons (starting at age six). Rates range from $130 to $390. ✉ *End of Kualapa Pl., Kapa'a* ☎ *808/822–4688* ⊕ *www.kauaihorses.com.*

Fodor's Choice ★ **Princeville Ranch Stables.** A longtime *kama 'āina* (resident) family operates Princeville Ranch. They originated the waterfall picnic tours, which run three or four hours and include a short but steep hike down to Kalihi-wai Falls, a dramatic three-tier waterfall, for swimming and picnicking. Princeville also has shorter, straight riding tours and private rides, and if they're moving cattle while you're visiting, you can sign up for a cattle drive. Prices range from $80 to $135. ✉ *West of Princeville Airport mauka between mile markers 27 and 28, Princeville* ☎ *808/826–6777* ⊕ *www.princevilleranch.com.*

MOUNTAIN TUBING

For the past 40 years, Hawai'i's sugarcane plantations have closed one by one. In the fall of 2009, Gay and Robinson announced the closure of Kaua'i's last plantation, leaving only one in Maui, the last in the state. The sugarcane irrigation ditches remain, striating these islands like spokes in a wheel. Inspired by the Hawaiian *'auwai*, which diverted water from streams to taro fields, these engineering feats harnessed the rain. One ingenious tour company on Kaua'i has figured out a way to make exploring them an adventure: float inflatable tubes down the route.

☺ **Kaua'i Backcountry Adventures.** Very popular with all ages, this laid-back adventure can book up two weeks in advance in busy summer months. Here's how it works: You recline in an inner tube and float down fern-lined irrigation ditches that were built more than a century ago—the engineering is impressive—to divert water from Mt. Wai'ale'ale to sugar and pineapple fields around the island. Simple as that. They'll even give you a headlamp so you can see as you float through five covered tunnels. The scenery from the island's interior at the base of

Mt. Wai'ale'ale on Līhu'e Plantation land is superb. Ages five and up are welcome. The tour takes about three hours and includes a picnic lunch and a swim in a swimming hole. You'll definitely want to pack water-friendly shoes (or rent some from the outfitter), sunscreen, a hat, bug repellent, and a beach towel. Tours cost $100 per person and are offered morning and afternoon, daily. ⊠ *3–4131 Kūhiō Hwy., across from gas station, Hanamā'ulu* ☎ *808/245–2506 or 888/270–0555* ⊕ *www.kauaibackcountry.com.*

SKYDIVING

If you're a full-throttle adrenaline junkie, it doesn't get any better than jumping out of an airplane over an island—oh, the views—and floating peacefully back down to earth tethered to a parachute. There aren't many options, though, on Kaua'i; in fact, there's just one.

Skydive Kauai. Ten thousand feet over Kaua'i and falling at a rate of 120 mph is probably as thrilling as it gets while airborne. First, there's the 25-minute plane ride to altitude in a Cessna 182, then the exhilaration of the first step into sky, the sensation of sailing weightless in the air over Kaua'i, and finally the peaceful buoyancy beneath the canopy of your parachute. A tandem free fall rates among the most unforgettable experiences of a lifetime. Wed that to the aerial view over Kaua'I, and you've got a winning marriage. Tandem dive is $229. ⊠ *Salt Pond Beach Park, Port Allen Airport* ☎ *808/335–5859* ⊕ *www.skydivekauai.com.*

TENNIS

If you're interested in booking some court time on Kaua'i, there are public tennis courts in Waimea, Kekaha, Hanapēpē, Kōloa, Kalaheo, Puhi, Līhu'e, Wailua Homesteads, Wailua Houselots, and Kapa'a New Park.

For specific directions or more information, call the **County of Kaua'i Parks and Recreation Office** (☎ *808/241–4463*). Many hotels and resorts have tennis courts on property; even if you're not staying there, you can still rent court time. Rates range from $10 to $15 per person per hour. On the South Side, try the **Grand Hyatt Kaua'I** (☎ *808/742–1234*) and **Kiahuna Swim and Tennis Club** (☎ *808/742–9533*). On the North Shore, try the **Princeville Racquet Club** (☎ *808/826–1230*).

ZIPLINE TOURS

The latest adventure on Kaua'i is "zipping," or "ziplining." It's so new that the vernacular is still catching up with it, but regardless of what you call it, chances are you'll scream like a rock-star fan while trying it. Strap on a harness, clip onto a cable running from one side of a river or valley to the other, and zip across. The step off is the scariest part.
■ TIP➔ Pack knee-length shorts or pants, athletic shoes, and courage for this adventure.

Fodor'sChoice **Just Live.** When Nichol Baier and Julie Lester started Just Live in 2003,
★ their market was exclusively school-age children, but soon they added
visitor tours. Experiential education through adventure is how they
describe it. Whatever you call it, sailing 70 feet above the ground
for 3½ hours will take your vacation to another level. This is the
only treetop zipline in the state where your feet never touch ground
once you're in the air: Seven zips and four canopy bridges make
the Tree Top Tour ($120) their most popular one. For the heroic
at heart, there's the Zipline Eco Adventure ($125), which includes
three ziplines, two canopy bridges, a climbing wall, a 100-foot rap-
pelling tower, and a "Monster Swing." If you're short on time—or
courage—you can opt for the Wikiwiki Zipline Tour ($79), which
includes three ziplines and two canopy bridges in under two hours.
They still incorporate team building in the visitor tours, although their
primary focus remains community programming. Enjoy knowing that
money spent here serves Kaua'i's children. ⊠ *Kōloa* ☎ *808/482–1295*
⊕ *www.justlive.org.*

★ **Outfitters Kaua'i.** This company added new zipline offerings in the summer of 2009. They still have a half-day, multisport adventure of ziplining, suspension bridge crossings, and aerial walkways with hiking in
between. Their most popular tour (Zipline Trek Nui Loa) features an
1,800-foot tandem zip—that's right, you don't have to go it alone.
Plus, a unique WaterZip cools things off if you work up a sweat. The
price is $148. A shorter version of this adventure—the Zipline Trek
Iki Mua—is available and runs $108. Outfitters Kaua'i also includes
ziplining as part of its Kipu Safari tour *(see Kayaking in chapter 4).*
⊠ *2827-A Po'ipū Rd., Po'ipū* ☎ *808/742–9667 or 888/742–9887*
⊕ *www.outfitterskauai.com.*

Princeville Ranch Adventures. The North Shore's answer to ziplining is a
nine-zipline course with a bit of hiking, and suspension bridge crossing thrown in for a half-day adventure. The 4½-hour Zip N' Dip tour
includes lunch and swimming at a waterfall pool, while the Zip Express
whizzes you through the entire course in three hours. Both excursions
conclude with a 1,200-foot tandem zip across a valley. Guides are
energetic and fun and can offer good dining and nightlife recommendations. This is as close as it gets to flying; just watch out for the albatross. Prices start at $125 for the Zip Express and $145 for the Zip
N' Dip. ⊠ *West of Princeville Airport on Rte. 56, between mile markers 27 and 28, Princeville* ☎ *808/826–7669 or 888/955–7669* ⊕ *www.
adventureskauai.com.*

Shops and Spas

WORD OF MOUTH

"Find out where you can get a lomilomi massage. OMG—I thought I'd died and gone to heaven."

—PamSF

Updated by
Lois Ann Ell

There aren't a lot of shops and spas on Kaua'i, but what you will find here are a handful of places very much worth checking out for the quality of their selection of items sold and services rendered. Many shops now make an effort to sell as many locally made products as possible. When buying an item, ask where it was made, or even who made it.

Often you will find that a product handcrafted on the island may not be that much more expensive than a similar product made overseas. You can also look for the purple "Kaua'i Made" sticker many merchants display.

Along with one major shopping mall, a few shopping centers, and a growing number of big-box retailers, Kaua'i has some delightful mom-and-pop shops and specialty boutiques with lots of character. The Garden Isle also has a large and talented community of artisans and fine artists, with galleries all around the island showcasing their creations. You can find many island-made arts and crafts in the small shops, and it's worthwhile to stop in at crafts fairs and outdoor markets to look for bargains and mingle with island residents.

If you're looking for a special memento of your trip that is unique to Kaua'i County, check out the distinctive Ni'ihau shell lei. The tiny shells are collected from beaches on Kaua'i and Ni'ihau, pierced, and strung into beautiful necklaces, chokers, and earrings. It's a time-consuming and exacting craft, and these items are much in demand, so don't be taken aback by the high price tags. Those made by Ni'ihau residents will have certificates of authenticity and are worth collecting. You often can find cheaper versions made by non-Hawaiians at crafts fairs.

Kaua'i is often touted as the healing island, and local spas try hard to fill that role. With the exception of the Hyatt's ANARA Spa, the facilities aren't as posh as some might want, but it's in the human element that Kaua'i excels. Island residents are known for their warmth, kindness, and humility, and you can find all these attributes in the massage therapists and technicians who work long hours at the resort spas. These professionals take their therapeutic mission seriously; they genuinely want you to experience the island's relaxing, restorative qualities. Private massage services abound on the island, and your spa therapist may offer the same services at a much lower price outside the resort, but if you're looking for a variety of health-and-beauty treatments, an exercise workout, or a full day of pampering, a spa will prove most convenient.

SHOPS

Stores are typically open daily from 9 or 10 AM to 5 PM, although some stay open until 9 PM, especially those near resorts. Don't be surprised if the posted hours don't match the actual hours of operation at the smaller shops, where owners may be fairly casual about keeping to a regular schedule.

THE NORTH SHORE

The North Shore has three main shopping areas, all conveniently located in towns off the highway. Hanalei has two shopping centers directly across from each other, which offer more than you would expect in a remote, relaxed town. Princeville Shopping Center is a bustling little mix of businesses, necessities, and some unique shops, often pricey. Kilauea is a bit more sprawled out and offers a charming, laid-back shopping scene with a neighborhood feel.

SHOPPING CENTERS

Ching Young Village. Despite a face-lift, this popular shopping center looks a bit worn, but that doesn't deter business. Hanalei's only grocery store, **Big Save**, is here along with a number of other shops useful to locals and visitors. These include **Hanalei Music's Strings and Things**, where you can buy Hawaiian sheet music, compact discs, handmade instruments, and knitting supplies as well as rent DVDs; **Village Variety**, which has a bit of everything; **Savage Pearls**, a fine jewelry store that specializes in Tahitian pearls and gifts; **Hot Rocket**, a teen-oriented surf-wear shop; **Hanalei Surf Company Back Door**, for beachwear and gear; **Hula Moon Gifts of Kaua'i**, which offers an assortment of island-theme treasures; **Divine Planet**, for exotic clothing, jewelry, and home furnishings (also in Kapa'a); **Village Snack & Bakery**, which sells excellent chocolate cake and coconut-cream pie, among other treats; and several restaurants. A few steps away are **Evolve Love Artists Gallery**, a good place to find high-quality work by local artisans, and **On the Road to Hanalei**, a neat boutique with gifts, clothing, jewelry, housewares, and collectibles from Indonesia. ⊠ *Makai, after mile marker 2, 5-1590 Kūhiō Hwy., Hanalei* ☎ *808/826–7222.*

Hanalei Center. Listed on the Historic Register, the old Hanalei school has been refurbished and rented out to boutiques and restaurants. You can dig through '40s and '50s vintage memorabilia in the **Yellow Fish Trading Company**, find Polynesian artifacts at Hawa'iki, or search for that unusual gift at **Sand People**. Buy beach gear at the classic **Hanalei Surf Company and Hanalei** Paddler as well as island wear at **Hula Beach Clothing** or women's clothing at **Tropical Tantrum**. Find a range of fine jewelry and paper art jewelry from Uganda at Jewel of Paradise. For the kids, pick up something at **Rainbow Ducks Toys & Clothing.** For a little exercise, catch a class at the **Hanalei Yoga** studio in the two-story modern addition to the center, which also houses **Papaya's**, a well-stocked health-food store. ⊠ *Mauka, after mile marker 2, 5-5161 Kūhiō Hwy., Hanalei* ☎ *808/826–7677.*

Princeville Shopping Center. The big draws at this small center are **Foodland**, a full-service grocery store, and **Island Ace Hardware**. This is the last stop for gas and banking on the North Shore. You'll also find five restaurants and live music on Friday afternoon, a sandal shop, a mail service center, a post office, an ice cream shop, a kiosk with a good collection of Hawaiian and contemporary artists called **Paradise**

Music, and **Magic Dragon Toy & Art Supply Co.,** a tiny but interesting toy-and-hobby shop. ⊠ *Makai, mile marker 28, 5-4280 Kūhiō Hwy., Princeville* ☎ *808/826–9497.*

GIFTS

Kong Lung Co. Sometimes called the Gump's of Kaua'i, this gift store sells elegant clothing, exotic glassware, ethnic books, gifts, and artwork— all very lovely and expensive. The shop is housed in a beautiful 1892 stone structure right in the heart of Kīlauea. It's the showpiece of the pretty, little Kong Lung Center, whose shops feature distinctive jewelry, handmade soaps and candles, hammocks, plants, excellent pizza and baked goods, artwork, and consignment clothing, among other items. Next door is Kīlauea's farmers' market, a good place to buy natural and gourmet foods, wines, and sandwiches. ⊠ *2484 Keneke St., Kīlauea* ☎ *808/828–1822.*

Village Variety Store. How about a fun beach towel for the folks back home? That's just one of the gifts you can find here, along with shell lei, Kaua'i T-shirts, macadamia nuts, and other great souvenirs at low prices. The store also has many small, useful items such as envelopes, housewares, and toiletries. ⊠ *Ching Young Village, Kūhiō Hwy., Hanalei* ☎ *808/826–6077.*

JEWELRY

Crystal & Gems Gallery. Sparkling crystals of every shape, size, type, and color are sold in this small, amply stocked boutique. The knowledgeable staff can help you choose crystals for specific healing purposes. ⊠ *4489 Aku Rd., Hanalei* ☎ *808/826–9304.*

THE EAST SIDE: KAPA'A AND WAILUA

Kapa'a is the most heavily populated area on Kaua'i, so it's not surprising that it has the most diverse shopping opportunities on the island. Unlike the North Shore's retail scene, shops here are not neatly situated in centers; they are spread out along a long stretch of road, with many local retail gems tucked away that you may not find if you're in a rush.

SHOPPING CENTERS

Coconut Marketplace. This visitor-oriented complex is on the busy Coconut Coast near resort hotels and condominiums. A variety of shops sell everything from snacks and slippers (as locals call flip-flop sandals) to scrimshaw. There are restaurants open from breakfast to evening and a free Polynesian show on Wednesday at 5 and Saturday at noon. ⊠ *4-484 Kūhiō Hwy., Kapa'a* ☎ *808/822–3641.*

Kaua'i Village Shopping Center. The buildings of this Kapa'a shopping village are in the style of a 19th-century plantation town. **ABC Discount Store** sells sundries; **Safeway** carries groceries and alcoholic beverages; **Longs Drugs** has a pharmacy, health and beauty products, and a good selection of Hawaiian merchandise; and **Papaya's** has health foods. There's also a **Vitamin World** and a **UPS store.** Other shops sell jewelry, art, gift items, and children's clothes and toys. Restaurants include Chinese, vegetarian, and Vietnamese options, and there's also a **Starbuck's** and an ice cream parlor. ⊠ *4-831 Kūhiō Hwy., Kapaʻa* ☎ *808/822–3777.*

Kinipopo Shopping Village. Kinipopo is a tiny little center on Kūhiō Highway. **Korean Barbeque** fronts the highway, as does **Goldsmith's Kauaʻi Gallery,** which sells handcrafted Hawaiian-style gold jewelry. **Monaco's** has authentic Mexican food, and **Icing on the Cake** is a new pastry shop specializing in cakes. Worth a stop is **Tin Can Mailman,** with its eclectic collection of used books, stamps and coins, rare prints, vintage maps, and other collectibles. ⊠ *4-356 Kūhiō Hwy., Kapaʻa.*

Waipouli Town Center. **Foodland** is the focus of this small retail plaza, one of three shopping centers anchored by grocery stores in Kapaʻa. You can also find a **Blockbuster** video outlet, **McDonald's, Pizza Hut, Fun Factory** video arcade, and **The Coffee Bean & Tea Leaf,** along with a local-style restaurant. ⊠ *4-901 Kūhiō Hwy.,Kapaʻa*

BOOKS

Tin Can Mailman Books and Antiques. Both new and used books can be found here, along with an extensive collection of Hawaiian and South Pacific literature. The shop also sells maps, tapa cloth from Fiji, and specialty gift items. ⊠ *Kinipopo Shopping Village, 4-356 Kūhiō Hwy., Kapaʻa* ☎ *808/822–3009.*

CLOTHING

★ **Bambulei.** Two 1930s-style plantation homes have been transformed into a boutique featuring vintage and contemporary clothing, antiques, jewelry, and accessories. Also featured are rare Hawaiian collectibles and furniture. ⊠ *4-369 Kūhiō Hwy., Wailua* ☎ *808/823–8641.*

Deja Vu Surf Outlet. This mom-and-pop operation has a great assortment of surf wear and clothes for outdoor fanatics, including tank tops, visors, swimwear, and Kauaʻi-style T-shirts at low prices. ⊠ *4-1419 Kūhiō Hwy., Kapaʻa* ☎ *808/822–4401.*

Divine Planet. This friendly, hip boutique sells unusual merchandise from India and other exotic Asian locales. Dangly earrings, loose clothing, beads, campy home furnishings, and other eclectic offerings make this fun shop worth a stop. If you miss it here, you can check out the Hanalei location. ⊠ *4-1351 Kūhiō Hwy., Kapaʻa* ☎ *808/821–1835* ⊠ *Ching Young Village, 5–1590 Kūhiō Hwy., Hanalei* ☎ *808/826–8970.*

Marta's Boat. This charming boutique sells handmade, one-of-a-kind clothing by husband-and-wife team Ambrose and Marta Curry. He creates silk-screen art with nontoxic paint on fabric in his studio next door; then she cuts and sews the fabric into bags and clothing for men, women, and children. ⊠ *4-770 Kūhiō Hwy., Kapaʻa* ☎ *808/822–3926.*

GALLERIES

ALOHA Images. ALOHA in this gallery's title stands for "Affordable Location Of Hawaiian Art." A self-proclaimed "candy store for art lovers," it has a large selection of Hawaiian-theme art, ranging from $50 up to the rare $9,000. ⊠ *4–1383 Kūhiō Hwy., Kapaʻa* ☎ *808/821–1382.*

Kela's Glass Gallery. The colorful vases, bowls, and other fragile items sold in this distinctive gallery are definitely worth viewing if you appreciate quality handmade glass art. It's expensive, but if something catches your eye, they'll happily pack it for safe transport home. ✉ *4-1354 Kūhiō Hwy., Kapaʻa* ☎ *808/822–4527.*

GIFTS

Vicky's Fabric Shop. This small shop is packed full of tropical prints, silks, slinky rayons, soft cottons, and other fine fabrics. A variety of sewing patterns and notions are featured, making it a must-stop for any seamstress. If you're seeking something that's truly one-of-a-kind, check out the selection of purses, aloha wear, and other quality hand-sewn items. ✉ *4-1326 Kūhiō Hwy., Kapaʻa* ☎ *808/822–1746.*

HOME DECOR

Otsuka's Furniture & Appliances. This family-owned furniture store has a surprisingly large clientele of visitors, who appreciate the wide selection of artwork, candles, tropical-print pillows, accessories, and knickknacks that are packed and shipped to the customer's home. ✉ *4-1624 Kūhiō Hwy., Kapaʻa* ☎ *808/822–7766.*

JEWELRY

Jim Saylor Jewelers. Jim Saylor has been designing beautiful keepsakes for over 30 years on Kauaʻi. Gems from around the world, including black pearls and diamonds, appear in his unusual settings. ✉ *1318 Kūhiō Hwy., Kapaʻa* ☎ *808/822–3591.*

Kauaʻi Gold/Kauaʻi Pearl. A wonderful selection of rare Niʻihau shell lei ranges in price from $20 to $200. To appreciate the craftsmanship, understand the sometimes-high prices, and learn to care for and preserve these remarkable necklaces, ask how they are made. The store also sells a selection of 14-karat gold jewelry and Tahitian black pearls. ✉ *Coconut Marketplace, 4-484 Kūhiō Hwy., Kapaʻa* ☎ *808/822–9361.*

MARKET

Kauaʻi Products Fair. Open daily, this outdoor market features fresh produce, tropical plants and flowers, aloha wear, jewelry, gifts, a Thai food eatery, and a shave ice stand. ✉ *Outside on north side of Kapaʻa, across from Otsuka's Furniture* ☎ *808/246–0988.*

THE EAST SIDE: LĪHUʻE

Līhuʻe is the business area on Kauaʻi, as well as home to all the big-box stores and the only real mall. Do not mistake this town as lacking in rare finds, however. Līhuʻe is steeped in history and diversity while simultaneously welcoming new trends and establishments.

SHOPPING CENTERS

Kilohana Plantation. This 16,000-square-foot Tudor mansion contains art galleries, a jewelry store, and Gaylord's restaurant. The house itself is filled with antiques from its original owner and is worth a look. The restored outbuildings house a crafts shop. Horse-drawn carriage rides and train rides on a restored railroad are available, with knowledgeable guides reciting the history of sugar on Kauaʻi. ✉ *3-2087 Kaumualiʻi Hwy., 1 mi west of Līhuʻe* ☎ *808/245–5608.*

Kukui Grove Center. This is Kauaʻi's only true mall. Besides **Sears** and **Kmart,** anchor tenants are **Longs Drugs, Macy's,** and **Star Market.**

Borders Books & Music, with its **Starbucks** coffee shop, is one of the island's most popular stores. The mall's stores offer women's clothing, surf wear, art, toys, athletic shoes, jewelry, and locally made crafts. Restaurants range from fast food and sandwiches to Mexican and Chinese. The center stage often has entertainment. ⊠ *3-2600 Kaumualiʻi Hwy., west of Lĩhuʻe* ☎ *808/245–7784.*

CLOTHING

Hilo Hattie, The Store of Hawaiʻi, Fashion Factory. This is the big name in aloha wear for tourists throughout the islands. You can visit the only store on Kauaʻi, a mile from Lĩhuʻe Airport, to pick up cool, comfortable aloha shirts and muʻumuʻus in bright floral prints, as well as other souvenirs. While here, check out the line of Hawaiian-inspired home furnishings. ⊠ *3252 Kūhiō Hwy., Lĩhuʻe* ☎ *808/245–3404.*

GIFTS

Fodor's Choice **Kapaia Stitchery.** Hawaiian quilts made by hand and machine, a beautiful selection of fabrics, quilting kits, and fabric arts fill this cute little red plantation-style structure. There are also many locally made gifts for sale. The staff is friendly and helpful, even though a steady stream of customers keeps them busy. ⊠ *Kūhiō Hwy., ½ mi north of Lĩhuʻe* ☎ *808/245–2281.*

★ **Kauaʻi Museum.** The gift shop at the museum sells some fascinating books, maps, and prints, as well as lovely feather lei hatbands, Niʻihau shell jewelry, handwoven *lau hala* hats, and koa wood bowls. Also featured are tapa cloth, authentic tikis (hand-carved wooden figurines), and other good-quality local crafts at reasonable prices. ⊠ *4428 Rice St., Lĩhuʻe* ☎ *808/246–2470.*

Kauaʻi Products Store. Seed lei, finely crafted koa-wood boxes, tropical-flower earrings, and Niʻihau lei are on hand in this boutique. Ninety percent of the products are handcrafted on Kauaʻi. Other gift options include a collection of local Hawaiian music CDs, koa-oil lamps, pottery, sculpture, paintings, and homemade fudge. ⊠ *Kukui Grove Center, 3-2600 Kaumualiʻi Hwy., Lĩhuʻe* ☎ *808/246–6753.*

HOME DECOR

Two Frogs Hugging. This spacious store has lots of interesting housewares, accessories, knickknacks, and hand-carved collectibles, as well as baskets and furniture with a primarily Indonesian influence. ⊠ *3215 Kūhiō Hwy., Lĩhuʻe* ☎ *808/246–8777.*

FOOD SPECIALTIES

Kauaʻi Fruit and Flower Company. At this shop near Lĩhuʻe and five minutes away from the airport, you can buy tropical cut flowers, fresh Hawaiian-grown sugarloaf pineapple, sugarcane, ginger, coconuts, local jams, jellies, and honey, plus Kauaʻi-grown papayas, bananas, and mangos in season. The fruit has been inspected and approved for shipment to take home out of Hawaiʻi; airlines do not charge for the fruit carry-ons. ⊠ *3-4684 Kūhiō Hwy., Kapaʻa* ☎ *808/245–1814 or 800/943–3108.*

6

THE SOUTH SHORE AND WEST SIDE

The South Shore, like the North Shore, has convenient shopping clusters, including Poʻipu Shopping Village and the new Kukuiʻula Shopping Village. There are many high-priced shops but some unique clothing and gift selections. By comparison, the West Side is years behind in development, offering charming, simple shops with authentic local flavor.

SHOPPING CENTERS

ʻEleʻele Shopping Center. Kauaʻi's West Side has a scattering of stores, including those at this no-frills strip-mall shopping center. It's a good place to rub elbows with local folk at **Big Save** grocery store or to grab a quick bite to eat at the casual **Grinds Cafe** or **Tois Thai Kitchen.** ⊠ *Rte. 50 near Hanapēpē, ʻEleʻele.*

Kukuiʻula Shopping Village. This is the South Shore's newest shopping center, with shops, exclusive galleries, restaurants, and cafés. While the complex debuted in late 2009, at this writing all 40 establishments were expected to be open by summer 2010. Traditional Hawaiian music is featured Monday and Wednesday from 5 to 7 PM and Hawaiian cultural and hula events are held Saturday from 11 AM to 2 PM. This open-air, plantation-style center is just beyond the roundabout as you enter Poʻipū. ⊠ *2829 Kalanikaumaka, Poʻipū* ☎ *808/ 742-0234* ⊕ *www. kukuiula.com* ☺ *Daily 10–9.*

Poʻipū Shopping Village. Convenient to nearby hotels and condos on the South Shore, the two-dozen shops here sell resort wear, gifts, souvenirs, and art. The upscale **Black Pearl Kauaʻi** and **Na Hoku** shops are particularly appealing jewelry stores. There are a couple of art galleries and several fun clothing stores, including **Bamboo Lace, Making Waves,** and **Blue Ginger.** Also worth a visit are **Sand Kids** and **Whaler's General Store.** Restaurants include **Keoki's Paradise, Roy's, Poʻipū Tropical Burgers,** and **Puka Dog Hawaiian Style Hot Dogs,** along with **Papalani Gelato.** A Tahitian dance troupe performs in the open-air courtyard Tuesday and Thursday at 5 PM. ⊠ *2360 Kiahuna Plantation Dr., Poʻipū Beach* ☎ *808/742–2831.*

Waimea Canyon Plaza. As Kekaha's retail hub and the last stop for supplies before heading up to Waimea Canyon, this tiny, tidy complex of shops is surprisingly busy. Look for local foods, souvenirs, and island-made gifts for all ages. ⊠ *Kōkeʻe Rd. at Rte. 50, Kekaha* ☎ *No phone.*

CLOTHING

Paradise Sportswear. This is the retail outlet of the folks who invented Kauaʻi's popular "red dirt" shirts, which are dyed and printed with the characteristic local soil. Ask the salesperson to tell you the charming story behind these shirts. Sizes from infants up to 5X are available. ⊠ *4350 Waialo Rd., Port Allen* ☎ *808/335–5670.*

FLOWERS

Kauaʻi Tropicals. You can have this company ship heliconia, anthuriums, ginger, and other tropicals in 5-foot-long boxes directly from its flower farm in Kalāheo. It accepts phone-in orders only. ⊠ *Kalāheo* ☎ *800/303–4385.*

Continued on page 166

ALL ABOUT LEI

Leis brighten every occasion in Hawai'i, from birthdays to bar mitz-vahs to baptisms. Creative artisans weave nature's bounty—flowers, ferns, vines, and seeds—into gorgeous creations that convey an array of heartfelt messages: "Welcome," "Congratulations," "Good luck," "Farewell," "Thank you," "I love you." When it's difficult to find the right words, a lei expresses exactly the right sentiments.

WHERE TO BUY THE BEST LEI

Some nice leis on Kauai can be found—believe it or not—in the major chain stores, including **Foodland** (✉ 5-4290 Kūhiū Hwy., Princeville, ☎ 808/862–7513), in the Princeville Shopping Center, and **Safeway** (✉ 4-831 Kūhiū Hwy., Po'ipū Beach), in the Kaua'i Village Shopping Center. Also fabulous leis can be found at the various roadside vendors you'll see as you drive around the island.

LEI ETIQUETTE

■ To wear a closed lei, drape it over your shoulders, half in front and half in back. Open leis are worn around the neck, with the ends draped over the front in equal lengths.

■ Pīkake, ginger, and other sweet, delicate blossoms are "feminine" leis. Men opt for cigar, crown flower, and ti leaf, which are sturdier and don't emit as much fragrance.

■ Leis are always presented with a kiss, a custom that supposedly dates back to World War II when a hula dancer fancied an officer at a U.S.O. show. Taking a dare from members of her troupe, she took off her lei, placed it around his neck, and kissed him on the cheek.

■ You shouldn't wear a lei before you give it to someone else. Hawaiians believe the lei absorbs your *mana* (spirit); if you give your lei away, you'll be giving away part of your essence.

ORCHID

Growing wild on every continent except Antarctica, orchids—which range in color from yellow to green to purple—comprise the largest family of plants in the world. There are more than 20,000 species of orchids, but only three are native to Hawai'i—and they are very rare. The pretty lavender vanda you see hanging by the dozens at local lei stands has probably been imported from Thailand.

MAILE

Maile, an endemic twining vine with a heady aroma, is sacred to Laka, goddess of the hula. In ancient times, dancers wore maile and decorated hula altars with it to honor Laka. Today, "open" maile leis usually are given to men. Instead of ribbon, interwoven lengths of maile are used at dedications of new businesses. The maile is untied, never snipped, for doing so would symbolically "cut" the company's success.

'ILIMA

Designated by Hawai'i's Territorial Legislature in 1923 as the official flower of the island of O'ahu, the golden 'ilima is so delicate it lasts for just a day. Five to seven hundred blossoms are needed to make one garland. Queen Emma, wife of King Kamehameha IV, preferred 'ilima over all other leis, which may have led to the incorrect belief that they were reserved only for royalty.

PLUMERIA

This ubiquitous flower is named after Charles Plumier, the noted French botanist who discovered it in Central America in the late 1600s. Plumeria ranks among the most popular leis in Hawai'i because it's fragrant, hardy, plentiful, inexpensive, and requires very little care. Although yellow is the most common color, you'll also find plumeria leis in shades of pink, red, orange, and "rainbow" blends.

PĪKAKE

Favored for its fragile beauty and sweet scent, pīkake was introduced from India. In lieu of pearls, many brides in Hawai'i adorn themselves with long, multiple strands of white pīkake. Princess Kaiulani enjoyed showing guests her beloved pīkake and peacocks at Āinahau, her Waikīkī home. Interestingly, pīkake is the Hawaiian word for both the bird and the blossom.

KUKUI

The kukui (candlenut) is Hawai'i's state tree. Early Hawaiians strung kukui nuts (which are quite oily) together and burned them for light; mixed burned nuts with oil to make an indelible dye; and mashed roasted nuts to consume as a laxative. Kukui nut leis may not have been made until after Western contact, when the Hawaiians saw black beads from Europe and wanted to imitate them.

FOOD SPECIALTIES

Kaua'i Coffee Visitor Center and Museum. Kaua'i produces more coffee than any other island in the state. The local product can be purchased from grocery stores or here at the source, where a sampling of the nearly one dozen coffees is available. Be sure to try some of the estate-roasted varieties. ✉ *870 Halawili Rd., off Rte. 50, west of Kalāheo* ☎ *808/335–0813 or 800/545–8605.*

GALLERIES

Fodor's Choice

★

Galerie 103. This new gallery sells art, but the owners want you to experience it as well. Sparse and dramatic, the main room consists of concrete floors and walls of featured pieces, from internationally acclaimed artists and local Kaua'i ones. Most of the artwork is contemporary or modern with a focus on environmental issues. ✉ *2829 Ala Kalanikaumaka, Kōloa* ☎ *808/742-0103* ⊕ *www.galerie103.com* ☼ *Daily 11–9.*

Pineapples & Palms Gallery. Located in old Kōloa town, this gallery sells photographs of Hawai'i, including landscapes, marine life, and black-and-white vintage hula photos. You can also purchase intricate shell-art pieces called "sailor's valentines." A large amount of the artwork is done by local artists on Kaua'i, though not all. ✉ *5420 Kōloa Rd., Kōloa* ☎ *808/742–1199* ⊕ *www.pineapplesandpalms.com.*

SPAS

Though most spas on Kaua'i are associated with resorts, none are restricted to guests only. And there's much by way of healing and wellness to be found on Kaua'i beyond the traditional spa—or even the day spa. More and more retreat facilities are offering what some would call alternative healing therapies. Others would say there's nothing alternative about them; you can decide for yourself.

Alexander Day Spa & Salon at the Kaua'i Marriott. This sister spa of Alexander Simson's Beverly Hills spa focuses on body care rather than exercise, so don't expect any fitness equipment or exercise classes. Tucked away in the back corner of the Marriott, the spa has a bit of the stilted formality found in the rest of the resort, but it is otherwise a sunny, pleasant facility. Massages are available in treatment rooms and on the beach, although the beach locale isn't as private as you might imagine. Wedding-day and custom spa packages can be arranged. ✉ *Kaua'i Marriott Resort & Beach Club, 3610 Rice St., Līhu'e* ☎ *808/246–4918* ⊕ *www.alexanderspa.com* ☞ *$65–$195 massage. Facilities: Hair salon, steam room. Services: Body treatments—including masks, scrubs, and wraps—facials, hair styling, makeup, manicures, massages, pedicures, waxing.*

Fodor's Choice

★

ANARA Spa. This luxurious facility is far and away the best on Kaua'i, setting a standard that no other spa has been able to meet. It has all the equipment and services you expect from a top resort spa, along with a pleasant, professional staff. Best of all, it has indoor and outdoor areas that capitalize on the tropical locale and balmy weather, further distinguishing it from the Marriott and Princeville spas. Its 46,500-square-foot space includes the Garden Treatment Village, an open-air courtyard with private thatched-roof huts, each featuring a relaxation area, misters, and

Anara Spa

an open-air shower in a tropical setting. Ancient Hawaiian remedies and local ingredients are featured in many of the treatments, such as a red-dirt clay wrap, coconut-mango facial, and a body brush scrub that polishes your skin with a mix of ground coffee, orange peel, and vanilla bean. The open-air lava-rock showers are wonderful, introducing many guests to the delightful island practice of showering outdoors. The spa, which includes a full-service salon, adjoins the Hyatt's legendary swimming pool. ⊠ *Grand Hyatt Kaua'i Resort and Spa, 1571 Po'ipū Rd., Po'ipū* ☎ *808/240–6440* ⊕ *www.anaraspa.com* ☞ *Massages start at $100. Facilities: Hair salon, outdoor hot tubs, sauna, steam room. Gym with cardiovascular machines, free weights, weight-training equipment. Services: Body scrubs and wraps, facials, manicures, massage, pedicures. Classes and programs: Aerobics, aquaerobics, body sculpting, fitness analysis, flexibility training, personal training, Pilates, step aerobics, sunrise walk, weight training, yoga.*

Angeline's Mu'olaulani Wellness Center. It doesn't get more authentic than this. In the mid-'80s Aunty Angeline Locey opened her Anahola home to offer traditional Hawaiian healing practices. Now her son and granddaughter carry on the tradition. There's a two-hour treatment ($150) that starts with a steam, followed by a sea-salt-and-clay body scrub and a two-person massage. The real treat, however, is relaxing on Aunty's open-air garden deck. Hot-stone lomi is also available. Aunty's mission is to promote a healthy body image; as such, au naturel is the accepted way here, so if you're nudity-shy, this may not be the place for you. On second thought, Aunty would say it most definitely is. *Mu'olaulani* translates to "a place for young buds to bloom." ☎ *808/822–3235* ⊕ *www.angelineslomikauai.com* ☞ *Facilities: Steam room. Services: Body scrubs and massage.*

Hanalei Day Spa. As you travel beyond tony Princeville, life slows down. The single-lane bridges may be one reason. Another is the Hanalei Day Spa (opened in 2004), an open-air, thatched-roof, Hawaiian-style hut nestled just off the beach on the grounds of Hanalei Colony Resort in Hā'ena. Though this no-frills day spa offers facials, waxing, wraps, scrubs, and the like, its specialty is massage: Ayurveda, Zen shiatsu, Swedish, and even a baby massage (and lesson for Mom, to boot). On Tuesday and Thursday, owner Darci Frankel teaches yoga, a discipline she started as a young child living in south Florida. That practice led her to start the Ayurveda Center of Hawaii, which operates out of the spa and offers an ancient Indian cleansing and rejuvenation program known as Pancha Karma. Think multiday wellness retreat. ⊠ *Hanalei Colony Resort, Rte. 560, 6 mi past Hanalei* ☎ *808/826–6621* ⊕ *www.hanaleidayspa.com* ☞ *Massage $90–$195. Services: Body scrubs and wraps, facials, massage, waxing. Classes and programs: Pancha Karma, yoga.*

★ **A Hideaway Spa**. This is the only full-service day spa on the laid-back West Side. It's in one of the restored plantation cottages that make up the guest quarters at Waimea Plantation Cottages, creating a cozy and comfortable setting you won't find elsewhere. The overall feel is relaxed, casual, and friendly, as you'd expect in this quiet country town. The staff is informal yet thoroughly professional. Beach yoga and massages

KAUA'I: THE HEALING ISLAND

If you look at a globe, you'll notice that, yes, Hawai'i is in the middle of the ocean, and then you'll realize that it's also a connecting point between East and West. Over the centuries, as people have migrated, the islands have become a melting pot not only of cultures but of healing practices as well. You'll find healing modalities from around the world on Kaua'i. Some practitioners have offices; many work out of their homes. ■ TIP➜ Virtually all will require a reservation—no walk-ins—except in yoga studios. Here is a sampling of the healing arts offered on Kaua'i. You can also visit ⊕ www.kauaihealing.org and ⊕ www.kauaihwa.org.

Acupuncture & Natural Healing Center. Acupuncture and complementary medicine by Latifa Amdur. ☎ 808/828–1155.

Bikram Yoga Kaua'i. A wide selection of daily classes in yoga and dance. Call for updated weekly schedule. ✉ 4504 Kukui St., Suite 10 ☎ 808/822–5053 ⊕ www. bikramyogaretreats.com.

Deborah Burnham, PT. Aqua-Cranial and CranialSacral therapies. ☎ 808/651–4534.

Dr. Carrie Brennan. Naturopathic physician in Kapa'a. ☎ 808/652–7581.

Dr. Leia Melead. Naturopathic physician and acupuncturist in Kapa'a. ☎ 808/822–2087.

Kaua'i Osteopathic, Inc. Lisa Chun, doctor of osteopathy, in Kōloa. ☎ 808/742–1200 ⊕ www.health-from-within.com.

Ken Solin. Certified advanced Rolf practitioner in Kapa'a. ☎ 808/651–6979.

Mana Massage. Various locations and out-call. Check Web site for special offers. ☎ 808/822–4746 ⊕ www. manamassage.com.

Pilates Kaua'i. Full studio offering private and semiprivate lessons in secluded setting. ☎ 808/639–3074.

Yoga Hanalei. Wide variety of daily classes at the Hanalei Center. ☎ 808/826–9642 ⊕ www. yogahanalei.com.

are available, as well as a full-service salon with hair, nails, and make-up services. Try the kava kava ginger wrap followed by the lomi 'ili'ili—hot stone massage. Ooh la la! ✉ *Waimea Plantation Cottages, 9400 Kaumuali'i Hwy., Waimea* ☎ *808/338–0005* ⊕ *www.ahideawayspa. com* ☞ *Massage $50–$170. Facilities: Outdoor hot tub, steam room. Services: Acupuncture, body scrubs and wraps, facials, hydrotherapy, massage. Classes and programs: Yoga.*

Princeville Health Club & Spa. Inspiring views of mountains, sea, and sky provide a lovely distraction in the gym area of this spa, which is well equipped but small and often overly air-conditioned. The treatment area is functional but lacks charm and personality. Luckily the gorgeous setting helps make up for it. This is the only facility of this kind on the North Shore, so it's well used, and the generally well heeled clientele pay attention to their gym attire. The adjacent Prince Club restaurant is a good spot to take in the scenery over a quiet lunch. It's $20 for a day pass. ✉ *Prince Golf Course clubhouse, 53-900 Kūhiō Hwy., Princeville* ☎ *808/826–5030*

⊕ *www.princeville.com* ☞ *Massage $50–$150. Gym with cardiovascular machines, free weights, weight-training equipment. Services: Body scrubs and wraps, facials, massage. Classes and programs: Aerobics, aquaerobics, personal training, Pilates, step aerobics, tai chi, yoga.*

Qi Center. Technically, the Qi Center of Kaua'i is not a spa. It does, however, concern itself with healing, and because its technique is so gentle, it is, in a sense, pampering. More than that, it can be life changing—even life saving. Hong Liu, a qigong grand master of the highest degree, opened the center in 2005 as part of his lifelong goal to share qigong with the West. The essence

> ## TRY A LOMI MASSAGE
>
> Living in ancient Hawai'i wasn't all sunbathing and lounging at the beach. Growing taro was hard work, you know. So, too, were building canoes, fishing for dinner, and pounding tapa for clothing, sails, and blankets. Enter *lomi-lomi*—Hawaiian-style massage. It's often described as being more vigorous, more rhythmical, and faster than Swedish massage, and it incorporates more elbow and forearm work. It might even involve chanting, music, and four hands (in other words, two people).

of qigong centers on building, increasing, and directing energy: physical, mental, and spiritual. Master Liu does not suggest qigong as an alternative to Western medicine but as an adjunct. The center in Līhu'e conducts all levels of qigong training as well as "humanitarian" (i.e., free) events for the community on such topics as the immune system, asthma, allergies, and heart and senior health. ⊠ *3343 Kanakolu St.* ☎ *808/639–4300.*

Tri Health Ayurveda Spa. The goal of this spa isn't a onetime massage for momentary bliss, although relaxation is a key ingredient. Rather, this spa's focus is a multiweek, multitreatment, intensive program designed to eliminate toxins stored in the body and increase the flow and energy of all systems. Treatments are designed around the ancient Ayurvedic tradition of heat to open the pores, oil to deliver nutrients to tissues and nerve endings, and massage (by two therapists working in synchronized movement) to accelerate circulation. Note: Because the massage strokes are long and can run the length of the body, there is no draping involved. Ayurvedic doctors, food, and treatments are available, as is lodging in the 10-bedroom retreat facility, on 25 acres hidden by design for privacy—hence, no glaring signs. Single sessions are available. ☎ *808/828–2104* ⊕ *www.trihealthayurveda.com* ☞ *Massage $130–$275. Facilities: Steam room. Services: Herbal body scrubs, massage. Classes and programs: Pancha Karma.*

Entertainment
and Nightlife

WORD OF MOUTH

"On Friday nights, Hanapēpē's art shops and other stores are open late, and there is live music. . . . We browsed through the shops and admired the beautiful jewelry and artwork, walked over the Hanapēpē swinging bridge, and then listened to a couple of bands."

—Ronda

Updated by
Michael Levine

Kaua'i has never been known for its nightlife. It's a rural island, where folks tend to retire early, and the streets are dark and deserted well before midnight. The island does have its nightspots, though, and the after-dark entertainment scene may not be expanding, but it is consistently present in areas frequented by tourists.

Most of the island's dinner and lū'au shows are held at hotels and resorts. Hotel lounges are a good source of live music, often with no cover charge, as are a few bars and restaurants around the island.

Check the local newspaper, *The Garden Island,* for listings of weekly happenings, or tune in to community radio station KKCR—found at 90.9, 91.9, or 92.7 on the FM dial, depending on where on the island you are at that moment—at 5:30 PM for the arts and entertainment calendar. Free publications such as *Kaua'i Gold, This Week on Kaua'i,* and *Essential Kaua'i* also list entertainment events. You can pick them up at Līhu'e Airport near the baggage claim area, as well as at numerous retail areas on the island.

ENTERTAINMENT

Although lū'au remain a primary source of evening fun for families on vacation, there are a handful of other possibilities. There are no traditional dinner cruises, but some boat tours do offer an evening buffet with music along Nāpali Coast. A few times a year, Women in Theater (WIT), a local women's theater group, performs dinner shows at the Hukilau Lānai in Wailua. You can always count on a performance of *South Pacific* at the Kaua'i Beach Resort, and the Kaua'i Community College Performing Arts Center draws well-known artists.

Kaua'i Community College Performing Arts Center. This is the main venue for island entertainment, hosting a concert music series, visiting musicians, dramatic productions, and special events such as the International Film Festival. ⊠ *3-1901 Kaumuali'i Hwy., Līhu'e* ☎ *808/245–8270* ⊕ *kauai. hawaii.edu/pac/.*

DINNER SHOW

South Pacific Dinner Show. It seems a fitting tribute to see the play that put Kaua'i on the map. Rodgers and Hammerstein's *South Pacific* has been playing at the Kaua'i Beach Resort to rave reviews since 2002. The full musical production, accompanied by a buffet dinner, features local Kaua'i talent. ⊠ *Jasmine Ballroom, Kaua'i Beach Resort, 4331 Kaua'i Beach Dr., Līhu'e* ☎ *808/346–6500* ⊕ *www.southpacifickauai. com* 🍴 *$85* ⊗ *Wed., doors open at 5:15 PM, show at 7.*

Hula is hot in Hawaiʻi, and on Kauaʻi the top places to see it include Smith's Tropical Paradise, Coconut Marketplace, and Poʻipū Shopping Village.

FESTIVAL

Bon Festival. Traditional Japanese celebrations in honor of loved ones who have died are held from late June through August at various Buddhist temples all over the island. It sounds somber, but it's really a community festival of dance. To top it off, you're welcome to participate. Dance, eat, play carnival games, and hear Japanese *taiko* drumming by Kauaʻi youth at one of the Bon folk dances, which take place on temple lawns every Friday and Saturday night from dusk to midnight. Some dancers wear the traditional kimono; others wear board shorts and a tank top. The moves are easy to follow, the event is lively and wholesome, and it's free. A different temple hosts a dance each weekend. Watch the local paper for that week's locale.

LŪʻAU

Although the commercial lūʻau experience is a far cry from the backyard lūʻau thrown by local residents to celebrate a wedding, graduation, or baby's first birthday, they're nonetheless entertaining and a good introduction to the Hawaiian food that isn't widely sold in restaurants. Besides the feast, there's often an exciting dinner show with Polynesian-style music and dancing. It all makes for a fun evening that's suitable for couples, families, and groups, and the informal setting is conducive to meeting other people. Every lūʻau is different, reflecting the cuisine and tenor of the host facility, so compare prices, menus, and entertainment before making your reservation. Most lūʻau on Kauaʻi are offered only on a limited number of nights each week, so plan ahead to get the lūʻau you want. We tend to prefer those *not* held on resort properties, because they feel a bit more authentic. *The lū'au shows listed below are our favorites.*

Grand Hyatt Kaua'i Lū'au. What used to be called Drums of Paradise has a new name and a new dance troupe but still offers a traditional lū'au buffet and an exceptional performance. This oceanfront lū'au comes with a view of majestic Keoneloa Bay. ⊠ *Grand Hyatt Kaua'i Resort & Spa, 1571 Po'ipū Rd., Po'ipū* ☎ *808/240–6456* ⊕ *www.hyatt.com/gallery/kauailuau/* ⊠ *$94* ☉ *Thurs. and Sun. 6–8:30.*

★ **Lū'au Kālamakū.** Set on historic sugar-plantation land, this new lū'au bills itself as the only "theatrical" lū'au on Kaua'i. The lū'au feast is served buffet-style, there's an open bar, and the performers aim to both entertain and educate about Hawaiian culture. Guests sit at tables around a circular stage; tables farther from the stage are elevated, providing unobstructed views. Additional packages offer visitors the opportunity to tour the 35-acre plantation via train or special romantic perks like a lei greeting and champagne. ⊠ *3-2087 Kaumuali'i St., Līhu'e* ☎ *877/622–1780* ⊕ *www.luaukalamaku.com* ⊠ *$99* ☉ *Tues. and Fri. check-in begins at 5, dinner at 6:30, show at 7:30.*

Fodor'sChoice   **Smith's Tropical Paradise Lū'au.** A 30-acre tropical garden provides the ★   lovely setting for this popular lū'au, which begins with the traditional blowing of the conch shell and *imu* (pig roast) ceremony, followed by cocktails, an island feast, and an international show in the amphitheater overlooking a torchlighted lagoon. It's fairly authentic and a better deal than the pricier resort events. ⊠ *174 Wailua Rd., Kapa'a* ☎ *808/821–6895* ⊕ *www.smithskauai.com* ⊠ *$78* ☉ *Sept.–May, Mon., Wed., and Fri. 5–9:15; June–Aug., weekdays 5–9:15.*

MUSIC

Check the local paper for outdoor reggae and Hawaiian-music shows, or one of the numbers listed below for more formal performances.

Hanalei Slack Key Concerts. Relax to the instrumental musical art form created by Hawaiian *paniolo* (cowboys) in the early 1800s. Shows are held at the Hanalei Family Community Center, which is *mauka* down a dirt access road across from St. Williams Catholic Church (Malolo Road) and then left down another dirt road. Look for a thatched-roof *hale* (house), several little green plantation-style buildings, and the brown double-yurt community center around the gravel parking lot. ⊠ *Hanalei Family Community Center, 5-5299 Kūhiō Hwy., Hanalei* ☎ *808/826–1469* ⊕ *www.hawaiianslackkeyguitar.com* ⊠ *$20* ☉ *Fri. at 4, Sun. at 3.*

Kaua'i Concert Association. This group offers a seasonal program at the Kaua'i Community College Performing Arts Center. A range of big-name artists, from Ricky Lee Jones to Taj Mahal, have been known to show up on Kaua'i for planned or impromptu performances. ⊠ *3-1901 Kaumuali'i Hwy., Līhu'e* ☎ *808/245–7464* ⊕ *www.kauai-concert.org.*

THEATER

Kaua'i Community Players. This talented local group presents plays throughout the year. ⊠ *Līhu'e Parish Hall, 4340 Nāwiliwili Rd., Līhu'e* ☎ *808/245–7700* ⊕ *www.kauaicommunityplayers.org.*

NIGHTLIFE

For every new venue that opens on Kaua'i, another one closes. Perhaps it's simply the result of the island's ubiquitous but little-known epidemic: paradise paralysis. Symptoms include a slight fragrance of coconut wafting from the pores, pink cheeks and nose, a relaxed gait, and a slight smile curving on the lips. Let's face it: Kaua'i lulls people into a stupor that puts them to bed before 10 PM. But if you are one of those immune to the disease, Kaua'i may have a place or two for you to while away your spare hours.

BARS AND CLUBS

Nightclubs that stay open until the wee hours are rare on Kaua'i, and the bar scene is pretty limited. The major resorts generally host their own live entertainment and happy hours. All bars and clubs that serve alcohol must close at 2 AM, except those with a cabaret license, which allows them to close at 4 AM. For information on events or specials, check out the local newspaper's nightlife section, Kaua'i Times (⊕ kauaitimes.net).

THE NORTH SHORE

Hanalei Gourmet. The sleepy North Shore stays awake—until 10:30, that is—each evening in this small, convivial setting inside Hanalei's restored old school building. The emphasis here is on local live jazz, rock, and folk music. ⊠ *5-5161 Kūhiō Hwy., Hanalei Center, Hanalei* ☎ *808/826–2524* ⊕ *www.hanaleigourmet.com.*

St. Regis Bar. This spacious lounge overlooking Hanalei Bay offers drinks daily from 3 to 10:30. Stop by between 5 and 10 for *pūpū* (hors d'oeuvres), acoustic guitar or piano music, and an ocean view. ⊠ *Princeville Resort, 5520 Ka Haku Rd., Princeville* ☎ *808/826–9644.*

Tahiti Nui. This venerable and decidedly funky institution in sleepy Hanalei stopped offering its famous lū'au when owner and founder Auntie Louise Marston died. The family still owns the place and is doing its best to keep the place hopping with nightly entertainment: Hawaiian music is featured early every night, and rock and roll usually follows, starting at around 9 PM, with the exception of Monday, which hosts karaoke. It's definitely a locals' spot. ⊠ *5-5134 Kūhiō Hwy., Hanalei* ☎ *808/826–6277.*

THE EAST SIDE

Duke's Barefoot Bar. This is one of the liveliest bars on Kalapakī Beach. Contemporary Hawaiian music is performed in the beachside bar on most Fridays and Saturdays, and upstairs a traditional Hawaiian trio plays nightly for diners. The bar closes at 11 most nights. ⊠ *3610 Rice St., Kalapakī Beach, Līhu'e* ☎ *808/246–9599* ⊕ *www.dukeskauai.com.*

Continued on page 180

7

MORE THAN A FOLK DANCE

Hula has been called "the heartbeat of the Hawaiian people" and also "the world's best-known, most misunderstood dance." Both are true. Hula isn't just dance. It is storytelling.

Chanter Edith McKinzie calls it "an extension of a piece of poetry." In its adornments, implements, and customs, hula integrates every important Hawaiian cultural practice: poetry, history, genealogy, craft, plant cultivation, martial arts, religion, protocol. So when 19th century Christian missionaries sought to eradicate a practice they considered depraved, they threatened more than just a folk dance.

With public performance outlawed and private hula practice discouraged, hula went underground for a generation, to rural villages. The fragile verbal link by which culture was transmitted from teacher to student hung by a thread. Even increasing literacy did not help because hula's practitioners were a secretive and protected circle.

As if that weren't bad enough, vaudeville, Broadway, and Hollywood got hold of the hula, giving it the glitz treatment in an unbroken line from "Oh, How She Could Wicky Wacky Woo" to "Rock-A-Hula Baby." Hula became shorthand for paradise: fragrant flowers, lazy hours. Ironically, this development assured that hundreds of Hawaiians could make a living performing and teaching hula. Many danced 'auana (modern form) in performance; but taught kahiko (traditional), quietly, at home or in hula schools.

Today, 30 years after the cultural revival known as the Hawaiian Renaissance, language immersion programs have assured a new generation of proficient—and even eloquent—chanters, songwriters, and translators. Visitors can see more, and more authentic, traditional hula than at any other time in the last 200 years.

Like the culture of which it is the beating heart, hula has survived.

Lei *po'o*. Head lei. In kahiko, greenery only. In 'auana, flowers.

Face emotes appropriate expression. Dancer should not be a smiling automaton.

Shoulders remain relaxed and still, never hunched, even with arms raised. No bouncing.

Eyes always follow leading hand.

Lei. Hula is rarely performed without a shoulder lei.

Arms and hands remain loose, relaxed, below shoulder level—except as required by interpretive movements.

Traditional hula skirt is loose fabric, smocked and gathered at the waist.

Hip is canted over weight-bearing foot.

Knees are always slightly bent, accentuating hip sway.

Kupe'e. Ankle bracelet of flowers, shells, or—traditionally—noise-making dog teeth.

In kahiko, feet are flat. In 'auana, they may be more arched, but not tiptoes or bouncing.

BASIC MOTIONS

Speak or Sing

Moon or Sun

Grass Shack or House

Mountains or Heights

Love or Caress

At backyard parties, hula is performed in bare feet and street clothes, but in performance, adornments play a key role, as do rhythm-keeping implements.

In hula kahiko (traditional style), the usual dress is multiple layers of stiff fabric (often with a pellom lining, which most closely resembles *kapa*, the paperlike bark cloth of the Hawaiians). These wrap tightly around the bosom but flare below the waist to form a skirt. In pre-contact times, dancers wore only kapa skirts. Monarchy-period hula is performed in voluminous Mother Hubbard muʻumuʻu or high-necked muslin blouses and gathered skirts. Men wear loincloths or, for monarchy period, white or gingham shirts and black pants—sometimes with red sashes.

In hula ʻauana (modern), dress for women can range from grass skirts and strapless tops to contemporary tea-length dresses. Men generally wear aloha shirts, but sometimes grass skirts over pants or even everyday gear. (One group at a recent competition wore wetsuits to do a surfing song!)

SURPRISING HULA FACTS

■ Grass skirts are not traditional; workers from Kiribati (the Gilbert Islands) brought this custom to Hawaiʻi.

■ In olden-day Hawaiʻi, *mele* (songs) for hula were composed for every occasion—name songs for babies, dirges for funerals, welcome songs for visitors, celebrations of favorite pursuits.

■ Hula *maʻi* is a traditional hula form in praise of a noble's genitals; the power of the *aliʻi* (royalty) to procreate gave *mana* (spiritual power) to the entire culture.

■ Hula students in old Hawaiʻi adhered to high standards: scrupulous cleanliness, no sex, daily cleansing rituals, certain food prohibitions, and no contact with the dead. They were fined if they broke the rules.

WHERE TO WATCH

■ Coconut Marketplace, ✉ 4-484 Kūhiō Hwy., Kapaʻa, 🕐 Sat. 1 PM.

■ Poʻipū Shopping Village, ✉ 2360 Kiahuna Plantation Dr., Poʻipū Beach, ☎ 808/742-7444 🕐 Tues. and Thurs. 5 pm.

■ Smith's Tropical Paradise, ✉ 174 Wailua Rd., Kapaʻa, ☎ 808/821-6895, 🕐 Mon., Wed., and Fri. 5–9:15. Dinner included.

■ Festivals: There are many festivals on the island year-round where you can see hula performed. For more information visit *www.kauaifestivals.com*.

Kaua'i: Undercover Movie Star

Though Kaua'i has played itself in the movies (you may remember Nicolas Cage frantically shouting, "Is it Kapa'a or Kapa'a-a?" into a pay phone in *Honeymoon in Vegas* [1992]), most of its screen time has been as a stunt double for a number of tropical paradises. The island's remote valleys and waterfalls portrayed the Venezuelan jungle in Kevin Costner's *Dragonfly* (2002) and a Costa Rican dinosaur preserve in Steven Spielberg's *Jurassic Park* (1993). Spielberg was no stranger to Kaua'i, having filmed Harrison Ford's escape via seaplane from Menehune Fishpond in *Raiders of the Lost Ark* (1981). The fluted cliffs and gorges of Kaua'i's rugged Nāpali Coast play the misunderstood beast's island home in *King Kong* (1976), and a jungle dweller of another sort frolicked on Kaua'i in *George of the Jungle* (1997). Harrison Ford returned to the island for 10 weeks during the filming of *Six Days, Seven Nights* (1998), a romantic adventure set in French Polynesia. Part-time Kaua'i resident Ben Stiller, as well as Robert Downey Jr. and Jack Black, used the island as a stand-in for the jungles of Vietnam in *Tropic Thunder* (2008).

But these are all relatively recent movies. What's truly remarkable is that Hollywood discovered Kaua'i in 1933 with the making of *White Heat*, which was set on a sugar plantation. In 1950, Esther Williams and Rita Moreno arrived to film *Pagan Love Song*, a forgettable musical. Then, it was off to the races, as Kaua'i saw no fewer than a dozen movies filmed on the island in the 1950s, not all of them Oscar contenders.

The movie that is still immortalized on the island in the names of restaurants, real estate offices, a hotel, and even a sushi item is *South Pacific* (1957). (You guessed it, right?) That mythical place called Bali Hai is never far away on Kaua'i. There's even an off-off-off-Broadway musical version performed today—some 50 years after the movie was released—at the Kaua'i Beach Resort in Līhu'e.

In the 1960s Elvis Presley filmed *Blue Hawaii* (1961) and *Girls! Girls! Girls!* (1962) on the island. A local movie tour likes to point out the stain on a hotel carpet where Elvis's jelly doughnut fell.

Kaua'i has welcomed a long list of Hollywood's A-List: John Wayne in *Donovan's Reef* (1963); Jack Lemmon in *The Wackiest Ship in the Army* (1961); Richard Chamberlain in *The Thorn Birds* (1983); Gene Hackman in *Uncommon Valor* (1983); Danny DeVito and Billy Crystal in *Throw Momma from the Train* (1987); and Dustin Hoffman, Morgan Freeman, Renee Russo, and Cuba Gooding Jr. in *Outbreak* (1995).

Yet the movie scene isn't the only screen on which Kaua'i has starred. A slew of TV shows, TV pilots, and made-for-TV movies make the list as well, including *Gilligan's Island, Fantasy Island, Starsky & Hutch, Baywatch-Hawai'i*—even reality TV shows *The Bachelor* and *The Amazing Race 3*.

For the record, just because a movie did some filming here doesn't mean the entire movie was filmed on Kaua'i. *Honeymoon in Vegas* filmed just one scene here, while the murder mystery *A Perfect Getaway* (2009) was set on the famous Kalalau Trail and featured beautiful Kauaian backdrops but was shot mostly in Puerto Rico.

Hukilau Lānai. This open-air bar and restaurant is on the property of the Kaua'i Coast Resort but operates independently. If the mood takes you, go on a short walk to the sea, or recline in big, comfortable chairs while listening to mellow jazz or Hawaiian slack key guitar. Live music plays Sunday, Tuesday, and Friday, though the bar is open every day but Monday. Freshly infused tropical martinis—perhaps locally grown lychee and pineapple or a Big Island vanilla-bean infusion—are house favorites. ⊠ *520 Aleka Loop, Kūhiō Hwy., Wailua* ☎ *808/822–0600* ⊕ *www.hukilaukauai.com.*

Rob's Good Times Grill. Let loose at this sports bar, which also houses Kaua'i's hottest DJs spinning Thursday through Saturday from 9 PM to 2 AM, with the occasional live band on Friday as well. Wednesday you can kick up your heels with salsa and country line dancing from 7:30 to 11 PM. Sunday, Monday, and Tuesday evenings are open mike for karaoke enthusiasts. ⊠ *4303 Rice St., Līhu'e* ☎ *808/246–0311.*

Tapaz Martini Lounge. This hip club just opened in 2009 and falls under the roof and management of the Kapa'a location of Pizzetta Italian restaurant. Open from 9 PM until 1:45 AM on Friday and Saturday, Tapaz is one of the few places you can go to hear young, local DJs and bands. For a quieter spot to grab a drink, head to the bar next door at Pizzetta. ⊠ *1387 Kūhiō Hwy., Kapa'a* ☎ *808/823–8882* ⊕ *www. pizzettarestaurant.com.*

Tradewinds—A South Seas Bar. This salty mariner's den is surprisingly located within the clichéd confines of a cheesy mall. Tradewinds has a tattered palm-frond roof and a tropical theme reminiscent of Jimmy Buffett, but you aren't likely to hear Buffett tunes here. In fact, you're more likely to meet Ernest Hemingway types. From karaoke to dart league competitions to live music, this little bar busts at the seams with local flavor. It's open daily from 10 AM to 2 AM but opens early (7 AM) on Sunday mornings, serving as a home away from home to displaced NFL fans. ⊠ *Coconut Marketplace, 484 Kūhiō Hwy., Kapa'a* ☎ *808/822–1621* ⊕ *www.tradewinds-kauai.com.*

Trees Lounge. Behind the hokey Coconut Marketplace and next to the Kaua'i Coast Resort in Kapa'a, you'll find Trees Lounge. For a while, this chic wood-filled bar and restaurant hosted good live music but didn't allow any dancing, to the chagrin of its patrons. Now with the proper liquor licenses in hand, Trees will let you move a little more than just tap your toes in your seat, but with an 11 PM last call, you may want to dine here and then head elsewhere to shake your coconuts. ⊠ *440 Aleka Pl. Kapa'a* ☎ *808/823–0600* ⊕ *www.treesloungekauai.com.*

THE SOUTH SHORE AND WEST SIDE

Keoki's Paradise. A young, energetic crowd makes this a lively spot on Thursday, Friday, and Saturday nights, with live music from 7 to 9. After 9 PM, when the dining room clears out, there's a bit of a bar scene for singles. The bar closes at 10:30 PM. ⊠ *Po'ipū Shopping Village, 2360 Kiahuna Plantation Dr., Po'ipū* ☎ *808/742–7534* ⊕ *www. keokisparadise.com.*

The Point at Sheraton Kaua'i. This is *the* place to be on the South Shore to celebrate sunset with a drink; the ocean view is unsurpassed. Starting at

8 or 9 PM on Friday, Saturday, Sunday, and Monday, there's live entertainment until 12:30 or 1 AM. The lineup isn't set in stone, so call before
you arrive to see who's playing that night. ⊠ *Sheraton Kaua'i Resort,
2440 Ho'onani Rd., Po'ipū* ☎ *808/742–1661* ⊕ *www.sheraton-kauai.
com/de_thepoint.htm.*

Waimea Brewing Company. Sip one of the award-winning beers at this
airy plantation-style house, located in a 100-year-old coconut grove
on the property of the Waimea Plantation Cottages that in late 2009
added a new moniker—the Grove Cafe. Home-brewed beer, outdoor
seating, and a wraparound lānai make this brewery-eatery an authentic
West Side experience. No promises, but there is usually live music on
Wednesday, Thursday, and Friday. ⊠ *9400 Kaumuali'i Hwy., Waimea*
☎ *808/338–9733.*

COFFEEHOUSES

The island has a few coffeehouses where you can keep the night's entertainment going by taking in some live music in a quiet setting.

Fodor'sChoice   **Caffé Coco.** Nestled in a bamboo forest draped in bougainvillea and
★   flowering vines and hidden from view off the Kūhiō Highway is a
charming little venue where local musicians perform nightly. Caffé Coco
offers pūpū (appetizers), entrées, and desserts. It may not have a liquor
license, but don't let that stop you from enjoying the local talent; just
bring your own wine or beer. The outdoor setting—twinkle lights and
tiki torches beneath a thatched hut—is what the Kaua'i of old must have
been like. There's hula every Friday, and a belly-dancing group performs
on Tuesday. It's open until 9 Tuesday through Sunday. ⊠ *4-369 Kūhiō
Hwy., Wailua* ☎ *808/822–7990.*

Fodor'sChoice   **Small Town Coffee.** This funky little coffeehouse is the best thing to hap-
★   pen to the East Side in years. Owner Annie Caporuscio had a vision
for a venue that supports music, community, and art. Poetry slams,
improv jazz, open-mike nights, comedy, and writing groups—you'll
find them all on this tiny lot across the street from the beach in Kapa'a.
You can't miss the bright blue facade of this two-story house or the
crowd hanging out beneath umbrellas on the front stoop. Open daily
at 5:30 AM, with nightly entertainment until 9 every night except Sunday, this café is abuzz with local talent and soulful conversation. And
it hasn't hurt business to offer free Wi-Fi either. ⊠ *4-1495 Kūhiō Hwy.,
Kapa'a* ☎ *808/821–1604.*

Where to Eat

WORD OF MOUTH

"On our first night with family, we always like to have a casual dinner in the tropical open-air setting at Keoki's. We really feel we've arrived in paradise . . . When just the two of us arrive, my husband and I enjoy pupus and drinks or dinner surrounded by orchids in the quieter Plantation Gardens in Kiahuna complex."

—jojo46

WHERE TO EAT PLANNER

Eating-Out Strategy

Where should we eat? With dozens of island eateries competing for your attention, it may seem like a daunting question. But our expert writers and editors have done most of the legwork—the dozens of selections here represent the best eating experience this island has to offer. Search "Best Bets" for top recommendations by price, cuisine, and experience. Or find a restaurant quickly—reviews are ordered alphabetically within their geographic area.

With Kids

Hawai'i is a kid-friendly destination in many regards, and that includes taking the little ones out to eat with you. Because of the overall relaxed vibe and casual dress here, you won't have to worry too much about your tot's table manners or togs—within reason, of course. Take advantage of treats and eating experiences unique to Hawai'i, such as shave ice, sunshine markets (perfect for picnic lunches or beach provisions), and lū'au.

Reservations

It's always a good idea to make reservations when you can, and if you plan to dine at one of Kaua'i's top eateries, reservations are essential. However, you'll find that many places on the island don't take reservations at all, and service is first come, first served.

What to Wear

Just about anything goes on Kaua'i. At lunch you can dine in your bathing suit, a sarong or T-shirt and shorts, and flip-flops at most places. Dinner is only a slight step up. That said, if you're out for a special occasion and want to don your fanciest duds, no one will look twice.

Smoking

Smoking is prohibited in all Hawai'i restaurants and bars.

Hours and Prices

Restaurants on Kaua'i significantly quiet down by 9 PM; the bar scene continues past midnight—but not much past. It seems as if the entire island is in bed before 10 PM to get up early the next day and play. In general, peak dining hours here tend to be on the earlier side, during sunset hours from 6 to 8 PM.

A tip of 18% to 20% is standard for good service.

WHAT IT COSTS					
	¢	$	$$	$$$	$$$$
AT DINNER	under $10	$10–$17	$18–$26	$27–$35	over $35

Restaurant prices are for a main course at dinner.

BEST BETS FOR KAUA'I DINING

Where can I find the best food the island has to offer? Fodor's writers and editors have selected their favorite restaurants by price, cuisine, and experience in the lists below. In the first column, the Fodor's Choice properties represent the "best of the best" across price categories. You can also search by area for excellent eats—just peruse our complete reviews on the following pages.

Fodor'sChoice ★

Bar Acuda, p. 186
Beach House, p. 199
Café Portofino, p. 196
Dondero's, p. 200

By Price

¢

Dani's Restaurant, p. 197
Eggbert's, p. 192
Hamura Saimin, p. 198
Hanamā'ulu Restaurant, p. 198
Mermaid's Café, p. 193
Papaya's, p. 193

$

Joe's on the Green, p. 205
Kalaheo Café & Coffee Co., p. 206
Kīlauea Fish Market, p. 189

Mema Thai Chinese Cuisine, p. 193
Po'ipū Tropical Burgers, p. 208
Toi's Thai Kitchen, p. 210
Verde, p. 195

$$

The Eastside, p. 192
Kaua'i Pasta, p. 192
Līhu'e Barbecue Inn, p. 199
Pomodoro Ristorante Italiano, p. 208
Wrangler's Steakhouse, p. 210

$$$

Bar Acuda, p. 186
Beach House, p. 199
Dondero's, p. 200
Hukilau Lana'i, p. 192
Plantation Gardens, p. 206
Scotty's Beachside BBQ, p. 195

$$$$

Roy's Po'ipū Bar & Grill, p. 209
Tidepools, p. 209

By Cuisine

HAWAIIAN

Dani's Restaurant ¢, p. 197
Hamura Saimin ¢, p. 198
Hanamā'ulu Restaurant ¢–$, p. 198

PLATE LUNCH

Dani's Restaurant ¢, p. 197
Kīlauea Fish Market $, p. 189
Bouchon's $$, p. 187
Hanamā'ulu Restaurant ¢–$, p. 198
Keoki's Paradise $$–$$$, p. 206
Restaurant Kintaro $$, p. 195

By Experience

MOST KID-FRIENDLY

Eggbert's ¢–$, p. 192
Keoki's Paradise $$–$$$, p. 206
Kīlauea Bakery and Pau Hana Pizza $$, p. 189
Pizzetta $, p. 206
Po'ipū Tropical Burgers $–$$, p. 208

MOST ROMANTIC

Beach House $$–$$$, p. 199
Café Portofino $$$–$$$$, p. 196
Dondero's $$–$$$, p. 200

BEST VIEW

Beach House $$–$$$, p. 199
Brennecke's Beach Broiler $$–$$$, p. 200
Bull Shed $$, p. 191
Café Portofino $$$–$$$$, p. 196

8

By Lois Ann Ell   In Kaua'i, if you're lucky enough to win an invitation to a potluck, baby lū'au, or beach party, don't think twice—just accept. The best grinds (food) are homemade, and so you'll eat until you're full, then rest, eat some more, and make a plate to take home, too.

But even if you can't score a spot at one of these parties, don't despair. Great local-style food is easy to come by at countless low-key places around the island, and as an extra bonus, these eats are often inexpensive, and portions are generous. Expect plenty of meat—usually deep-fried or marinated in a teriyaki sauce and grilled *pulehu*-style (over an open fire)—and starches. Rice is standard, even for breakfast, and often served alongside potato-macaroni salad, another island specialty. Another local favorite is *poke*, made from chunks of raw tuna or octopus seasoned with sesame oil, soy sauce, onions, and pickled seaweed. It's a great *pūpū* (appetizer) when paired with a cold beer.

Kaua'i's cultural diversity is apparent in its restaurants, which offer authentic Vietnamese, Chinese, Korean, Japanese, Thai, Mexican, Italian, and Hawaiian specialties. Less specialized restaurants cater to the tourist crowd, serving standard American fare—burgers, pizza, sandwiches, surf-and-turf combos, and so on. Kapa'a offers the best selection of restaurants, with options for a variety of tastes and budgets; most fast-food joints are in Lihū'e.

THE NORTH SHORE

Because of the North Shore's isolation, restaurants have enjoyed a captive audience of visitors who don't want to make the long, dark trek into town for dinner. As a result, dining in this region has been characterized by expensive fare that isn't especially tasty, either. Fortunately, the situation is slowly improving as new restaurants open and others change hands or menus.

Still, dining on the North Shore can be pricier than other parts of the island, and not especially family-friendly. Most of the restaurants are found either in Hanalei town or the Princeville resorts. Consequently, you'll encounter delightful mountain and ocean views, but just one restaurant with oceanfront dining.

$$–$$$
MEDITERRANEAN
Fodor's Choice
★

✕ **Bar Acuda.** This tapas bar is a very welcome addition to the Hanalei dining scene, rocketing right to top place in the categories of tastiness, creativity, and pizzazz. Owner-chef Jim Moffat's brief menu changes weekly: You might find sea bass, polenta, fried fish cakes, grilled veggies, a fresh mozzarella salad, and sausages with onions, all served with fresh bread. The small servings are intended to be shared, tapas-style. The food is consistently remarkable, with subtly intense sauces that further elevate the outstanding cuisine. It's super casual, but chic, with a nice porch for outdoor dining, and the service is discreet but

Dining is a scenic affair at the St. Regis Princeville Resort, whose restaurants overlook Hanalei Bay and Mt. Makana.

thorough. ⊠ *Hanalei Center, 5-5161 Kūhiō Hwy., Hanalei* ☎ *808/826–7081* ⊕ *www.restaurantbaracuda.com* ▬ *MC, V* ⊗ *Closed Mon.*

$$
JAPANESE

✕ **Bouchon's.** This second-story restaurant and sushi bar, known until recently as Sushi Blues, has a nice ambience, with copper tabletops, lovely views of mountains streaked with waterfalls, and photos of international jazz greats lining the staircase. Regular entertainment, a full bar, and a sake menu add to its appeal. Choose from steaks, seafood dishes, and specialty sushi items such as the Las Vegas Roll, which is filled with tuna, yellowtail, and avocado and fried in a tempura batter. ⊠ *Ching Young Village, 5-5190 Kūhiō Hwy., Hanalei* ☎ *808/826–9701* ▬ *AE, D, DC, MC, V.*

$–$$
AMERICAN

✕ **Hanalei Gourmet.** This spot in Hanalei's restored old schoolhouse offers dolphin-safe tuna, low-sodium meats, fresh-baked breads, and homemade desserts as well as a casual atmosphere where both families and the sports-watching crowds can feel equally comfortable. Early birds can order coffee and toast or a hearty breakfast. Lunch and dinner menus feature sandwiches, burgers, filling salads, and nightly specials of fresh local fish. They also will prepare a picnic and give it to you in an insulated backpack. A full bar and frequent live entertainment keep things hopping even after the kitchen closes. Thursday evenings fill up for fish taco night. ⊠ *5-5161 Kūhiō Hwy., Hanalei* ☎ *808/826–2524* ⊕ *www.hanaleigourmet.com* ▬ *D, DC, MC, V.*

$$$$
ECLECTIC

✕ **Kaua'i Grill.** Savor an artful meal created by world-renowned chef Jean-Gorges Vongerichten, surrounded by a dramatic Hanalei Bay scene by night. Located at the new St. Regis Princeville Resort, Kaua'i Grill has dark wood decor and an ornate red chandelier, the centerpiece of

Where to Eat on the North Shore

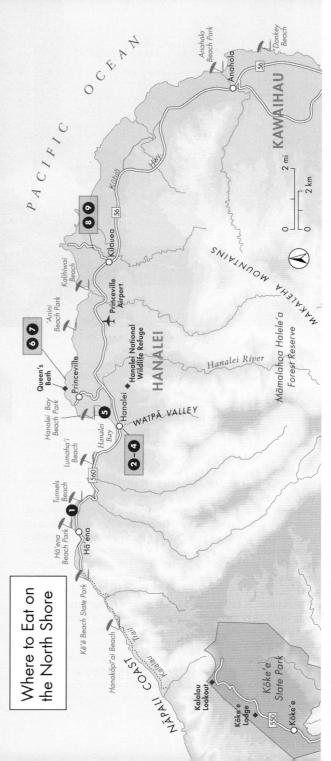

Bar Acuda **4**
Bouchon's **3**
Hanalei Gourmet **2**
Kaua'i Grille **7**

Kīlauea Bakery
and Pau Hana Pizza ... **9**
Kīlauea Fish Market ... **8**

Makana Terrace **6**
Mediterranean Gourmet ... **1**
Postcards Café **5**

BUDGET-FRIENDLY EATS: NORTH SHORE

It's not easy to find cheap food on the North Shore, but these little eateries serve up dinner for two for under $20.

■ **Foodland.** In a pinch, you can pick up pretty good packaged sushi and ready-to-eat hot entrées and sandwiches at the Foodland grocery store. ⊠ *Princeville Shopping Center, 5–4280 Kūhiō Hwy., Princeville* ☎ *808/826–9880.*

■ **Neide's Salsa & Samba.** This is one of the best low-cost eateries, with unusual and tasty Brazilian food to take out or eat in a casual garden setting at the Hanalei Center. ⊠ *5-5161 Kūhiō Hwy., Hanalei* ☎ *808/826–1851.*

■ **Panda's Kitchen.** Chinese food—including noodle dishes, stir-fries, spring rolls, and other basics—is served in this tiny eatery with limited

outdoor seating adjacent to Ching Young Village. ⊠ *5-5190 Kūhiō Hwy., Hanalei* ☎ *808/826–7388.*

■ **Papaya's.** Health foods, such as rice dishes, soups, and salads, are served in the back of this natural-foods store at the Hanalei Center; takeout only. ⊠ *5-5161 Kūhiō Hwy., Hanalei* ☎ *808/826–0089* ⊕ *www.papayasnaturalfoods.com.*

■ **Hanalei Pizza.** Excellent pizza (the pesto with whole-wheat crust is a winner), salads, and a few pasta dishes can be taken out or enjoyed at inside and outside tables at Ching Young Village. ⊠ *5-5190 Kūhiō Hwy., Hanalei* ☎ *808/826–9494.*

■ **Tropical Taco.** This is a satisfactory choice for a quick take-out meal of basic Mexican food. ⊠ *5-5088 Kūhiō Hwy., Hanalei* ☎ *808/827–8226* ⊕ *www.tropicaltaco.com.*

8

the room. The attention here is on the flavors of robust meat and local, fresh seafood. Most dishes are plainly grilled, accompanied by exotic sauces and condiments. The specials change frequently and use as many Hawaiian-grown ingredients as possible. Expect attentive service with the somewhat stiff feel of an exclusive hotel, and an expertly created meal. ⊠, *5520 Ka Haku Rd.* ☎ *808/826–9644* ⚷ *Reservations essential* 🍴 *AE, D, DC, MC, V* ☯ *No lunch. Closed Sun.–Mon.*

$$ ✕ **Kīlauea Bakery and Pau Hana Pizza.** This bakery has garnered tons of
AMERICAN well-deserved good press for its starter of Hawaiian sourdough made with guava as well as its specialty pizzas topped with such yummy ingredients as smoked ono (a Hawaiian fish), Gorgonzola-rosemary sauce, barbecued chicken, goat cheese, and roasted onions. Open from 6:30 AM, the bakery serves coffee drinks, delicious fresh pastries, bagels, and breads in the morning. Late risers, beware: Breads and pastries sell out quickly on weekends. Pizza, soup, and salads can be ordered for lunch or dinner. If you want to hang out or do the coffee-shop bit in Kīlauea, this is the place. A pretty courtyard with covered tables is a pleasant place to linger. ⊠ *Kong Lung Center, 2490 Keneke St., Kīlauea* ☎ *808/828–2020* 🍴 *MC, V.*

$ ✕ **Kīlauea Fish Market.** If you're not in a hurry, this tiny restaurant serves
SEAFOOD up fresh fish in quality preparations, including tucked into hearty wraps and salads, stir-fried, and grilled with tasty sauces made from scratch. All fish and vegetables are locally purchased. The 'ahi wrap is the most

popular selection, while the chicken plate lunch, with a choice of brown or white rice, is the best deal for the budget conscious. After placing your order inside, you can eat outside at covered tables, or take out. ⊠ *Kīlauea Lighthouse Rd., Kīlauea* ☎ *808/828–6244* ▭ *MC, V* ☺ *Closed Sun.*

$$$$
MODERN
HAWAIIAN

✕ **Makana Terrace.** Enjoy breakfast, lunch, or dinner in front of one of the most exquisite views of Hanalei Bay. There's no doubt it's pricey, but you're paying for the view—sit on the terrace if you can—and for an attentive staff. There is a focus on local, Hawaiian-grown foods here, including the fish plate of a fresh Pacific catch, which is your best bet for lunch. Feast at the extensive breakfast buffet for $25 per person from 6:30 to 11:00 AM, but it's traditional fare: nothing spectacular or exotic. For a special evening, splurge on the surf and turf (around $45) and time your dinner around sunset for an unforgettable Hawaiian vista. ⊠ *5520 Ka Haku Rd., Princeville* ☎ *808/826–9644* ▭ *AE, D, DC, MC, V.*

$$–$$$
ECLECTIC

✕ **Mediterranean Gourmet.** This restaurant is nearly at the end of the road, but if you happen to be in the area, it's well worth a stop. Owner-chef Imad Beydoun, a native of Beirut, serves such classics as hummus, stuffed grape leaves, and baba ghanoush alongside traditional favorites like rib-eye steak and rosemary rack of lamb. Pacific Rim influences can be found in dishes like 'ahi baked in banana leaf. The seafood paella, a hearty stew of clams, scallops, mussels, shrimp, fish, and saffron rice, topped with Dungeness crab and a lobster tail, is an excellent choice. Belly-dancing performances on Thursday nights might distract you from the lovely ocean views. ⊠ *Hanalei Colony Resort, 5-7130 Kūhiō Hwy., Ha'ena* ☎ *808/826–9875* ⊕ *www.kauaimedgourmet.com* ▭ *MC, V* ☺ *Closed Sun.*

$$–$$$
HAWAIIAN

✕ **Postcards Café.** With its postcard artwork, beamed ceilings, and light interiors, this traditional plantation-cottage restaurant has a menu consisting mostly of organic, additive-free vegetarian foods and fish. But don't get the wrong idea—this isn't simple cooking: Choices might include carrot-ginger soup, taro fritters, fresh fish served with peppered pineapple-sage sauce, or blackened 'ahi. Desserts are made without refined sugar. Try the chocolate silk pie made with barley malt chocolate, pure vanilla, and creamy tofu with a crust of graham crackers, sun-dried cherries, and crushed cashews. This is probably your best bet for dinner in Hanalei town. ⊠ *5-5075A Kūhiō Hwy., Hanalei* ☎ *808/826–1191* ⊕ *www.postcardscafe.com* ▭ *AE, MC, V* ☺ *No lunch.*

WORD OF MOUTH

"Postcards Café in Hanalei. When you're on the North Shore, absolutely be sure to go here for dinner. They are open 6 to 9 PM and serve outstanding, mostly organic food. The preparations are unique and so, so delicious. If you get there around 6 you'll even see them cutting the herbs and lettuce from the garden. It's in a small, intimate house."
–MelissaMorgan

THE EAST SIDE

Since the East Side is the island's largest population center, it makes sense that it should boast the widest selection of restaurants. It's also a good place to get both cheaper meals and the local-style cuisine that residents favor.

Most of the eateries are found along Kūhiō Highway between Kapa'a and Wailua; a few are tucked into shopping centers and resorts. In Līhu'e, it's easier to find lunch than dinner because many restaurants cater to the business crowd.

You'll find all the usual fast-food joints in both Kapa'a and Līhu'e, as well as virtually every ethnic cuisine available on Kaua'i. While fancy gourmet restaurants are less abundant in this part of the island, there's plenty of good, solid food, and a few stellar attractions. But unless you're staying on the East Side, or passing through, it's probably not worth the long drive from the North Shore or Po'ipū resorts to eat here.

KAPA'A AND WAILUA

In recent years, the most affordable, hip new eateries on the island have opened in Kapa'a. Unlike the resort-dominated South and North shores, Kapa'a is local, fun, and eclectic, with hamburger stands on the side of the road, vegetarian venues, and swanky bars serving up artful appetizers. Diversity is the key to this area; there is something for everyone, especially those on a budget.

$$
STEAKHOUSE

✕ **Bull Shed**. The A-frame structure makes this popular restaurant look distinctly rustic from the outside. Inside, light-color walls and a full wall of glass highlight an ocean view that is one of the best on Kaua'i. Come early for a window seat and watch the surf crashing on the rocks while you study the menu. The food is simple and basic—think white bread and iceberg lettuce—but they know how to do surf and turf. You can try both in one of several combo dinner platters or order fresh island fish and thick steaks individually. The restaurant is best known for its prime rib and Australian rack of lamb. Longtime visitors and locals love this place, which hasn't changed much in 20 years. Arrive by 5:30 for early-bird specials. ✉ 796 *Kūhiō Hwy., Kapa'a* ☎ 808/822–3791 or 808/822–1655 ⊕ *www.bullshedrestaurant.com* ▭ AE, D, DC, MC, V ☉ *No lunch.*

$-$$
CAFÉ

✕ **Caffé Coco**. A restored plantation cottage set back off the highway and surrounded by tropical foliage is the setting for this island café. You'll know it by its bright lime-green storefront. An attached black-light art gallery and a vintage apparel shop called Bambulei make this a fun stop for any meal. Outdoor seating in the vine-covered garden is pleasant during nice weather, although on calm nights it can get buggy. Acoustic music is offered regularly, attracting a laid-back local crowd. Potstickers filled with tofu and chutney, 'ahi wraps, Greek and organic salads, fresh fish and soups, and a daily list of specials are complemented by a full espresso bar and wonderful desserts. Allow plenty of time, because the tiny kitchen can't turn out meals quickly. ✉ 4-369 *Kūhiō Hwy., Wailua* ☎ 808/822–7990 ▭ MC, V ☉ *Closed Mon.*

8

$$–$$$
PACIFIC RIM

✗ **The Eastside.** Excellent service, an open-air casual atmosphere, and live music are great perks of this new hot spot. The reason people flock here is the food. 'Ahi ceviche served in a coconut with baked plantains, mahimahi wrapped in delicate potato slices with a curried jade pesto sauce, and fresh watermelon and tangerine martinis are

WORD OF MOUTH

"Hukilau Lana'i (in Kapa'a): had an outstanding meal here. Of course, made better by the company. Their grilled 'ono with mac nut brown butter sauce was to die for." –china_cat

some of the staples on the menu its loyal customers dine here for. It's run by brothers John Pfleuger and Dylan Scott; both have extensive restaurant experience and run a seamless operation in the central spot in Kapa'a town. ✉ *4-1380 Kūhiō Hwy. Kapa'a* ☎ *808/823–9500* ⊕ *www.theeastsidekauai.com* ☰ *MC, V* ⊗ *Closed Sun.–Mon.*

¢–$
AMERICAN
🍴

✗ **Eggbert's.** If you're big on breakfasts, try Eggbert's, which serves breakfast items until 3 PM daily. In the Coconut Marketplace, this family-friendly restaurant has a sunny interior, lots of windows, and lānai seating. It's a great spot for omelets, banana pancakes, and eggs Benedict in two sizes. Lunch selections include sandwiches, burgers, stir-fry, and fresh fish. Take-out orders are also available. ✉ *Coconut Marketplace, 4-484 Kūhiō Hwy., Kapa'a* ☎ *808/822–3787* ☰ *MC, V.*

$$–$$$
AMERICAN
Fodor'sChoice
★

✗ **Hukilau Lana'i.** Relying heavily on superfresh island fish and locally grown vegetables, this restaurant offers quality food that is competently and creatively prepared. The fish—grilled, steamed, or sautéed and served with succulent sauces—shines here. Other sound choices are the savory meat loaf and prime rib. Chicken and a few pasta dishes round out the menu. The 'ahi nachos appetizer is not to be missed, nor is the warm chocolate dessert soufflé. The spacious dining room looks out to the ocean, and it's lovely to eat at the outdoor tables when the weather is nice. Overall, it's one of the best choices on the East Side. *Kauai'i Coast Resort* ✉ *Coconut Marketplace, 520 Aleka Loop, Kapa'a* ☎ *808/822–0600* ⊕ *www.hukilaukauai.com* ☰ *AE, D, DC, MC, V* ⊗ *No lunch. Closed Mon.*

$–$$
ITALIAN

✗ **Kaua'i Pasta.** If you don't mind a no-frills atmosphere for affordable five-star food, this is the place. The husband of the husband-and-wife team that runs the restaurant left his executive-chef position at Roy's to open a catering business. He leased a kitchen that happened to have a small dining area, and rather than let it go to waste, they open for dinner every evening except Monday. Specials, written on the whiteboard at the entrance, are always satisfying and delicious. The locals have this place figured out; they show up in droves. The food's fabulous, and the price is right. The Līhu'e branch also serves lunch. ✉ *4-939B Kūhiō Hwy., Kapa'a* ☎ *808/822–7447* ⊕ *www.kauaipastarestaurants.com* ☰ *MC, V* ⊗ *Closed Mon.*

$$–$$$
ECLECTIC

✗ **Lemongrass Grill.** The inside of Kapa'a's Lemongrass Grill may remind you of a Pacific Rim–theme rustic tavern, with its stained wood interior, numerous paintings and carvings, and food that is as fresh as it can get. There's something for everybody here: salads, poultry, steaks and ribs, vegetarian fare, and, of course, a wide selection of seafood, all with an

Some of the best eats on Kaua'i come from the sea. Ask what the local catch of the day is for the freshest option.

island flair. Specials include a heaping seafood platter featuring lobster tails, scallops, shrimp scampi, the fish of the day, and an assortment of vegetables—they say it's "for two," but it could easily feed three or four. Service is laid-back but friendly. ⊠ 4-885 Kūhiō Hwy., Kapa'a ☎ 808/821–2888 ▭ AE, D, MC, V ☺ No lunch.

$ ╳ **Mema Thai Chinese Cuisine.** Refined and intimate, Mema Thai serves its
THAI dishes on crisp white linens accented by tabletop orchid sprays. Menu items such as broccoli with oyster sauce and cashew chicken reveal Chinese origins, but the emphasis is on Thai dishes. A host of curries—red, green, yellow, and house—made with coconut milk and kaffir-lime leaves run from mild to mouth searing. The traditional green-papaya salad adds a cool touch for the palate. ⊠ Wailua Shopping Plaza, 369 Kūhiō Hwy., Kapa'a ☎ 808/823–0899 ▭ AE, D, DC, MC, V ☺ No lunch weekends.

¢ ╳ **Mermaid's Café.** Sit and watch as your meal is prepared at this café
ECLECTIC in Kapa'a. The small yet diverse menu of sophisticated dishes features homemade sauces and local ingredients. Try the 'ahi nori wrap with fresh seared tuna, rice, cucumber, and wasabi cream sauce with pickled ginger and soy sauce—their most popular pick. Other dishes include rice, fresh vegetables, and either tofu or chicken served with a peanut sauce or coconut curry sauce. Everything can be made either vegetarian or vegan. The fish is caught daily by local fisherman, and produce is grown on the island. ⊠ 1384 Kūhiō Hwy., Kapa'a ☎ 808/821–2026 ▭ MC, V.

¢ ╳ **Papaya's.** Kaua'i's largest natural-foods market contains a buffet-style
VEGETARIAN café with good food at low prices. Food items change daily, but there's always a hot and cold salad bar, and favorites like taro burgers for

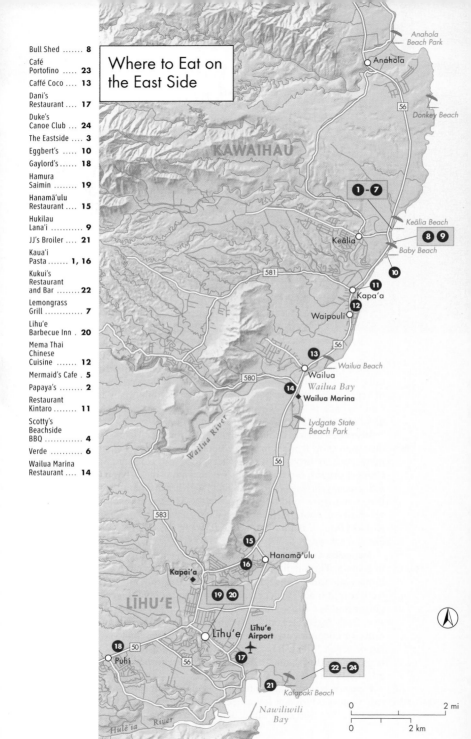

Where to Eat on the East Side

lunch and dinner. Meals are made with fresh organic lettuce and vegetables, most grown nearby. You can order takeout or eat at a covered table in the courtyard. ⊠ *Kauaʻi Village Shopping Center, 4-831 Kūhiō Hwy., Kapaʻa* ☎ *808/823–0190* ⊕ *www.papayasnaturalfoods.com* ⊟ *AE, D, MC, V* ⊗ *Closed Sun.*

$$ / JAPANESE ╳ **Restaurant Kintaro.** If you want to eat someplace that's a favorite with locals, visit Kintaro's. But be prepared to wait, because the dining room and sushi bar are always busy. Try the Bali Hai, a roll of eel and smoked salmon, baked and topped with wasabi mayonnaise. For an "all-in-one-dish" meal, consider the *Nabemono,* a single pot filled with a healthful variety of seafood and vegetables. *Teppanyaki* dinners are meat, seafood, and vegetables flash-cooked on tabletop grills in an entertaining display. Tatami-mat seating is available behind shoji screens that provide privacy for groups. Like many longtime restaurants, it's an enduring favorite that doesn't always live up to expectations. ⊠ *4-370 Kūhiō Hwy., Wailua* ☎ *808/822–3341* ⊟ *AE, D, DC, MC, V* ⊗ *No lunch. Closed Sun.*

$$–$$$ / AMERICAN ╳ **Scotty's Beachside BBQ.** Ribs and other succulent smoked meats are the stars at this casual upstairs restaurant that has a large, often noisy dining room and lovely ocean view. While the BBQ is best here, the menu also has grilled steak, shrimp, chicken, and burgers. You can choose your BBQ sauce and two side dishes; the coleslaw and baked beans are noteworthy. If you still have room for dessert, try the make-your-own s'mores. ⊠ *4-1546 Kūhiō Hwy., Kapaʻa* ☎ *808/823–8480* ⊕ *www.scottysbbq.com* ⊟ *AE, D, MC, V* ⊗ *Closed Sun.*

¢–$ / MEXICAN ╳ **Verde.** Combining classic Mexican food with chili-based sauces and creations from the chef's hometown of New Mexico, Verde's menu includes tostadas, enchiladas, and tacos served with fresh fish or slow-cooked beef or chicken. The seared tuna tacos with red chili aioli and the stacked enchilada, with chicken or beef short ribs smothered in red or green chili sauce, are favorites. Beers and margaritas served with premium tequila complement the spicy sauces perfectly. Don't be misled by the location of this spot—a small space in a shopping complex. ⊠ *4-1101 Kūhiō Hwy., Kapaʻa* ☎ *808/821–1400* ⊕ *www.verdehawaii.com* ⊟ *MC, V* ⊗ *Closed Mon.–Tues.*

$–$$ / SEAFOOD ╳ **Wailua Marina Restaurant.** Offering the island's only river view, this marina restaurant—an island fixture for almost 40 years—is a good spot to stop for lunch after a boat ride up the Wailua River to the Fern Grotto, and worth a visit on its own merit. With more than 40 selections, the menu is a mix of comfort food and more sophisticated dishes;

8

Nothing beats shave ice (no, not "shaved" ice) on a hot Hawaiian day.

portions are gigantic. The chef is fond of stuffing: You'll find stuffed baked pork chops, stuffed chicken baked in plum sauce, and 'ahi stuffed with crab. The steamed mullet is a classic island dish. ⊠ *Wailua River State Park, Wailua Rd., Wailua* ☎ *808/822–4311* ▭ *AE, D, DC, MC, V* ⊘ *Closed Mon.*

LĪHU'E

You will probably find yourself in Līhu'e at least a few times during your stay. When it comes to restaurants, Līhu'e is somewhat extreme. There are some remarkable (and expensive) restaurants and some great low-cost eateries that feed the business lunch crowd—but not much in between. If you are in town for lunch, don't pass up some of the authentic, local spots.

$$$–$$$$
ITALIAN
Fodor's Choice
★

✕ **Café Portofino.** The menu at this authentic northern Italian restaurant is as impressive as the views of Kalapakī Bay and the Hā'upu range. Owner Giuseppe Avocadi's flawless dishes have garnered a host of culinary awards and raves from dining critics. The fresh 'ahi carpaccio is a signature dish, and pasta, scampi, and veal are enhanced by sauces that soar like Avocadi's imagination. Linger over coffee and ice-cream-filled profiteroles or traditional tiramisu while enjoying harp music. Excellent service and a soothing, dignified ambience complete the delightful dining experience, making this one of your best bets for a quality meal in Līhu'e. ⊠ *Kaua'i Marriott Resort & Beach Club, 3610 Rice St., Līhu'e* ☎ *808/245–2121* ⊕ *cafeportofino.com* ▭ *AE, D, DC, MC, V* ⊘ *No lunch.*

SHAVE ICE

Nothing goes down quite as nicely as shave ice on a hot day. This favorite island treat has been likened to a sno-cone, but that description doesn't do a good shave ice justice. Yes, it is ice served up in a cone-shaped cup and drenched with sweet syrup, but the similarities end there. As its name implies, the ice should be feathery, light—the texture of snowflakes, not frozen slush. And alongside the standard cherry and grape, you'll find all sorts of exotic island flavorings, such as passion fruit, pineapple, coconut, mango, and, of course, a rainbow mix.

Not all shave ice meets these high standards, and when you're hot, even the average ones taste great. But a few places are worth seeking out. On the East Side, the best is **Hawaiian Blizzard** (Kapa'a Shopping Center, 4-1105 Kūhiō Hwy.), a true shave ice stand that opens up midday in front of the Big Save grocery store in Kapa'a. In Līhu'e, try **Halo Halo Shave Ice** (2956 Kress St.). And on the hot, dry West Side, make a beeline for **Jo-Jo's Clubhouse** (mile marker 23, Kaumuali'i, Hwy. 50), on the main drag in Waimea. All three places have benches where you can sit and slurp.

¢ ✕ **Dani's Restaurant.** Kaua'i residents frequent this big, sparsely furnished eatery near the Līhu'e Fire Station for hearty, local-style food at breakfast and lunch. Dani's is a good place to try lū'au food without commercial lū'au prices. You can order Hawaiian-style *laulau* (pork and taro leaves wrapped in ti leaves and steamed) or *kālua* pig, slow roasted in an underground oven. Other island-style dishes include Japanese-prepared *tonkatsu* (pork cutlet) and teriyaki beef, and there's always the all-American New York steak. Omelets are whipped up with fish cake, *kālua* pig, or seafood; everything is served with rice. ⊠ *4201 Rice St., Līhu'e* ☎ *808/245–4991* ▭ *MC, V* ☺ *No dinner. Closed Sun.*

HAWAIIAN

$$$ ✕ **Duke's Canoe Club.** Surfing legend Duke Kahanamoku is immortalized in this casual restaurant set on Kalapakī Bay. Guests can admire surfboards, photos, and other memorabilia marking his long tenure as a waterman. It's an interesting collection, and an indoor garden and waterfall add to the pleasing sights. You'll find simple fare ranging from fish tacos and stir-fried cashew chicken to hamburgers, served 11 AM to 11 PM. At dinner, fresh fish prepared in a variety of styles is the best choice. Duke's claims to have the biggest salad bar on the island, though given the lack of competition, that isn't saying much. A happy-hour drink and appetizer is a less expensive way to enjoy the moonrises and ocean views here—though it can get pretty crowded. The Barefoot Bar is a hot spot for after-dinner drinks, too. ⊠ *Kaua'i Marriott Resort & Beach Club, 3610 Rice St., Līhu'e* ☎ *808/246–9599* ⊕ *www.dukeskauai.com* ▭ *AE, D, DC, MC, V.*

SEAFOOD

$$$–$$$$ ✕ **Gaylord's.** Located in what was at one time Kaua'i's most expensive plantation estate, Gaylord's pays tribute to the elegant dining rooms of 1930s high society. The candlelit tables sit on a cobblestone patio surrounding a fountain and overlooking a wide lawn. The innovative menu features classic American cooking with an island twist. Try wonton-wrapped prawns with a wasabi plum sauce, New Zealand venison,

ECLECTIC

8

blackened prime rib, or fresh fish specials. Lunches are a mix of salads, sandwiches, and pasta, enjoyed in a leisurely fashion. The lavish Sunday brunch may include such specialties as sweet-potato hash and Cajun 'ahi in addition to the standard omelets and pancakes. Before or after dining you can wander around the estate grounds or take a horse-drawn carriage ride.

The unique setting makes up for the culinary gaps. ⊠ *Kilohana Plantation, 3-2087 Kaumuali'i Rd., Līhu'e* ☎ *808/245–9593* ⊕ *gaylordskauai. com* ▭ *AE, D, DC, MC, V.*

¢–$
HAWAIIAN
✕ **Hamura Saimin.** Folks just love this funky old plantation-style diner. Locals and tourists stream in and out all day long, and Neighbor Islanders stop in on their way to the airport to pick up take-out orders for friends and family back home. *Saimen* is the big draw, and each day the Hiraoka family dishes up about 1,000 bowls of steaming broth and homemade noodles, topped with a variety of garnishes. The barbecued chicken and meat sticks take on a smoky flavor during grilling. The landmark eatery is also famous for its *liliko'i* (passion fruit) chiffon pie. ■TIP→ As one of the few island eateries open late, until 11 pm on weeknights and midnight on Friday and Saturday, it's favored by night owls. ⊠ *2956 Kress St., Līhu'e* ☎ *808/245–3271* ▭ *No credit cards.*

¢–$
JAPANESE
✕ **Hanamā'ulu Restaurant, Tea House, Sushi Bar, and Robatayaki.** Business is brisk at this landmark Kaua'i eatery. The food is a mix of Japanese, Chinese, and local-style cooking, served up in hearty portions. The ginger chicken and fried shrimp are wildly popular, as are the fresh sashimi and sushi. Other choices include tempura, chicken *katsu* (fried Japanese-style), beef broccoli, and *robatayaki* (grilled seafood and meat). The main dining room is rather unattractive, but the private rooms in back look out on the Japanese garden and fishponds and feature traditional seating on tatami mats at low tables. These tearooms can be reserved and are favored for family events and celebrations. ⊠ *1-4291 Kūhiō Hwy., Rte. 56, Hanamā'ulu* ☎ *808/245–2511* ▭ *MC, V* ⊘ *Closed Mon.*

$
AMERICAN
✕ **JJ's Broiler.** This spacious, low-key restaurant serves hearty fare, with dinner specials such as lobster and Slavonic steak, a broiled sliced tenderloin dipped in buttery wine sauce. On sunny afternoons, ask for a table on the lānai overlooking Kalapakī Bay and try one of the generous salads. The pricier upstairs section is currently closed due to the economy, but you can still order much of the menu on the restaurant's lower level, which is open-air and casual. JJ's is a relaxed place to enjoy lunch, dinner, or just sit at the bar for a drink, with one of the best ocean views in Līhu'e. ⊠ *Anchor Cove, 3146 Rice St., Nāwiliwili* ☎ *808/246–4422* ▭ *D, MC, V.*

$$–$$$
ECLECTIC
✕ **Kukui's Restaurant and Bar.** The healthful choices and cross-cultural flavors on Kukui's menu are well matched with its casual, open-air setting. The meals have hints of Hawaiian, Asian, and contemporary

American cuisines. Slow-roasted prime rib, fresh catch, *huli huli* chicken (a Hawaiian version of barbecued chicken), penne with sun-dried tomato and macadamia pesto, and a surf-and-turf option are representative of the well-rounded fare. A prime rib and king crab buffet ($45) is served on Friday and Saturday nights in addition to the regular menu. An extensive breakfast buffet ($20) is offered every morning, or choose from the à la carte menu. Newly renovated with a modern theme in 2009, there

> **BUDGET-FRIENDLY: SOUTH SHORE & WEST SIDE**
>
> ■ **Grind's Cafe and Espresso.** ⊠ *Rte. 50, 'Ele'ele* ☎ *808/335–6027* ⊕ *www.grindscafe.net.*
>
> ■ **Puka Dog.** ⊠ *2650 Kiahuna Plantation Dr., Kōloa* ☎ *808/742–6044* ⊕ *www.pukadog.com.*
>
> ■ **Wong's Chinese Restaurant.** ⊠ *Kaumuali'i Hwy., Hanapēpē* ☎ *808/335–5066.*

is also now a hip sushi bar called Toro Tei—try "da spida roll," a crispy fried shrimp roll with crab, cucumber, sprouts, and avocado. You can also order from the bar menu. ⊠ *Kaua'i Marriott Resort & Beach Club, 3610 Rice St., Līhu'e* ☎ *808/245–5050* ⊕ *kukuiskauaimarriott.com* ⊟ *AE, D, DC, MC, V.*

$–$$
AMERICAN

✕ **Līhu'e Barbecue Inn.** Few Kaua'i restaurants are more beloved than this family-owned eatery, a mainstay of island dining since 1940. The menu runs from traditional American to Asian. Try the baby-back ribs, macadamia-nut chicken, or Cajun seafood medley with king crab, or choose a full Japanese dinner from the other side of the menu. If you can't make up your mind, strike a compromise with the inn's tri-sampler. Opt for the fruit cup—fresh, not canned—instead of soup or salad, and save room for a hefty slice of homemade cream pie, available in all sorts of flavors. ⊠ *2982 Kress St., Līhu'e* ☎ *808/245–2921* ⊟ *MC, V* ⊗ *Closed Sun.*

THE SOUTH SHORE AND THE WEST SIDE

Although the South Shore and West Side are lumped together, they're two different worlds when it comes to dining. Most South Shore restaurants are more upscale and located within the Po'ipū resorts, whereas West Side eateries tend to be more local-style and are generally found along Kaumuali'i Highway.

If you're looking for a gourmet meal in a classy setting, the South Shore is where you'll find it. Po'ipū has a number of excellent restaurants in dreamy settings and decidedly fewer family-style, lower-priced eateries.

Pickings start to get slimmer the farther west you travel, and dining choices often are dictated by what's open. Fortunately, West Side restaurants are generally worth patronizing, so you won't go too far wrong if your hunger demands to be satisfied while you're out enjoying the sights.

$$–$$$
AMERICAN
Fodor's Choice
★

✕ **Beach House.** This restaurant pairs a dreamy ocean view with impressive cuisine. Few Kaua'i experiences are more delightful than sitting at one of the outside tables and savoring a delectable meal while the sun sinks into the glassy blue Pacific. It's the epitome of tropical dining,

8

and no other restaurant on Kaua'i can offer anything quite like it. Chef Todd Barrett's menu changes often, but the food is consistently creative and delicious. A few trademark dishes appear regularly, such as Chinese-style roast duck, mint-coriander lamb rack, fire-roasted 'ahi, and lemongrass and kaffir-lime sea scallops. Seared macadamia-nut-crusted mahimahi, a dish ubiquitous on island menus, gets a refreshing new twist when served with a *liliko'i* (passion fruit)–lemongrass beurre blanc. Save room for the signature molten chocolate desire, a decadent finale at this pleasing and deservedly popular restaurant. ⊠ *5022 Lāwa'i Rd., Kōloa* ☎ *808/742–1424* ⊕ *www.the-beach-house.com* ⌂ *Reservations essential* ⊟ *AE, DC, MC, V* ⊗ *No lunch.*

> ## WORD OF MOUTH
>
> "If I could pick only one [restaurant] it would be the Beach House. The location and the sunset, as well as the food and excellent service make it very special. I did pick it—and then I picked it again." –GBC

$$–$$$ **✕ Brennecke's Beach Broiler.** Brennecke's is decidedly casual and fun, with
STEAKHOUSE a busy bar, windows overlooking the beach, and a cheery blue-and-white interior. It specializes in big portions of a wide range of offerings, including New York steaks, crab legs, shrimp, and the fresh catch of the day. Can't decide? You can create your own combination meal. This place is especially good for happy hour (3 PM to 5 PM), as the drink and pūpū menus are tomes. The standard surf and turf is not remarkable in any way, but the ocean view is nice. There's a take-out deli downstairs. ⊠ *2100 Ho'ōne Rd., Po'ipū* ☎ *808/742–7588* ⊕ *www.brenneckes.com* ⊟ *AE, D, DC, MC, V.*

$$–$$$ **✕ Casablanca at Kiahuna.** Outdoor dining in a pleasant garden setting
MEDITERRANEAN and consistently good food make this restaurant at the Kiahuna Swim and Tennis Club worth a visit. The Moroccan lamb (only offered in winter months) is noteworthy, or try the fresh mozzarella wrapped in prosciutto and served with poached figs in a distinctive pork-fig sauce. A tapas menu rounds out the offerings. ⊠ *2290 Po'ipū Rd., Po'ipū* ☎ *808/742–2929* ⊕ *www.casablancakauai.com* ⊟ *MC, V* ⊗ *No dinner Sun.–Mon.*

$$ **✕ Casa di Amici.** Tucked away in a quiet neighborhood above Po'ipū
ITALIAN Beach, this "House of Friends" has live classical piano music on weekends and an outside deck open to sweeping ocean views. Entrées from the internationally eclectic menu include a saffron-vanilla paella risotto made with black tiger prawns, fresh fish, chicken breast, and homemade Italian sausage. For dessert, take the plunge with a baked Hawai'i: a chocolate-macadamia-nut brownie topped with coconut and passion-fruit sorbet and flambéed Italian meringue. The food and setting are pleasant, but service can be maddeningly slow, especially when you're really hungry. ⊠ *2301 Nalo Rd., Po'ipū* ☎ *808/742–1555* ⊕ *www.casadiamici.com* ⊟ *D, DC, MC, V* ⊗ *No lunch.*

$$–$$$ **✕ Dondero's.** The inlaid marble floors, ornate tile work, and Italianate
ITALIAN murals that compose the elegant interior at this restaurant compete with
Fodor'sChoice a stunning ocean view. And in addition to the beautiful setting, Don-
★ dero's offers outstanding food, a remarkable wine list, and impeccable

Continued on page 205

LŪʻAU: A TASTE OF HAWAIʻI

The best place to sample Hawaiian food is at a backyard lūʻau. Aunts and uncles are cooking, the pig is from a cousin's farm, and the fish is from a brother's boat.

But even locals have to angle for invitations to those rare occasions. So your choice is most likely between a commercial lūʻau and a Hawaiian restaurant.

Most commercial lūʻau will offer you little of the authentic diet; they're more about umbrella drinks, laughs, spectacle, and fun. Expect to spend some time and no small amount of cash.

For greater authenticity, folksy experiences, and rock-bottom prices, visit a Hawaiian restaurant (most are in anonymous storefronts in residential neighborhoods). Expect rough edges and some effort negotiating the menu.

In either case, much of what is known today as Hawaiian food would be as foreign to a 16th-century Hawaiian as risotto or chow mien. The pre-contact diet was simple and healthy—mainly raw and steamed seafood and vegetables. Early Hawaiians used earth ovens and heated stones to cook seafood, taro, sweet potatoes, and breadfruit and seasoned their food with sea salt and ground kukui nuts. Seaweed, fern shoots, sweet potato vines, coconut, banana, sugarcane, and select greens and roots rounded out the diet.

Successive waves of immigrants added their favorites to the ti leaf–lined table. So it is that foods as disparate as salt salmon and chicken long rice are now Hawaiian—even though there is no salmon in Hawaiian waters and long rice (cellophane noodles) is Chinese.

AT THE LŪʻAU: KĀLUA PORK

The heart of any lūʻau is the *imu*, the earth oven in which a whole pig is roasted. The preparation of an imu is an arduous affair for most families, who tackle it only once a year or so, for a baby's first birthday or at Thanksgiving, when many Islanders prefer to imu their turkeys. Commercial lūʻau operations have it down to a science, however.

THE ART OF THE STONE

The key to a proper imu is the *pohaku*, the stones. Imu cook by means of long, slow, moist heat released by special stones that can withstand a hot fire without exploding. Many Hawaiian families treasure their imu stones, keeping them in a pile in the backyard and passing them on through generations.

PIT COOKING

The imu makers first dig a pit about the size of a refrigerator, then lay down *kiawe* (mesquite) wood and stones, and build a white-hot fire that is allowed to burn itself out. The ashes are raked away, and the hot stones covered with banana and ti leaves. Well-wrapped in ti or banana leaves and a net of chicken wire, the pig is lowered onto the leaf-covered stones. *Laulau* (leaf-wrapped bundles of meats, fish, and taro leaves) may also be placed inside. Leaves—ti, banana, even ginger—cover the pig followed by wet burlap sacks (to create steam). The whole is topped with a canvas tarp and left to steam for the better part of a day.

OPENING THE IMU

This is the moment everyone waits for: The imu is unwrapped like a giant present and the imu keepers gingerly wrestle out the steaming pig. When it's unwrapped, the meat falls moist and smoky-flavored from the bone, looking and tasting just like Southern-style pulled pork, but without the barbecue sauce.

WHICH LŪʻAU?

Grand Hyatt Kauaʻi Lūʻau. Choose this oceanfront lūʻau if it's a romantic evening you're after.

Lūʻau Kālamakū. This lūʻau is on a former sugar plantation and has a more theatrical style than the resort type.

Paʻina o Hanalei. Lavish, with upscale Pacific Rim cuisine.

Smith's Tropical Paradise. Our top pick, set on a lovely 30-acre tropical garden.

MEA 'AI 'ONO. GOOD THINGS TO EAT.

LAULAU
Steamed meats, fish, and taro leaf in ti-leaf bundles: fork-tender, a medley of flavors; the taro resembles spinach.

Laulau

LOMI LOMI SALMON
Salt salmon in a piquant salad or relish with onions, tomatoes.

POI (DON'T CALL IT LIBRARY PASTE.)
Islanders are beyond tired of jokes about poi, a paste made of pounded taro root.

Lomi Lomi Salmon

Consider: The Hawaiian Adam is descended from *kalo* (taro). Young taro plants are called "keiki"–children. Poi is the first food after mother's milk for many Islanders. 'Ai, the word for food, is synonymous with poi in many contexts.

Not only that, we like it. "There is no meat that doesn't taste good with poi," the old Hawaiians said.

But you have to know how to eat it: with something rich or powerfully flavored. "It is salt that makes the poi go in," is another adage. When you're served poi, try it with a mouthful of smoky kālua pork or salty lomi lomi salmon. Its slightly sour blandness cleanses the palate. And if you don't like it, smile and say something polite. (And slide that bowl over to a local.)

Poi

8

E HELE MAI 'AI! COME AND EAT!

Hawaiian restaurants tend to be inconveniently located in well-worn storefronts with little or no parking, outfitted with battered tables and clattering Melmac dishes, open odd (and usually limited) hours and days, and often so crowded you have to wait. But they personify aloha, invariably run by local families who welcome tourists who take the trouble to find them.

Many are cash-only operations and combination plates are a standard feature: one or two entrées, a side such as chicken long rice, choice of poi or steamed rice and—if the place is really old-style—a tiny portion of coarse Hawaiian salt and some raw onions for relish.

Most serve some foods that aren't, strictly

speaking, Hawaiian, but are beloved of kama'āina, such as salt meat with watercress (preserved meat in a tasty broth), or *akubone* (skipjack tuna fried in a tangy vinegar sauce).

Our favorite: **Dani's Restaurant** (⊠ 4201 Rice St., Līhu'e, ☎ 808/245–4991).

MENU GUIDE

Much of the Hawaiian language encountered during a stay in the Islands will appear on restaurant menus and lists of lū'au fare. Here's a quick primer.

'ahi: *yellowfin tuna.*

aku: *skipjack, bonito tuna.*

'ama'ama: *mullet; it's hard to get but tasty.*

bento: *a box lunch.*

chicken lū'au: *a stew made from chicken, taro leaves, and coconut milk.*

haupia: *a light, pudding-like sweet made from coconut.*

imu: *the underground ovens in which pigs are roasted for lū'au.*

kālua: *to bake underground.*

kaukau: *food. The word comes from Chinese but is used in the Islands.*

kimchee: *Korean dish of pickled cabbage made with garlic and hot peppers.*

Kona coffee: *coffee grown in the Kona district of the Big Island.*

laulau: *literally, a bundle. Laulau are morsels of pork, chicken, butterfish, or other ingredients wrapped with young taro leaves and then bundled in ti leaves for steaming.*

liliko'i: *passion fruit, a tart, seedy yellow fruit that makes delicious desserts, juice, and jellies.*

lomi lomi: *to rub or massage; also a massage. Lomi lomi salmon is fish that has been rubbed with onions and herbs; commonly served with minced onions and tomatoes.*

lū'au: *a Hawaiian feast; also the leaf of the taro plant used in preparing such a feast.*

lū'au leaves: *cooked taro tops with a taste similar to spinach.*

mahimahi: *mild-flavored dolphinfish, not the marine mammal.*

mai tai: *potent rum drink with orange and lime juice, from the Tahitian word for "good."*

malasada: *a Portuguese deep-fried doughnut without a hole, dipped in sugar.*

manapua: *dough wrapped around diced pork or other fillings.*

manō: *shark.*

niu: *coconut.*

'ōkolehao: *a liqueur distilled from the ti root.*

onaga: *pink or red snapper.*

ono: *a long, slender mackerel-like fish; also called wahoo.*

'ono: *delicious; also hungry.*

'opihi: *a tiny shellfish, or mollusk, found on rocks; also called limpets.*

pāpio: *a young ulua or jack fish.*

pohā: *Cape gooseberry. Tasting a bit like honey, the pohā berry is often used in jams and desserts.*

poi: *a paste made from pounded taro root, a staple of the Hawaiian diet.*

poke: *chopped, pickled raw tuna or other fish, tossed with herbs and seasonings.*

pūpū: *Hawaiian hors d'oeuvre.*

saimin: *long thin noodles and vegetables in broth, often garnished with small pieces of fish cake, scrambled egg, luncheon meat, and green onion.*

sashimi: *raw fish thinly sliced and usually eaten with soy sauce.*

tī leaves: *a member of the agave family. The fragrant leaves are used to wrap food while cooking and removed before eating.*

uku: *deep-sea snapper.*

ulua: *a member of the jack family that also includes pompano and amberjack. Also called crevalle, jack fish, and jack crevalle.*

CLOSE UP

The Plate-Lunch Tradition

To experience island history firsthand, take a seat at one of Hawai'i's ubiquitous "plate lunch" eateries, and order a segmented Styrofoam plate piled with rice, macaroni salad, and maybe some fiery pickled vegetable condiment. On the sugar plantations, native Hawaiians and immigrant workers from many different countries ate together in the fields, sharing food from their "kaukau kits," the utilitarian version of the Japanese *bento* lunchbox. From this "melting pot" came the vibrant language of pidgin and its equivalent in food: the plate lunch.

At beaches and events, you will probably see a few tiny kitchens-on-wheels, another excellent venue for sampling plate lunches. These portable restaurants are descendants of "lunch wagons" that began selling food to plantation workers in the 1930s. Try the deep-fried chicken *katsu* (rolled in Japanese panko bread crumbs and spices). The marinated beef teriyaki is another good choice, as is miso butterfish. The noodle soup, *saimin,* with its Japanese fish stock and Chinese red-tinted barbecue pork, is a distinctly local medley. Koreans have contributed spicy barbecue *kal-bi* ribs, often served with chili-laden *kimchi* (pickled cabbage). Portuguese bean soup and tangy Filipino *adobo* stew are also favorites. The most popular Hawaiian contribution to the plate lunch is the *laulau,* a mix of meat and fish and young taro leaves, wrapped in more taro leaves and steamed.

service, making this Kaua'i's best restaurant. Chef Vincent Pecoraro combines old-world techniques with new energy to create menu selections as enticing as the surroundings. Pistachio-crusted rack of lamb with a root-vegetable fritter and pancetta mashed sweet potatoes, and lobster piccata on a bed of fettuccine with sun-dried tomatoes and a truffle cream sauce thrill the palate and delight the eye. Order a light, traditional tiramisu or chocolate crème brûlée with fresh raspberries so you can linger over coffee. The waitstaff deserves special praise for its thoughtful, discreet service. ⊠ *Grand Hyatt Kaua'i Resort and Spa, 1571 Po'ipū Rd., Kōloa* ☎ *808/240–6456* ▭ *AE, D, DC, MC, V* ☉ *No lunch.*

$ ✕ **The Grove Café at Waimea Brewing Company.** Housed within the Waimea
AMERICAN Plantation Cottages, this brewpub-restaurant is spacious, with hardwood floors and open-air decks. Dine indoors amid rattan furnishings or at a bar decorated with petroglyphs and colored with Kaua'i red dirt. Local-style dishes such as Korean garlic chicken, beef short ribs, and fresh fish are highlights. It is now open for breakfast starting at 6 AM and has live music on Thursday and Friday nights. It's a good place to stop while traveling to or from Waimea Canyon, and the microbrews are worth a try. ⊠ *9400 Kaumuali'i Hwy., Waimea* ☎ *808/338–9733* ▭ *AE, D, MC, V.*

¢–$ ✕ **Joe's on the Green.** Eat an open-air breakfast or lunch with an expansive vista of Po'ipū. Located on the Kiahuna Golf Course, this res-
AMERICAN taurant boasts such favorites as eggs Benedict, tofu scramble, and banana-macadamia-nut pancakes. For lunch, try the Reuben sandwich or ribs, or build your own salad. The "small plates" menu and happy-hour drink specials are available from 3 to 7, including favorites such

8

ROMANTIC DINING

Whether you're already feeling sparks or trying to fan banked embers into flame, a romantic meal can help things along. Fortunately, Kaua'i has a number of restaurants that are conducive to love.

For divine sunsets, **The Beach House** (☎ 808/742–1424), in Kōloa, is tops, as it puts you right on the water. **Café Portofino** (☎ 808/245–2121), in Līhu'e, with its second-story view of Kalapaki Bay and harp music, practically caters to couples.

Tops overall, though, is **Dondero's** (☎ 808/240–6456), in Kōloa, where the food, service, and elegant setting come together to create a special evening. If it's a nice evening, by all means opt for the veranda.

Be sure to make reservations, and don't plan on pinching pennies. If you're on a budget, pick up some take-out food and spread a blanket on the beach for a sunset picnic and dessert beneath brilliant stars.

as herb and garlic chicken skewers, seared 'ahi tacos, and homemade chili nachos, all accompanied by live Hawaiian music. With a casual atmosphere and generous portions, Joe's is a refreshing alternative to the pricier hotel brunch venues in this area. ⊠ *2545 Kiahuna Plantation Dr., Po'ipū* ☎ *808/742–9696* ▭ *MC, V* ⊙ *No dinner.*

¢–$
AMERICAN
✕ **Kalaheo Café & Coffee Co.** Right off the highway in Kalāheo, locals love this café, especially for breakfast. It's a casual atmosphere, except on weekend mornings when it can get very busy. Order up front and then find a seat inside or out on the lānai. Favorites include the Kahili Breakfast, scrambled eggs served with Portuguese sausage, ham, and green onions; and the Longboard sandwich, with fried egg, bacon, lettuce, tomato, and melted provolone cheese. Lots of local products are used here, including Anahola Granola, local fish and Kaua'i coffee, which you can buy by the pound. *2-2560 Kaumuali'i Hwy., Rte. 50, Kalāheo* ☎ *808/332–5858* ⊕ *www.kalaheo.com* ▭ *MC, V.*

$$–$$$
STEAK
✕ **Keoki's Paradise.** Built to resemble a dockside boathouse, this active, boisterous place fills up quickly at night thanks to the live music. Seafood appetizers span the tide from sashimi to Thai shrimp sticks, crab cakes, and scallops crusted in *panko* (Japanese-style bread crumbs). The day's fresh catch is available in half a dozen styles and sauces. And there's a sampling of beef, chicken, and pork-rib entrées for the committed carnivore. A lighter menu is available at the bar for lunch and dinner. ⊠ *Po'ipū Shopping Village, 2360 Kiahuna Plantation Dr., Kōloa* ☎ *808/742–7534* ⊕ *www.keokisparadise.com* ▭ *AE, D, DC, MC, V.*

$
ITALIAN
✕ **Pizzetta.** Solid food characterizes this family-style Italian restaurant, which serves up hearty portions of pasta, lasagna, and eggplant Parmesan, along with calzones, pizza with numerous toppings, and salads. The atmosphere is casual and lively and the food is good, especially for the price. Neighborhood delivery is available. ⊠ *5408 Kōloa Rd., Kōloa* ☎ *808/742–8881* ▭ *MC, V.*

$$–$$$
ITALIAN
✕ **Plantation Gardens.** A historic plantation manager's home has been converted to a restaurant that serves seafood and kiawe-grilled meats

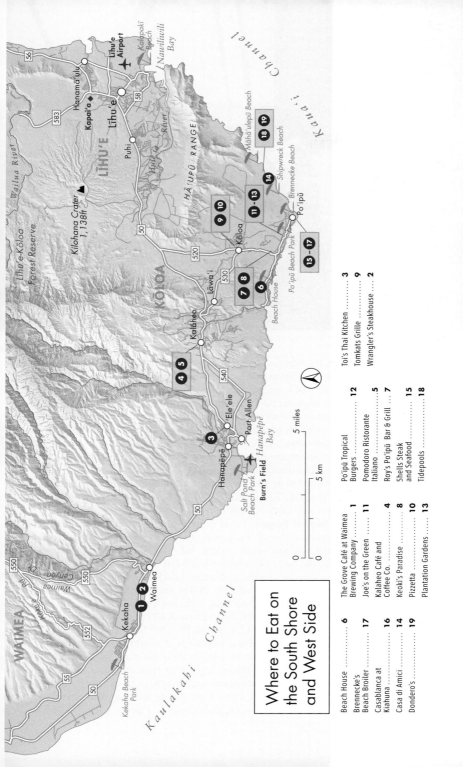

Where to Eat on the South Shore and West Side

Beach House **6**
Brennecke's
Beach Broiler **17**
Casablanca at
Kiahuna **16**
Casa di Amici **14**
Dondero's **19**

The Grove Café at Waimea
Brewing Company **1**
Joe's on the Green **11**
Kalaheo Café and
Coffee Co. **4**
Keoki's Paradise **8**
Pizzetta **10**
Plantation Gardens **13**

Po'ipū Tropical
Burgers **12**
Pomodoro Ristorante
Italiano **5**
Roy's Po'ipū Bar & Grill ... **7**
Shells Steak
and Seafood **15**
Tidepools **18**

Toi's Thai Kitchen **3**
Tomkats Grille **9**
Wrangler's Steakhouse **2**

The Beach House on the South Shore is a prime spot to watch the sun set.

with a Pacific Rim and Italian influence. You'll walk through a tropical setting of torchlighted orchid gardens and lotus-studded koi ponds to a cozy, European-style dining room. The menu is based on fresh, local foods: fish right off the boat, herbs and produce picked from the plantation's gardens, fruit delivered by neighborhood farmers. The result is cuisine with an island flair—seafood *laulau* (seafood wrapped in ti leaves and steamed) served with mango chutney—offered alongside the traditional sugarcane-skewered pork tenderloin. Definitely save room for dessert: The warm pineapple upside-down cake is a dream. In short, the food is excellent and the setting charming. ⊠ *Kiahuna Plantation, 2253 Poʻipū Rd., Kōloa* ☎ *808/742–2121* ⊕ *www.pgrestaurant.com* ▤ *AE, DC, MC, V* ☻ *No lunch.*

$–$$
AMERICAN
☺

✕ **Poʻipū Tropical Burgers.** Families may find themselves returning for multiple meals at this all-day casual restaurant, with its children's menu, simple food, and low prices. Veggie, fish, and gourmet half-pound beef burgers are the mainstay, with fresh fish and other specials added at dinner and sandwiches, soups, and hearty salads rounding out the choices. Bottomless soft drinks and milk shakes are a nice touch for the kids; adults can order wine, draft beer, and exotic drinks. Dining rooms at both locales are airy, cheerful, and casual. ⊠ *Poʻipū Shopping Village, 2360 Kiahuna Plantation Dr., Kōloa* ☎ *808/742–1808* ▤ *MC, V.*

$$
ITALIAN

✕ **Pomodoro Ristorante Italiano.** Two walls of windows brighten this intimate second-story restaurant in the heart of Kalāheo, where you'll find good food at reasonable prices. Begin with prosciutto and melon, then proceed directly to the multilayer meat lasagna, a favorite of the chefs—two Italian-born brothers. Other highlights include eggplant or veal parmigiana, chicken saltimbocca, and scampi in a garlic, caper, and white

Mahimahi is a popular fish dish on Kaua'i. The Beach House adds a macadamia nut crust for local flavor.

wine sauce. ⊠ *Upstairs at Rainbow Plaza, Kaumuali'i Hwy., Rte. 50, Kalāheo* ☎ *808/332–5945* ▭ *MC, V* ⊘ *Closed Sun. No lunch.*

$$$–$$$$
MODERN
HAWAIIAN

╳ **Roy's Po'ipū Bar & Grill.** Hawai'i's culinary superstar, Roy Yamaguchi, is fond of sharing his signature Hawaiian fusion cuisine by cloning the successful Honolulu restaurant where he got his start. You'll find one of these copycat eateries on Kaua'i's South Side in a shopping-center locale that feels too small and ordinary for the exotic food. The menu changes daily, and the hardworking kitchen staff dreams up 15 to 20 (or more) specials each night—an impressive feat. Though the food reflects the imaginative pairings and high-quality ingredients of the original Roy's and the presentation is spectacular, the atmosphere is a little different. As with most other restaurant branches, it just doesn't have the heart and soul of the original. ⊠ *Po'ipū Shopping Village, 2360 Kiahuna Plantation Dr., Kōloa* ☎ *808/742–5000* ▭ *AE, D, DC, MC, V* ⊘ *No lunch.*

$$$–$$$$
STEAKHOUSE

╳ **Shells Steak and Seafood.** Chandeliers made from shells light the dining room and give this restaurant its name. The menu is upscale surf and turf, with prime cuts of steak and fresh fish enhanced by tropical spices and sauces. Shells is one of three signature restaurants in the Sheraton's Oceanfront Galleria. Each of these restaurants has been designed to embrace the view of the Pacific Ocean from sunrise to starlight. ⊠ *Sheraton Kaua'i Resort, 2440 Ho'onani Rd., Po'ipū Beach, Kōloa* ☎ *808/742–1661* ▭ *AE, D, DC, MC, V* ⊘ *No lunch.*

$$$–$$$$
SEAFOOD

╳ **Tidepools.** The Grand Hyatt Kaua'i is notable for its excellent restaurants, which differ widely in their settings and cuisine. This one is definitely the most tropical and campy, sure to appeal to folks seeking a bit of island-style romance and adventure. Private grass-thatch huts seem to float on a koi-filled pond beneath starry skies, while torches flicker in the lushly landscaped grounds nearby. The equally distinctive food has an island flavor that comes from the chef's advocacy of Hawai'i regional cuisine and extensive use of Kaua'i-grown products. You won't go wrong ordering the fresh-fish specials or one of the signature dishes, such as wok-seared soy-, sake-, and ginger-marinated 'ahi; grilled mahimahi; or pan-seared beef tenderloin. Start with Tidepools' pūpū platter for two—with a lobster cake, peppered beef fillet, and 'ahi sashimi—to wake up your taste buds. If you're still hungry at the end of the meal, the ginger crème brûlée is sure to satisfy. ⊠ *Grand Hyatt Kaua'i Resort and Spa, 1571 Po'ipū Rd., Kōloa* ☎ *808/240–6456 Ext. 4260* ⊟ *AE, D, DC, MC, V* ☉ *No lunch.*

¢–$

THAI

✕ **Toi's Thai Kitchen.** Country-style Thai cuisine, hearty portions, reasonable prices, and a casual dining room make this family-run eatery a solid choice on the restaurant-sparse West Side. Most dishes can be prepared vegetarian-style or with beef, pork, chicken, or seafood. Try Toi's Temptation, a hearty mix of meats, pineapple, potatoes, and lemongrass in a sauce of red-chili-heated coconut milk, or one of the excellent curries. Meals include a green papaya or lettuce salad and warm tapioca or black rice pudding. ⊠ *Ele'ele Shopping Center, 4469 Waialo Rd. Ele'ele* ☎ *808/335–3111* ⊟ *MC, V.*

$–$$

AMERICAN

✕ **Tomkats Grille.** Tropical ponds, a waterfall, a large bar area, and a porch overlooking an inner courtyard give this grill a casual island vibe. Try the macadamia-nut-crusted "katch of the day" with a passion-fruit butter glaze or the homemade chili and burger. Wash it down with a glass of wine or one of 15 ales, stouts, ports, and lagers. Plenty of Tomkats' Nibblers—such as buffalo wings and sautéed shrimp—enliven happy hour from 3 to 6 PM. ⊠ *Old Kōloa Town, 5402 Kōloa Rd., Kōloa* ☎ *808/742–8887* ⊕ *www.tomkatsgrille.com* ⊟ *MC, V.*

$$–$$$

STEAKHOUSE

✕ **Wrangler's Steakhouse.** Denim-covered seating, decorative saddles, and a stagecoach in a loft helped to transform the historic Ako General Store in Waimea into a West Side steak house. You can eat under the stars on the deck out back or inside the old-fashioned, wood-paneled dining room. The 16-ounce New York steak comes sizzling, and the rib eye is served with capers. A tasty salad is part of each meal. Those with smaller appetites might consider the vegetable tempura or the 'ahi served on penne. Local folks love the special lunch: soup, rice, beef teriyaki, and shrimp tempura served in a three-tier *kaukau* tin, or lunch pail, just like the ones sugar-plantation workers once carried. A gift shop has local crafts (and sometimes a craftsperson doing demonstrations). ⊠ *9852 Kaumuali'i Hwy., Waimea* ☎ *808/338–1218* ⊟ *AE, MC, V* ☉ *Closed Sun.*

Where to Stay

WORD OF MOUTH

"If you are on Kaua'i for several days, splitting your time between the North and South shores would be nice, in order to allow leisurely visits to Waimea Canyon as well as the sites to the north. If your goal is to relax and stay put at the resort, I would select the South Shore."

—okoshi2002

WHERE TO STAY PLANNER

Hotels and Resorts

If you want to golf, play tennis, or hang at a spa, stay at a resort. You'll also be more likely to find activities for children at resorts, including camps that allow parents a little time off. The island's hotels tend to be smaller and older, with fewer on-site amenities. Some of the swankiest places to stay on the island are the St. Regis Princeville Resort on the North Shore, where rooms run more than $900 per night in high season, and the Grand Hyatt Kaua'i on the South Shore for a bit less; of course, those with views of the ocean book faster than those without.

B&Bs and Inns

The island's bed-and-breakfasts allow you to meet local residents and more directly experience the aloha spirit. Many have oceanfront settings and breakfasts with everything from tropical fruits and juices, Kaua'i coffee, and macadamia waffles to breads made with local bananas and mangoes. Some have pools, hot tubs, services such as *lomilomi* massage, and breakfasts delivered to your lānai. Some properties have stand-alone units on-site.

Condos and Vacation Rentals

Condos and vacation rentals on Kaua'i tend to run the gamut from fabulous luxury estates to scruffy little dives. It's buyer-beware in this totally unregulated sector of the visitor industry, though the County of Kaua'i is in the process of developing new regulations for these types of properties, particularly those in agricultural and rural areas. If you're planning to stay at one of these, be sure to contact the operator prior to traveling to ensure it's still open.

Properties managed by individual owners can be found on online vacation-rental directories such as CyberRentals and Vacation Rentals By Owner, as well as on the Kaua'i Visitors Bureau's Web site. There are also several Kaua'i-based management companies with vacation rentals.

Reservations

The rule on Kaua'i—and for Hawaii in general—is book as far in advance as possible. Rooms go most quickly during holidays, but there really isn't any low season to speak of. Some places allow 24 hours' notice to cancel; others require a week or will penalize you the cost of one night. Most hotels allow children under a certain age to stay in their parents' room at no extra charge, but others charge for them as extra adults; find out the cutoff age for discounts.

Prices

The prices used to establish price categories in this guide are the rack rates given by the hotels at this writing. The tax added to your room rate is 13.96%.

WHAT IT COSTS					
	¢	$	$$	$$$	$$$$
FOR TWO PEOPLE	under $100	$100–$180	$181–$260	$261–$340	over $340

Hotel prices are for two people in a standard double room in high season. Condo price categories reflect studio and one-bedroom rates.

BEST BETS FOR KAUA'I LODGING

Where can you find the best lodging experiences this island has to offer? Fodor's writers and editors have selected their favorite hotels, resorts, condos, vacation rentals, and B&Bs by price and experience in the lists below. In the first column, the Fodor's Choice properties represent the "best of the best" across price categories.

Fodor's Choice ★

Grand Hyatt Kaua'i Resort and Spa, p. 226

Waimea Plantation Cottages, p. 232

By Price

¢

Kōke'e Lodge, p. 232

Mana Yoga Vacation Rentals, p. 216

$

Garden Island Inn, p. 223

Hotel Coral Reef, p. 222

Kalaheo Inn, p. 232

Kaua'i Sands, p. 222

North Country Farms, p. 216

Po'ipū Crater Resort, p. 228

Rosewood Bed and Breakfast, p. 223

$$

Best Western Plantation Hale Suites, p. 219

Garden Isle Cottages, p. 226

Po'ipū Plantation Resort, p. 230

Po'ipū Shores, p. 230

$$$

Aston Aloha Beach Hotel, p. 219

Kaua'i Coast Resort, p. 222

Hanalei Bay Resort, p. 214

Hanalei Colony Resort, p. 215

Kaua'i Beach Resort, p. 223

Makahuena at Po'ipū, p. 228

Waimea Plantation Cottages, p. 232

$$$$

Grand Hyatt Kaua'i Resort and Spa, p. 226

St. Regis Princeville Resort, p. 216

Whalers Cove, p. 231

By Experience

BEST BEACH

Aston Aloha Beach Hotel $$$, p. 219

Aston Islander on the Beach $$-$$$, p. 219

Kaua'i Marriott Resort & Beach Club $$-$$$, p. 225

Outrigger at Lae Nani $$-$$$, p. 223

Waimea Plantation Cottages $$-$$$, p. 232

BEST B&BS AND INNS

Aloha Cottages $, p. 218

Garden Island Inn ¢-$, p. 223

Kalaheo Inn ¢-$, p. 232

Po'ipū Plantation Resort $-$$, p. 230

Rosewood Bed and Breakfast ¢-$, p. 223

BEST SPA

Grand Hyatt Kaua'i Resort and Spa $$$$, p. 226

Hanalei Colony Resort $$$-$$$$, p. 215

Kaua'i Beach Resort $$-$$$, p. 223

Kaua'i Marriott Resort & Beach Club $$-$$$, p. 225

St. Regis Princeville Resort $$$$, p. 216

Waimea Plantation Cottages $$-$$$, p. 232

MOST KID-FRIENDLY

Aston Aloha Beach Hotel $$-$$$, p. 219

Grand Hyatt Kaua'i Resort and Spa $$$$, p. 226

Hotel Coral Reef $-$$, p. 222

Kaua'i Marriott Resort & Beach Club $$-$$$, p. 225

North Country Farms $, p. 216

MOST ROMANTIC

Aloha Cottages $, p. 218

Grand Hyatt Kaua'i Resort and Spa $$$$, p. 226

Hanalei Bay Resort $$$-$$$$, p. 214

Hanalei Colony Resort $$$-$$$$, p. 215

St. Regis Princeville Resort $$$$, p. 216

9

Updated
by Charles
Roessler

The Garden Isle has lodgings for every taste, from swanky resorts to rustic cabins, and from family-friendly condos to romantic bed-and-breakfasts. The savvy traveler can also find inexpensive places that are convenient, safe, and accessible to Kaua'i's special places and activities.

When you're choosing a place to stay, location is an important consideration. Kaua'i may seem small on a map, but because it's circular with no through roads, it can take more time than you think to get from place to place. If at all possible, stay close to your desired activities. This way, you'll save time to squeeze in all the things you'll want to do.

Time of year is also a factor. If you're here in winter or spring, consider staying on the South Shore, as the surf on the North Shore and East Side tends to be rough, making many ocean beaches too rough for swimming or water sports.

Before booking accommodations, think hard about what kind of experience you want to have for your island vacation. There are several top-notch resorts to choose from, and Kaua'i also has a wide variety of condos, vacation rentals, and bed-and-breakfasts. The Kaua'i Visitors Bureau provides a comprehensive listing of accommodation choices to help you decide.

THE NORTH SHORE

The North Shore is mountainous and wet, which accounts for its rugged, lush landscape. Posh resorts and condominiums await you at Princeville, a community with dreamy views, excellent golf courses, and lovely sunsets. It maintains the lion's share of North Shore accommodations—primarily luxury hotel rooms and condos built on a plateau overlooking the sea. Hanalei, a bayside town in a broad valley, has a smattering of hotel rooms and numerous vacation rentals, many within walking distance of the beach. Prices tend to be high in this resort area. If you want to do extensive sightseeing on other parts of the island, be prepared for a long drive—one that's very dark at night.

$$$–$$$$
RENTAL

🖼 **Hanalei Bay Resort.** This time-share condominium resort has a lovely location overlooking Hanalei Bay and Nāpali Coast. Three-story buildings angle down the cliffs, making for some steep walking paths. Units are extremely spacious, with high, sloping ceilings and large private lānai. Rattan furniture and island art add a casual feeling to rooms. Studios have small kitchenettes not meant for serious cooking. The larger units have full kitchens. The resort's upper-level pool is one of the nicest on the island, with authentic lava-rock waterfalls, an open-air hot tub, and a kid-friendly sand "beach." The friendly tropical bar offers breakfast, lunch, and dinner items and some live music. The tennis courts are on-site. **Pros:** beautiful views; tennis courts on property; tropical pool. **Cons:** steep walkways; long walk to beach. ✉ *5380*

WHERE TO STAY IN KAUA'I

	Local Vibe	Pros	Cons
The North Shore	Properties here have the "wow" factor with ocean and mountain beauty; laid-back Hanalei and Princeville set the high-end pace.	When the weather is good (summer) this side has it all. Epic winter surf, gorgeous waterfalls, and verdant vistas create some of the best scenery in Hawai'i.	Lots of rain (being green has a cost) means you may have to travel south to find the sun; expensive restaurants and shopping offer few deals.
The East Side	The most reasonably priced area to stay for the practical traveler; lacks the pizzazz of expensive resorts on North and South shores; more traditional Hawaiian hotels.	The best travel deals show up here; more direct access to the local population; plenty of decent restaurants with good variety, along with delis in food stores.	Beaches aren't the greatest (rocky, reefy) at many of the lodging spots; bad traffic at times; some crime issues in parks.
The South Shore	Resort central; plenty of choices where the consistent sunshine is perfect for those who want to do nothing but play golf or tennis and read a book by the pool.	Beautiful in its own right; many enchanted evenings with stellar sunsets; summer surf easier for beginners to handle.	Some areas are deserty with scrub brush; construction can be brutal on piece of mind.
The West Side	There are few options for lodging in this mostly untourist-like setting with contrasts such as the extreme heat of a July day in Waimea to a frozen winter night up in Kōke'e.	A gateway area for exploration into the wilds of Kōke'e or for boating trips on the Nāpali Coast; main hub for boat and helicopter trips; outstanding sunsets.	Least convenient side for most visitors; daytime is languid and dry; river runoff can ruin ocean's clarity.

9

Honoiki Rd., Princeville ☎ *808/826–6522 or 866/507–1428* ⊕ *www.hanaleibayresort.com* ↩ *134 units* ☖ *In-room: a/c, safe, kitchen, refrigerator. In-hotel: restaurant, bar, tennis courts, pools, beachfront, children's programs (ages 5–12), laundry facilities* ▭ *AE, D, DC, MC, V.*

$$$–$$$$
RENTAL 🖼 **Hanalei Colony Resort.** This 5-acre property, the only true beachfront resort on Kaua'i's North Shore, is a laid-back, go-barefoot kind of place sandwiched between towering mountains and the sea. Its charm is in its simplicity. There are no phones, TVs, or stereos in the rooms, but you can get complimentary wireless Internet access in the resort's oceanfront common room. Each of the two-bedroom units can sleep a family of four, although this place is popular with the honeymoon crowd. The units are well maintained, with Hawaiian-style furnishings, full kitchens, and lānai. Amenities, such as cocktail receptions and cultural activities, vary from season to season. There's an art gallery, spa, and restaurant on-site. **Pros:** oceanfront setting; private; quiet; seventh night free. **Cons:** remote location; damp in winter. ⊠ *5-7130 Kūhiō Hwy., Hā'ena* ☎ *808/826–6235 or 800/628–3004* ⊕ *www.hcr.com* ↩ *48 units* ☖ *In-room: no a/c, no phone, kitchen, no TV. In-hotel: restaurant, bar, pool, spa, beachfront, laundry facilities, Wi-Fi* ▭ *AE, MC, V.*

$
RENTAL

⬚ **Hanalei Inn.** If you're looking for low-priced lodgings a block from gorgeous Hanalei Bay, look no further, as this is the only choice. While the accommodations are simple, they are clean, and the location is ideal. Each studio features a private bath and full kitchen, as well as a queen-size bed. There's also HDTV and Wi-Fi in every room. Outside, share the picnic table, hammocks, soda machine, pay phone, and barbecue with other guests. **Pros:** quick walk to beach. **Cons:** strict cancellation policy; very modest amenities; daytime traffic noise. ⌧ *5-5468 Kūhiō Hwy., Hanalei* ☎ *808/826–9333* ⊕ *www.hanaleiinn.com* ⭢ *4 studios* ⌂ *In-room: a/c, kitchen, Wi-Fi* ▭ *AE, D, DC, MC, V.*

¢
RENTAL

⬚ **Mana Yoga Vacation Rentals.** If you enjoy yoga, or just a rural environment, these lodgings (a studio and two-bedroom unit) offer peace and quiet, mountain views, and all the amenities of home, as well as the services of yoga instructor and massage therapist Michaelle Edwards, who has a yoga studio on-site. Three-night minimum stay. **Pros:** mountain views; yoga and massage on-site; beach accoutrements available. **Cons:** no beach; isolated; 5-minute drive to restaurants and shops. ⌧ *3812 Ahonui Pl., Princeville* ☎ *808/826–9230* ⊕ *www.manayoga.com* ⭢ *2 units* ⌂ *In-room: no a/c, DVD. In-hotel: bicycles, laundry facilities, Wi-Fi, no-smoking rooms* ▭ *MC, V.*

$
RENTAL
☾

⬚ **North Country Farms.** These comfortable lodgings are tucked away on a tidy, 4-acre organic fruit, flower, and vegetable farm just east of Kīlauea. Although simple, they're clean and provide everything a couple or family might need, including kitchenettes. Owner Lee Roversi and her children are warm, friendly, and creative. You'll enjoy the thoughtful selection of videos, games, puzzles, and reading material. The setting is rural and quiet, with lush tropical landscaping around the two units. You are welcome to pick fresh produce. Several nice beaches are just a few minutes' drive away. **Pros:** delightful setting; pick fresh fruit and vegetables; warm and friendly hostess. **Cons:** no beach; no resort-type amenities. ⌧ *Kahili Makai, Box 723, Kīlauea* ☎ *808/828–1513* ⊕ *www. northcountryfarms.com* ⭢ *2 cottages* ⌂ *In-room: no a/c, kitchen.*

$$$$
RESORT

⬚ **St. Regis Princeville Resort.** Built into the cliffs above Hanalei Bay, this sprawling Starwood resort offers expansive views of the sea and mountains, including Makana, the landmark peak immortalized as the mysterious Bali Hai island in the film *South Pacific*. Reopened in October 2009 with the high-end St. Regis brand, the spacious guest rooms reflect an ocean ambience with subtle earth tones. Little details make a difference, such as lighted closets, dimmer switches on all lamps, original artwork, and a wine cellar. Bathrooms are all elegant marble with a privacy window—flip a switch and it goes from clear to opaque so you can see the sights outside without becoming an attraction yourself. Two restaurants serve excellent food with excellent views, and the rebuilt pool is lavish with extremely comfortable lounge furniture. The St. Regis Bar hosts nightly entertainment and the huge windows showcase gorgeous sunsets and a breathtaking view of Hanalei Bay. The new in-house spa connotes a Zen-like atmosphere with traditional Hawaiian healing and Western techniques. There's shuttle service to the resort's two top-ranked golf courses and tennis center. **Pros:** great views; excellent restaurants; attractive lobby; strong focus on service. **Cons:** minimal

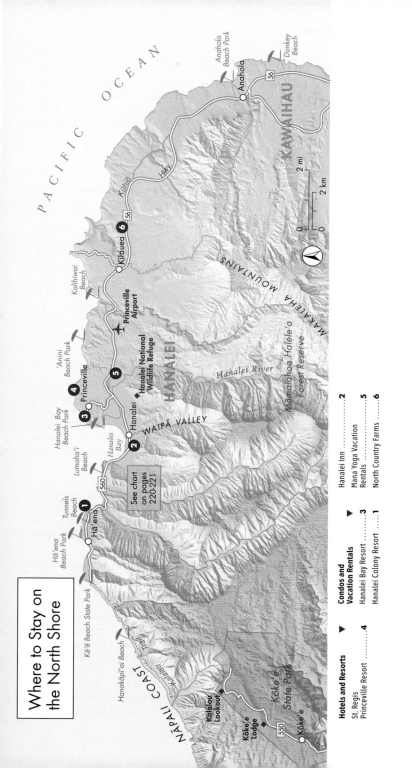

Where to Stay on the North Shore

PACIFIC OCEAN

Hā'ena Beach Park
Ke'e Beach State Park
Hanakāpī'ai Beach
NĀPALI COAST
Kalalau Trail

Kalalau Lookout
Kōke'e Lodge
Kōke'e State Park
550
Kōke'e

Tunnels Beach
Hā'ena
560
1

Lumaha'i Beach
Hanalei Bay
Hanalei Bay Beach Park
Hanalei
WAIPĀ VALLEY
2

See chart on pages 220-221

3
Princeville
4

'Anini Beach Park

Hanalei River
Hanalei National Wildlife Refuge
5
HANALEI
Princeville Airport
✈

Kalihiwai Beach
Kīlauea
56
6

Māmalahoa Halele'a Forest Reserve
MAKALEIHA MOUNTAINS

Kūhiō Hwy.

Anahola
56
KAWAIHAU
Anahola Beach Park
Donkey Beach

N
0   2 km
0   2 mi

Hotels and Resorts ▼
St. Regis Princeville Resort **4**

Condos and Vacation Rentals ▼
Hanalei Bay Resort **3**
Hanalei Colony Resort **1**

Hanalei Inn **2**
Mana Yoga Vacation Rentals **5**
North Country Farms **6**

grounds; reefy beach for swimming. ⊠ *5520 Ka Haku Rd., Princeville* ☎ *877/787–3447 or 808/826–9644* ⊕ *www.stregisprinceville.com* ↝ *201 rooms, 51 suites* ♨ *In-room: a/c, safe, DVD, Wi-Fi. In-hotel: 4 restaurants, room service, bars, 2 golf courses, 4 tennis courts, pools, gym, spa, beachfront, water sports, children's programs (ages 5–12), laundry service, Internet terminal, Wi-Fi, parking (paid), no-smoking rooms.* ▭ *AE, D, DC, MC, V.*

THE EAST SIDE

Location, location, location. The East Side, or Coconut Coast, is a good centralized home base if you want to see and do it all. This is one of the few resort areas on Kaua'i where you can actually walk to the beach, restaurants, and stores from your condo, hotel, or vacation-rental unit. It's not only convenient but comparatively cheap. You pay less for lodging, meals, services, merchandise, and gas here—mainly because the coral-reef coastline isn't as ideal as the sandy-bottom bays that front the fancy resorts. We think the shoreline is just fine. There are pockets in the reef to swim in, and the coast is uncrowded and boasts spectacular views. Warning: Traffic on the main highway can be maddening, and access can be challenging. New traffic and access relief is promised soon. All in all, it's a good choice for families because the prices are right and there's plenty to keep everyone happy and occupied.

KAPA'A AND WAILUA

Since Kapa'a is the island's major population center, this area, including Waipouli and Wailua, has a lived-in, real-world feel. This is where you'll find some of the best deals on accommodations and a wider choice of inexpensive restaurants and shops than in the resort areas. The beaches here are so-so for swimming but nice for sunbathing, walking, and watching the sun and moon rise.

The Wailua area is rather compact and is quite walkable, especially if you avoid the highway, which can be busy and clogged. The resorts here are attractive to middle-class travelers seeking a good bang for their buck. Wailua has rich historic significance among the ancient Hawaiians. Their royalty lived here and ancient sacred grounds, called *heiau*, are clearly marked.

$ 🏠 **Aloha Cottages.** Owners Charlie and Susan Hoerner restored a three-
B&B/INN   bedroom plantation home on Kapa'a's Baby Beach to reflect the charm of yesteryear with the conveniences of today. Think plank flooring, gingerbread, and stained glass alongside a Wolf stove, Bosch dishwasher, and granite countertops. The orientation is due east; you won't have to leave your bed—or living room or lānai—to watch the sun rise, the whales breach, or the full moon rise. In addition to the main house, there's a cozy bungalow called Moonrise Cottage in back that's perfect for honeymooners. Rent both (weekly rentals only) to sleep a total of eight. Credit cards are accepted via PayPal only. **Pros:** comfortable, homelike ambience; good for large groups; safe children's beach. **Cons:** can be windy in winter; not great for adult swimming. ⊠ *1041*

Moana Kai Rd., Kapa'a ☎ *808/823–0933 or 877/915–1015* ⊕ *www. alohacottages.com* ☞ *2 cottages* ☆ *In-room: no a/c, kitchen. In-hotel: beachfront* ⊟ *MC, V.*

$$–$$$
RESORT

☼

▦ **Aston Aloha Beach Hotel.** Nestled between Wailua Bay and the Wailua River, this low-key, low-rise resort is an easy, convenient place to stay. Families will enjoy being within walking distance of Lydgate Beach Park. It's also close to shops and low-cost restaurants. Rooms are in two wings and have beach, mountain, or ocean views. The resort also offers one-bedroom beach cottages with kitchenettes. **Pros:** excellent cultural program; walk to beach and park; convenient locale. **Cons:** exiting hotel parking lot onto highway can be difficult; restaurant meals are average. ✉ *3-5920 Kūhiō Hwy., Kapa'a* ☎ *808/823–6000 or 888/823–5111* ⊕ *www.astonhotels.com* ☞ *216 rooms, 10 suites, 24 beach cottages* ☆ *In-room: a/c, safe, Internet (some). In-hotel: restaurant, tennis court, pools, gym* ⊟ *AE, D, DC, MC, V.*

$$–$$$
HOTEL

▦ **Aston Islander on the Beach.** A Hawai'i-plantation-style design gives this 6-acre beachfront property a pleasant, low-key feeling. Rooms are spread over eight three-story buildings, with lānai that look out on lovely green lawns. Rooms have showers and tubs. A free-form pool sits next to a golden-sand beach that's perfect for a quiet stroll. **Pros:** convenient location; kids stay free; online rate deals. **Cons:** smallish pool; no restaurant on the property. ✉ *440 Aleka Pl., Kapa'a* ☎ *808/822–7417 or 866/774–2924* ⊕ *www.astonhotels.com* ☞ *198 rooms, 2 suites* ☆ *In-room:a/c, safe, refrigerator, Internet. In-hotel: bar, pool, beachfront, laundry facilities* ⊟ *AE, D, DC, MC, V.*

$$–$$$
RESORT

▦ **Aston Kaua'i Beach at Maka'iwa.** Formerly known as the Kaua'i Coconut Beach Resort, this popular oceanfront hotel was bought and refurbished by Courtyard by Marriott in 2005, then sold to ResortQuest in 2006, and is now operated by Aston. The bright, spacious rooms face the ocean or pool and have been outfitted with modern amenities, including free wireless high-speed Internet access. Each oceanfront room has a large lānai. The 11-acre site has always been desirable, nestled as it is among ancient coconut groves and close to a coastal bike and walking path, shops, restaurants, the ocean, and the airport. The new owners wisely kept the best of the old resort, including its sunset torchlighting ceremony. **Pros:** convenient location; online room deals; pleasant grounds. **Cons:** swimming at the beach is poor and sometimes litter washes in. ✉ *650 Aleka Loop, Kapa'a* ☎ *808/822–3455 or 800/760–8555* ⊕ *www.astonhotels.com* ☞ *311 rooms* ☆ *In-room:a/c, safe, Wi-Fi. In-hotel: restaurant, tennis court, pool, beachfront, no-smoking rooms* ⊟ *AE, D, DC, MC, V.*

$$
RENTAL

▦ **Best Western Plantation Hale Suites.** These attractive plantation-style one-bedroom units have well-equipped kitchenettes and garden lānai. Rooms are clean and pretty, with white-rattan furnishings and pastel colors. You couldn't ask for a more convenient location for dining, shopping, and sightseeing: It's across from Waipouli Beach and near Coconut Marketplace. Request a unit away from noisy Kūhiō Highway. **Pros:** bright, spacious units; three pools; walking distance to shops, restaurant, beach. **Cons:** traffic noise in mountain-view units; coral reef makes ocean swimming challenging. ✉ *484 Kūhiō Hwy., Kapa'a*

9

	Property Name	Worth Noting	Cost $	Pools	Beach	Golf Course	Tennis Courts	Gym	Spa	Children's Programs	Rooms	Restaurants	Other	Location
	The North Shore													
	Hotels and Resorts													
4	St. Regis Princeville Resort	Extravagant	$$$$	1	yes	yes	4	yes	yes	5–12	252	4	Shops	Princeville
	Rentals													
3	Hanalei Bay Resort	Great views	$$$–$$$$	2	yes		8		mass.	5–12	134	1	kitchens	Princeville
1	Hanalei Colony Resort	Go-barefoot kind of place	$$$–$$$$	1	yes				yes		48	1	no A/C	Hā'ena
2	Hanalei Inn	Great location	$								4		kitchens	Hanalei
5	Mana Yoga Vacation Rentals	Views, yoga	¢								2		kitchens	Princeville
6	North Country Farms	Rural	$								2		no A/C	Kīlauea
	The East Side													
	Hotels and Resorts													
11	Aston Aloha Beach Hotel	Beach cottages available	$$–$$$	2			1	yes			250	1		Kapa'a
6	Aston Islander on the Beach	Plantation-style design	$$$–$$$	1	yes						200			Kapa'a
3	Aston Kaua'i Beach at Maka'iwa	Popular nightly lū'a'u	$$–$$$	1	yes		1				311	1		Kapa'a
1	Hotel Coral Reef	Good location, low price	$–$$	yes	yes			yes			24		no A/C	Kapa'a
12	Kaua'i Beach Resort	Uncrowded beach	$$–$$$	4	yes	yes	4	yes	yes		357	3		Līhu'e
14	Kaua'i Marriott Resort & Beach Club	26,000-square-ft pool	$$$	1	yes	yes	7	yes	yes	5–12	599	5	shops	Līhu'e
15	Kaua'i Palms Hotel	Close to airport	¢								33			Līhu'e
7	Kaua'i Sands	Hawai'i-owned and -operated	$	2	yes			yes			202		kitchens	Kapa'a
	Rentals													
4	Best Western Plantation Hale Suites	Beach across the street	$$	3							110		kitchens	Kapa'a
10	Kapa'a Sands	Hawai'i-owned and -operated	$	1	yes						21		no A/C	Kapa'a
5	Kaua'i Coast Resort	Uncrowded beach	$$–$$$	1	yes		1	yes	yes		108		kitchens	Kapa'a
8	Outrigger at Lae Nani	Cultural programs	$$–$$$	1	yes		1				84	1	no A/C	Kapa'a

	#	Name	Comments	Price								Units		Notes	Location
		B&Bs													
	2	Aloha Cottages	Oceanfront	$								2		no A/C	Kapa'a
	13	Garden Island Inn	Beach across the street	¢–$								25			Lihu'e
	9	Rosewood Bed and Breakfast	Located on a plantation	¢–$								8		no A/C	Kapa'a
		The South Shore													
		Hotels and Resorts													
★	17	Grand Hyatt Kaua'i Resort and Spa	5 acres of swimming lagoons	$$$$	1	yes	yes	4	yes	yes	3–12	639	6	shops	Po'ipū
	14	Ko'a Kea Hotel and Resort	High-end	$$$$	1	Yes			yes	yes		121			Po'ipū
	11	Sheraton Kaua'i Resort	Ocean wing right on water	$$–$$$	2	yes		3	yes	mass.	5–12	402	4		Po'ipū
		Rentals													
	6	Garden Isle Cottages	Beautiful ocean view	$$								4		no A/C	Po'ipū
	16	Hideaway Cove	Quiet	$–$$								7		kitchens	Po'ipū
	5	Kaua'i Cove Cottages	Excellent snorkeling	¢–$								3		kitchens	Po'ipū
	15	Makahuena at Po'ipū	Close to the center of Po'ipū	$$$	1			1				78		no A/C	Po'ipū
	8	Outrigger Kiahuna Plantation	Popular with families	$$$–$$$$	1	yes	Yes	6				332	1	no A/C	Po'ipū
	10	Po'ipū Crater Resort	Close to beach	$	1							30		no A/C	Po'ipū
	7	Po'ipū Kapili	Deluxe penhouse suites available	$$–$$$	1			2				60		no A/C	Po'ipū
	12	Po'ipū Plantation Resort	Full breakfast included	$–$$	1							13			Po'ipū
	13	Po'ipū Shores	Excellent whale-watching	$$	1							39		no A/C	Po'ipū
	6	Suite Paradise Po'ipū Kai	Short walk to beach	$$–$$$	6			9				130	1	kitchens	Po'ipū
	4	Whalers Cove	Rocky beach	$$$–$$$$	1	yes						39		no A/C	Po'ipū
		The West Side													
		Hotels and Resorts													
	3	Kalaheo Inn	Close to town	¢–$								14		kitchens	Kalaheo
		Rentals													
	1	Kōke'e Lodge	Rustic wilderness cabins	¢								12	1	no A/C	Kōke'e
★	2	Waimea Plantation Cottages	Good for large groups	$$–$$$	1	yes			yes			48	1	no A/C	Waimea

☎ *808/822–4941 or 800/775–4253* ⊕ *www.plantation-hale.com* ⬎ *110 units* ⚐ *In-room: a/c, safe, kitchen, Internet. In-hotel: pools, laundry facilities, Wi-Fi* ▭ *AE, D, DC, MC, V.*

$–$$
HOTEL
♻

◫ **Hotel Coral Reef.** Coral Reef has been in business since the 1960s and is something of a beachfront landmark. It went through a major renovationin 2006, and now the accommodations are on a par with the prime location. Besides remodeling the rooms, the owners added a large pool that looks onto the ocean. The two two-room units are good for families. **Pros:** nice pool; sauna; oceanfront setting; convenient location. **Cons:** located in a busy section of Kapaʻa; ocean swimming is marginal, few resort amenities. ✉ *1516 Kūhiō Hwy., Kapaʻa* ☎ *808/822–4481 or 800/843–4659* ⊕ *www.hotelcoralreefresort.com* ⬎ *24 suites* ⚐ *In-room: a/c, safe, refrigerator (some). In-hotel: pool, gym, beachfront, laundry facilities* ▭ *AE, D, MC, V.*

$
RENTAL

◫ **Kapaʻa Sands.** An old rock etched with *kanji*, Japanese characters, reminds you that the site of this condominium gem was formerly occupied by a Shinto temple. Two-bedroom rentals—equipped with full kitchens and private lānai—are a fair deal. Some studios feature pull-down Murphy beds to create more daytime space. Ask for an ocean-front room to get the breeze. **Pros:** discounts for extended stays; walking distance to shops, restaurants, and beach; turtle and monk-seal sightings common. **Cons:** no-frills lodging; traffic noise in mountain-facing units. ✉ *380 Papaloa Rd., Kapaʻa* ☎ *808/822–4901 or 800/222–4901* ⊕ *www.kapaasands.com* ⬎ *21 units* ⚐ *In-room: no a/c, kitchen. In-hotel: pool, beachfront* ▭ *MC, V.*

$$–$$$
RENTAL

◫ **Kauaʻi Coast Resort.** Fronting an uncrowded stretch of beach, this three-story, primarily time-share resort is convenient and a bit more upscale than nearby properties. The fully furnished one- and two-bedroom condo units, each with a private lānai and well-equipped kitchen, are housed in three buildings. They are decorated in rich woods, tropical prints, and Hawaiian-quilt designs. The 8-acre property looks out on the ocean and offers a heated pool with waterscapes, a day spa, a children's pool, a good restaurant, and an oceanside hot tub. It's in the Coconut Marketplace, so it's within walking distance of shops and restaurants. **Pros:** lovely pool; excellent restaurant; convenient. **Cons:** area is a bit touristy. ✉ *520 Aleka Loop, Kapaʻa* ☎ *808/822–3441 or 866/678–3289* ⊕ *www.shellhospitality.com* ⬎ *108 units* ⚐ *In-room: a/c, safe, kitchen, refrigerator, Internet. In-hotel: restaurant, tennis court, pool, gym, spa, beachfront* ▭ *AE, D, DC, MC, V.*

$
HOTEL

◫ **Kauaʻi Sands.** This oceanfront inn is an example of what island accommodations were like before the arrival of the megaresorts. This is basic, no-frills lodging. Furnishings are spare, simple, and clean. It's so retro it's unintentionally hip. A big grassy courtyard opens to the beach, and there's plenty of dining and shopping at the Coconut Marketplace. **Pros:** convenient location. **Cons:** coral reef makes ocean swimming marginal; modest property; no resort amenities. ✉ *420 Papaloa Rd., Kapaʻa* ☎ *808/822–4951 or 800/560–5553* ⊕ *www.kauaisandshotel. com* ⬎ *200 rooms, 2 suites* ⚐ *In-room: a/c, kitchen (some). In-hotel: pools, gym, beachfront, laundry facilities, no-smoking rooms* ▭ *AE, D, DC, MC, V.*

$$–$$$ [image] **Outrigger at Lae Nani.** Ruling Hawaiian chiefs once returned from
RENTAL ocean voyages to this spot, now host to condominiums comfortable
enough for minor royalty. Hotel-sponsored Hawaiiana programs and
a booklet for self-guided historical tours are nice extras. Units are all
uniquely decorated, with bright, full kitchens and expansive lānai. Your
view of landscaped grounds is interrupted only by a large pool before
ending at a sandy, swimmable beach. You can find plenty of dining and
shopping at the nearby Coconut Marketplace. **Pros:** nice swimming
beach; walking distance to playground; attractively furnished. **Cons:**
occasional odors from nearby sewage-treatment plant. ⊠ *410 Papaloa
Rd., Kapa'a* ☎ *808/822–4938 or 800/688–7444* ⊕ *www.outrigger.com*
⤻ *84 units* ⚿ *In-room: no a/c, safe, kitchen. In-hotel: tennis court, pool,
beachfront, laundry facilities* ▭ *AE, D, DC, MC, V.*

¢–$ [image] **Rosewood Bed and Breakfast.** This charming bed-and-breakfast on a
B&B/INN macadamia-nut plantation estate offers five separate styles of accommodations, including a two-bedroom Victorian cottage; a three-bedroom,
two-bath home; a little one-bedroom grass-thatch cottage; a bunkhouse
with three rooms and a shared bath; and the traditional main plantation home with two rooms, each with private bath. The bunkhouse and
thatched cottage feature outside hot-cold private shower areas hidden
from view by a riot of tropically scented foliage and a fence. The entire
property has Wi-Fi. **Pros:** varied accommodations; good breakfast;
attractive grounds. **Cons:** some traffic noise; no beach. ⊠ *872 Kamalu
Rd., Kapa'a* ☎ *808/822–5216* ⊕ *www.rosewoodkauai.com* ⤻ *3 cottages, 3 rooms in bunkhouse, 2 rooms in main house* ⚿ *In-room: no a/c,
no phone, kitchen. In-hotel: no-smoking rooms* ▭ *No credit cards.*

LĪHU'E

Līhu'e is not the most desirable place to stay on Kaua'i, in terms of scenic beauty, although it does have its advantages, including easy access
to the airport. Restaurants and shops are plentiful, and there's lovely
Kalapakī Bay for beachgoers. Aside from the Marriott and the Kaua'i
Beach Resort, most of the limited lodging possibilities are smaller and
aimed at the cost-conscious traveler.

¢–$ [image] **Garden Island Inn.** Bargain hunters love this three-story inn near
B&B/INN Kalapakī Bay and Anchor Cove shopping center. You can walk across
the street and enjoy the majesty of Kalapakī Beach or check out the
facilities and restaurants of the Marriott. It's clean and contemporary
island-style, and the innkeepers are friendly, sharing fruit and beach
gear. **Pros:** walk to beach, restaurants, and shops; good for families,
extended stays, and budget travel. **Cons:** some traffic noise; near a busy
harbor; limited grounds; no pool. ⊠ *3445 Wilcox Rd., Kalapakī Beach,
Līhu'e* ☎ *808/245–7227 or 800/648–0154* ⊕ *www.gardenislandinn.
com* ⤻ *21 rooms, 2 suites, 2 condos* ⚿ *In-room: a/c, kitchen, refrigerator, Wi-Fi. In-hotel: Wi-Fi, no-smoking rooms* ▭ *AE, DC, MC, V.*

$$–$$$ [image] **Kaua'i Beach Resort.** This hotel has had a number of different owners
RESORT and is now under the management of Aqua Hotels and Resorts. This
follows a $14 million renovation in 2006 that upgraded the amenities
and now offers a luxurious, upscale ambience. The rooms are extremely

9

Where to Stay on the East Side

KAWAIHAU

Keālia Beach

Keālia

Baby Beach

581

1 Kapaʻa

2
Waipouli
3

4

5

56

7 **6**
Wailua
8
580

10

Wailua Bay

See chart on pages 220-221

♦ **Wailua Marina**

11

Lydgate State Beach Park

56

9

Wailua River

583

12

Hanamāʻulu

Kapaiʻa ♦

LĪHUʻE

Līhuʻe
15

✈ Līhuʻe Airport

50
Puhi
56

Kalapakī Beach

13
14

Nawiliwili Bay

0 _____ 2 mi
0 _____ 2 km

Huleʻia River

Hotels and Resorts ▼

Aston Aloha Beach Hotel ..**11**

Aston Islander
on the Beach **6**

Aston Kauaʻi
Beach at Makaʻiwa **3**

Hotel Coral Reef **1**

Kauaʻi
Beach Resort **12**

Kauaʻi Marriott Resort
& Beach Club **14**

Kauaʻi Palms Hotel **15**

Kauaʻi Sands **7**

**Condos and
Vacation Rentals** ▼

Best Western Plantation
Hale Suites **4**

Kapaʻa Sands **10**

Kauaʻi Coast Resort **5**

Outrigger at Lae Nani **8**

B&Bs ▼

Garden Island Inn **13**

Aloha Cottages **2**

Rosewood
Bed and Breakfast **9**

comfortable, with a relaxed tropical theme, and the oceanfront grounds are beautifully landscaped; the sand-bottom pool with 12-foot waterfall is a highlight, as is the South Pacific Dinner Show on Wednesdays. It's an excellent choice for those seeking a convenient location, as it's near the airport, without the noise. **Pros:** nice pool, quiet, resort amenities. **Cons:** not a good swimming beach, restaurants are unimpressive. ✉ *4331 Kauai Beach Drive., Līhu'e* ☎ *888/805–3843* ⊕ *www. kauaibeachresorthawaii.com* ⇨ *350 rooms, 7 suites* ♿ *In-room: a/c, safe,. In-hotel: 3 restaurants, room service, pools, spa, beachfront, no-smoking rooms* ▭ *AE, D, DC, MC, V.*

$$–$$$ 🏨 **Kaua'i Marriott Resort & Beach Club.** An elaborate tropical garden,
RESORT waterfalls right off the lobby, Greek statues and columns, and an enor-
☺ mous 26,000-square-foot swimming pool characterize the grand—and grandiose—scale of this resort on Kalapakī Beach, which looks out at the dramatic Hā'upu mountains. This resort has it all—fine dining, shopping, a spa, golf, tennis, and water activities of all kinds. Rooms have bright, contemporary tropical decor, and most have expansive ocean views. It's comfortable and convenient, with free airport shuttle service. Many of the rooms have been converted to time-shares, too. **Pros:** oceanfront setting; good restaurants; convenient location. **Cons:** distant airport noise; inconvenient parking. ✉ *3610 Rice St., Kalapakī Beach, Līhu'e* ☎ *808/245–5050 or 800/220–2925* ⊕ *www. kauaimarriott.com* ⇨ *356 rooms, 11 suites, 232 time-share units* ♿ *In-room: a/c, refrigerator. In-hotel: 5 restaurants, room service, golf courses, tennis courts, pool, fitness center, spa, beachfront, children's programs (ages 5–12)* ▭ *AE, D, DC, MC, V.*

¢ 🏨 **Kaua'i Palms Hotel.** This low-cost alternative is priced right for the
HOTEL frugal traveler. It's close to the airport and a convenient place to leave your items as you daytrip to all sides of the island. The small physical footprint almost compels you to get out and explore during your stay since the hotel itself has little to offer on its own. The rooms are simple, clean, and small, but new flat-screen TVs help pass the time in the evening. It's not really designed with families in mind, but a couple with one child can make this hotel work. **Pros:** clean; inexpensive; centrally located. **Cons:** back-street ambience; bare-bones amenities; smallish rooms. ✉ *2931 Kalena St., Līhu'e* ☎ *808/246–0908* ⊕ *www. kauaipalmshotel.com* ⇨ *33 rooms* ♿ *In-room: a/c (some), no phone, safe, kitchen (some), refrigerator, Wi-Fi (some). In-hotel: laundry facilities, Wi-Fi, parking (free), no-smoking rooms* ▭ *AE, D, DC, MC, V.*

THE SOUTH SHORE

Sunseekers usually head south to the condo-studded shores of Po'ipū, where three- and four-story complexes line the coast and the surf is generally ideal for swimming. As the island's primary resort community, Po'ipū has the bulk of the island's accommodations, and more condos than hotels, with prices in the moderate to expensive range. Although it accommodates many visitors, its extensive, colorful landscaping and low-rise buildings save it from feeling dense and overcrowded, and it has a delightful coastal promenade perfect for sunset strolls. Surprisingly, the South

Shore doesn't have as many shops and restaurants as one might expect for such a popular resort region, but there are still ample choices. ■TIP→ The area's beaches are among the best on the island for families, with sandy shores, shallow waters, and grassy lawns adjacent to the sand.

$$
RENTAL

🏠 **Garden Isle Cottages.** Tropical fruit trees and flower gardens surround these spacious oceanside cottages. Contemporary Hawaiian furnishings include some rattan; amenities include kitchens with microwaves, ceiling fans, and washers and dryers. The restaurants of nearby Po'ipū are a five-minute walk away. The best part of staying here is the ocean view. **Pros:** gorgeous view; oceanfront setting; comfortable accommodations. **Cons:** no sandy beach; cleaning fee. ⊠ 2658 Pu'uholo Rd., Kōloa ☎ 808/639–9233 or 800/742–6711 ⊕ www.oceancottages.com ⌨ 2 cottages ♿ In-room: a/c, kitchen. In-hotel: laundry facilities ⊟ No credit cards.

$$$$
RESORT
☺
Fodor's Choice
★

🏠 **Grand Hyatt Kaua'i Resort and Spa.** Dramatically handsome, this classic Hawaiian low-rise is built into the cliffs overlooking an unspoiled coastline. It's open, elegant, and very island-style, making it our favorite of the megaresorts. It has four very good restaurants, including Dondero's, the best on Kaua'i. Spacious rooms, two-thirds with ocean views, have a plantation theme with bamboo and wicker furnishings and island art. Five acres of meandering fresh- and saltwater-swimming lagoons—a big hit with kids—are beautifully set amid landscaped grounds. While adults enjoy treatments at the first-rate Anara Spa, kids can check out Camp Hyatt. **Pros:** fabulous pool; excellent restaurants; Hawaiian ambience. **Cons:** poor swimming beach; small, dreary balconies. ⊠ 1571 Po'ipū Rd., Kōloa ☎ 808/742–1234 or 800/633–7313 ⊕ www.grandhyattkauai.com ⌨ 602 rooms, 37 suites ♿ In-room: a/c, safe, refrigerator, Wi-Fi(some). In-hotel: 6 restaurants, room service, bars, golf course, tennis courts, pool, gym, spa, beachfront, children's programs (ages 3–12) ⊟ AE, D, DC, MC, V.

$–$$
RENTAL

🏠 **Hideaway Cove.** On a quiet side street ending in a cul-de-sac, Hideaway Cove is very quiet, even though it's one block from the ocean's edge in the heart of Po'ipū. What was once two homes has been converted to seven complete vacation homes. Owner Herb Lee appointed each with resort-quality furniture and furnishings—even original artwork. The two-bedroom Seabreeze villa comes with a hot tub on the lānai. The three-bedroom Oceanview villa connects via an internal staircase with the two-bedroom Aloha villa to provide a large five-bedroom home with two complete living areas—perfect for two families traveling together. Rates drop with a seven-night stay, effectively making the seventh night free. **Pros:** high-quality furnishings; private lānai; hot tub or Jacuzzi in each unit. **Cons:** not on the ocean; high cleaning fee. ⊠ 2307 Nalo Rd., Po'ipū ☎ 808/635–8785 or 866/849–2426 ⊕ www.hideawaycove.com ⌨ 7 units ♿ In-room: a/c, kitchen. In-hotel: laundry facilities ⊟ AE, D, MC, V.

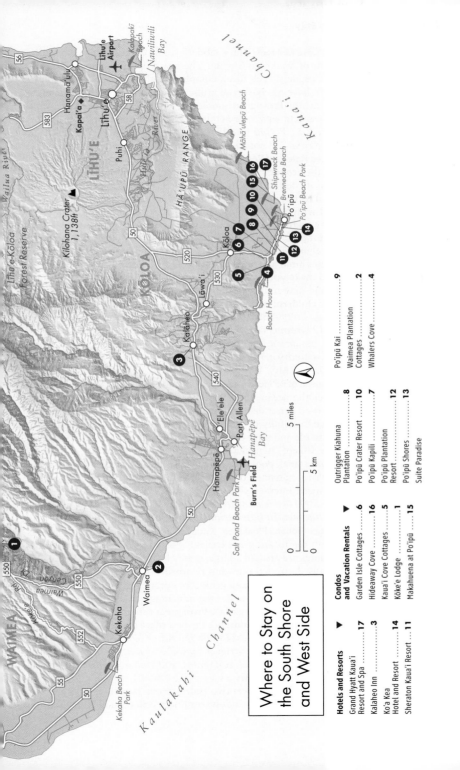

Where to Stay on the South Shore and West Side

Hotels and Resorts ▼

Grand Hyatt Kaua'i Resort and Spa ... **17**
Kalaheo Inn ... **3**
Ko'a Kea Hotel and Resort ... **14**
Sheraton Kaua'i Resort ... **11**

Condos and Vacation Rentals ▼

Garden Isle Cottages ... **6**
Hideaway Cove ... **16**
Kaua'i Cove Cottages ... **5**
Kōke'e Lodge ... **1**
Makahuena at Po'ipū ... **15**

Outrigger Kiahuna Plantation ... **8**
Po'ipū Crater Resort ... **10**
Po'ipū Kapili ... **7**
Po'ipū Plantation Resort ... **12**
Po'ipū Shores ... **13**
Suite Paradise

Po'ipū Kai ... **9**
Waimea Plantation Cottages ... **2**
Whalers Cove ... **4**

¢–$ ⊡ **Kaua'i Cove Cottages.** Three modern studio cottages sit side by side at
RENTAL   the mouth of Waikomo Stream. The airy tropical-theme studios have
cathedral ceilings; each has a complete kitchen. Private patios on the
ocean side have gas barbecue grills. There's a $50 to $75 cleaning fee
upon departure. **Pros:** great snorkeling in the nearby ocean cove. **Cons:**
major construction possible in this area; decor borders on kitsch. ⊠ *2672
Pu'uholo Rd., Po'ipū* ☎ *808/651–0279 or 800/624–9945* ⊕ *www.
kauaicove.com* ⤳ *3 cottages* ⚘ *In-room: a/c, kitchen* ⊟ *D, MC, V.*

$$$$ ⊡ **Ko'a Kea Hotel and Resort.** This luxury boutique hotel opened in April
HOTEL   2009 on the grounds of the former Poipu Beach Hotel, a Kaua'i favorite before its destruction by Hurricane 'Iniki in 1992. Its crisp, well-
appointed rooms include an espresso maker and a large flat-screen TV.
Designed with honeymooners and sophisticated adults in mind, it's a
high-end experience without the hustle of many larger resorts—a great
place to forget it all. The pool and beachfront are clean and cool, as is
the general interior—contemporary Asian touches with white, blue, and
sandy tones amid a gentle ocean theme. The view of surfers from your
lānai will make you envious of surfdom. **Pros:** incredibly comfortable
beds; brand-new ambience; good food at Red Salt restaurant. **Cons:** not
much for children; wind noise in hallways can be distracting. ⊠ *2251
Po'ipū Rd., Po'ipū* ☎ *808/828–8888 or 888/898–8858* ⊕ *www.koakea.
com* ⤳ *121 rooms* ⚘ *In-room: a/c, phone, safe, refrigerator, Wi-Fi.
In-hotel: restaurant, bar, pool, spa, beachfront, water sports, laundry
facilities, laundry service, Wi-Fi, parking (free), no-smoking rooms.*
⊟ *AE, D, DC, MC, V.*

$$$ ⊡ **Makahuena at Po'ipū.** Situated close to the center of Po'ipū, on a rocky
RENTAL   point over the ocean, the Makahuena is near Shipwreck and Po'ipū
beaches. It's a better deal for the price than some of the nearby proper-
ties. Large, tastefully decorated one-, two-, and three-bedroom suites
with white-tile and sand-color carpets are housed in white-wood build-
ings on well-kept lawns. Each unit has a kitchen and washer and dryer;
there's also a small pool and shared barbecue area on the property. **Pros:**
reasonable rates; tennis court; scenic setting. **Cons:** no swimming beach;
no high-speed Internet. ⊠ *1661 Pe'e Rd., Po'ipū* ☎ *808/742–2482 or
800/367–5004* ⊕ *www.castleresorts.com* ⤳ *78 units* ⚘ *In-room: no a/c,
kitchen, Internet. In-hotel: tennis court, pool* ⊟ *AE, MC, V.*

$$$–$$$$ ⊡ **Outrigger Kiahuna Plantation.** Kaua'i's largest condo project is lacklus-
RENTAL   ter, though the location is excellent. Forty-two plantation-style, low-
rise buildings arc around a large, grassy field leading to the beach. The
individually decorated one- and two-bedroom units vary in style, but
all are clean, have lānai, and get lots of ocean breezes. This is a popular
destination for families who take advantage of the swimming beach
and lawn for picnics and games. **Pros:** great sunset and ocean views are
bonuses in some units. **Cons:** not the best place to stay if you're looking
for a romantic getaway. ⊠ *2253 Po'ipū Rd., Kōloa* ☎ *808/742–6411 or
800/688–7444* ⊕ *www.outrigger.com* ⤳ *333 units* ⚘ *In-room: no a/c,
kitchen, Internet. In-hotel: restaurant, golf course, tennis courts, pool,
beachfront* ⊟ *AE, DC, MC, V.*

$ ⊡ **Po'ipū Crater Resort.** These two-bedroom condominium units are fairly
RENTAL   spacious, and the large windows and high ceilings add to the sense of

Grand Hyatt Kauai Resort and Spa

Grand Hyatt Kauai Resort and Spa

Waimea Plantation Cottages

space and light. They're also well furnished, with full kitchens and all the comforts of home. The condos are set within a nicely landscaped resort built on an extinct volcanic crater known as Piha Keakua, or "place of the gods." It's one of the best-priced properties with ocean proximity, located just 700 yards from Keoniloa Bay (Shipwrecks),

which is a famous bodysurfing spot with a snapping shore break. **Pros:** attractive and well kept; pretty setting. **Cons:** beach isn't good for swimming; few resort amenities. ⊠ *2330 Hoohu Rd., Poʻipū* ☎ *808/742–7260* ⊕ *www.suite-paradise.com* ⟿ *30 units* ⚙ *In-room: no a/c, kitchen. In-hotel: tennis court, pool, laundry facilities* ⊟ *AE, DC, MC, V.*

$$–$$$
RENTAL

⌂ **Poʻipū Kapili.** Spacious one- and two-bedroom condo units are minutes from Poʻipū's restaurants and beaches. White-frame exteriors and double-pitched roofs complement the tropical landscaping. Interiors include full kitchens and entertainment centers. Choose from garden and across-the-street-to-the-ocean views. Three deluxe 2,600-square-foot penthouse suites have enormous lānai, private elevators, and cathedral ceilings. You can mingle at a weekly coffee hour held beside the ocean-view pool or grab a good read from the resort library. Fresh seasonings are ready to be picked from the herb garden, and there's a barbecue poolside. In winter you can whale watch as you cook. **Pros:** units are roomy; good guest services; property is small. **Cons:** units are ocean-view, but not oceanfront. ⊠ *2221 Kapili Rd., Kōloa* ☎ *808/742–6449 or 800/443–7714* ⊕ *www.poipukapili.com* ⟿ *60 units* ⚙ *In-room: no a/c, kitchen, Internet. In-hotel: tennis courts, pool, laundry facilities* ⊟ *MC, V.*

$–$$
RENTAL

⌂ **Poʻipū Plantation Resort.** Plumeria, ti, and other tropical foliage create a lush landscape for this resort, which has one bed-and-breakfast-style plantation home and nine one- and two-bedroom cottage apartments. All cottage units have wood floors and full kitchens and are decorated in light, airy shades. The 1930s plantation home has two rooms with private baths and two suites. A full complimentary breakfast is served daily for those staying in the main house. A minimum three-night stay is required, but rates decrease with the length of stay. **Pros:** attractively furnished; full breakfast at the bed-and-breakfast. **Cons:** three-night minimum; no Internet in room. ⊠ *1792 Peʻe Rd., Poʻipū* ☎ *808/742–6757 or 800/634–0263* ⊕ *www.poipubeach.com* ⟿ *4 suites, 9 cottages* ⚙ *In-room: a/c, kitchen (some). In-hotel: laundry facilities, Wi-Fi* ⊟ *D, MC, V.*

$$
RENTAL

⌂ **Poʻipū Shores.** Sitting on a rocky point above pounding surf, this is a perfect spot for whale or turtle watching. Weddings are staged on a little lawn beside the ocean, and a sandy swimming beach is a 10-minute walk away. There are three low-rise buildings, with a pool in front of the middle one. Condo units are individually owned and decorated. All have large windows, and many of them have bedrooms on the ocean side; each unit either shares a sundeck or has a lānai. **Pros:** every unit faces the water; oceanfront pool; wildlife viewing. **Cons:** units vary widely in style; no resort amenities. ⊠ *1775 Peʻe Rd.,*

Kōloa ☎ *808/742–7700 or 800/367–5004* ⊕ *www.castleresorts.com* ⇨ *39 units* ⚪ *In-room: no a/c, kitchen, Internet. In-hotel: pool, laundry facilities* ⊟ *AE, MC, V.*

$$–$$$
RESORT

🏨 **Sheraton Kaua'i Resort.** The resort's ocean-wing accommodations here are so close to the water you can practically feel the spray of the surf as it hits the rocks below. Beachfront rooms have muted sand and eggshell colors, which complement the soothing atmosphere of this quiet, calm resort. Brighter palettes enliven the garden rooms. Dining rooms, king beds, and balconies differentiate the suites. Hawaiian artisans stage crafts demonstrations under a banyan tree in the central courtyard. The dining Galleria was designed so that all restaurants take advantage of the endless ocean horizon. **Pros:** ocean-view pool; quiet; nice dining views. **Cons:** no swimming beach; rather staid ambience. ✉ *2440 Ho'onani Rd., Po'ipū Beach, Kōloa* ☎ *808/742–1661 or 888/488–3535* ⊕ *www.sheraton-kauai.com* ⇨ *394 rooms, 8 suites* ⚪ *In-room: a/c, safe, refrigerator, Wi-Fi. In-hotel: 4 restaurants, room service, bar, tennis courts, pools, gym, beachfront, children's programs (ages 5–12), laundry facilities, Internet terminal* ⊟ *AE, D, DC, MC, V.*

$$–$$$
RENTAL

🏨 **Suite Paradise Po'ipū Kai.** Condominiums, many with cathedral ceilings and all with big windows overlooking the lawns, give this property the feeling of a spacious, quiet retreat inside and out. Large furnished lānai have views to the ocean and across the 110-acre grounds. All the condos are furnished with modern kitchens. Some units are two-level; some have sleeping lofts. One- to four-bedroom units are also available. A two-night minimum stay is required. Walking paths connect to both Brennecke and Shipwreck beaches. **Pros:** close to nice beaches; full kitchens; good rates for the location. **Cons:** units aren't especially spacious; beaches not ideal for swimming. ✉ *1941 Po'ipū Rd., Kōloa* ☎ *808/742–6464 or 800/367–8020* ⊕ *www.suite-paradise.com* ⇨ *130 units* ⚪ *In-room: a/c (some), kitchen, Internet. In-hotel: restaurant, tennis courts, pools* ⊟ *AE, D, DC, MC, V.*

$$$–$$$$
RENTAL

🏨 **Whalers Cove.** Perched about as close to the water's edge as they can get, these two-bedroom condos are the most luxurious on the South Shore. The rocky beach is good for snorkeling, and a short drive or brisk walk will get you to a sandy stretch. A handsome koa-bedecked reception area offers services for the plush units. Two barbecue areas, big picture windows, spacious living rooms, lānai, and modern kitchens with washer-dryers make this a home away from home. **Pros:** extremely luxurious; outstanding setting; fully equipped units. **Cons:** rocky beach not ideal for swimming. ✉ *2640 Pu'uholo Rd., Kōloa* ☎ *808/742–7571 or 800/225–2683* ⊕ *www.whalerscoveresort.com* ⇨ *39 units* ⚪ *In-room: no a/c, kitchen (some), Internet. In-hotel: pool, beachfront, laundry facilities* ⊟ *AE, MC, V.*

9

THE WEST SIDE

If you want to do a lot of hiking or immerse yourself in the island's history, find a room in Waimea (though this is not a resort area, so be aware that the pickings are slim). You won't find a lot of restaurants and shops, but you will encounter dark skies, quiet days, miles of largely deserted beach, and a rural environment.

¢–$
B&B/INN
Kalaheo Inn. It isn't easy to find lodgings on the West Side, but this old-fashioned inn does the job in Kalaheo town, where accommodations are otherwise unavailable. You can choose from studios or one, two-, and three-bedroom suites. The suites also have a fridge and microwave, and a few have gas stoves if you want to eat at home. The rooms are very basic but clean, with pillow-top beds for extra comfort. This property is a ways from the beach, but there's a great little hilltop 9-hole golf course just up the road, and it's an easy drive to Kokeʻe State Park. One nice touch is the tropical fruit picked on-site and offered free to guests, local-style. **Pros:** some units have kitchens; walking distance to restaurants. **Cons:** no beach; some traffic noise; no-frills lodgings. ⊠ *4444 Papalina Rd., Kalaheo* ☎ *808/332–6023 or 888/332–6023* ⊕ *www.kalaheoinn.com* ⊅ *14 units* ♿ *In-room: no a/c, kitchen, refrigerator, DVD. In-hotel: laundry facilities, parking (free), no-smoking rooms* ⊟ *MC, V.*

¢
RENTAL
Kokeʻe Lodge. If you're an outdoors enthusiast, you can appreciate Kauaʻi's mountain wilderness from the 12 rustic cabins that make up this lodge. They are austere, to say the least, but more comfortable than a tent, and the mountain setting is grand. Wood-burning stoves ward off the chill and dampness (wood is a few dollars extra). If you aren't partial to dormitory-style sleeping, request the cabins with two bedrooms; both styles sleep six and have kitchenettes. The lodge restaurant serves a light breakfast and lunch between 9 and 5 daily. **Pros:** outstanding setting; more refined than camping; cooking facilities. **Cons:** very austere; no restaurants for dinner; remote. ⊠ *3600 Kokeʻe Rd., at mile marker 15, Kekaha* ☏ *Box 819, Waimea 96796* ☎ *808/335–6061* ⊅ *12 cabins* ♿ *In-room: no a/c, no phone, kitchen (some), no TV. In-hotel: restaurant* ⊟ *D, DC, MC, V.*

$$–$$$
RENTAL
Fodorˢ Choice
★
Waimea Plantation Cottages. History buffs will adore these reconstructed and restored sugar-plantation cottages, which were originally built in the early 1900s. The one- to five-bedroom cottages are tucked among coconut trees along a lovely stretch of coastline on the sunny West Side. (Note that swimming waters here are sometimes murky, depending on weather conditions.) ■ TIP→ It's a great property for family reunions or other large gatherings. These cozy little homes, complete with porches, feature plantation-era furnishings, modern kitchens, and cable TV. Barbecues, hammocks, porch swings, a gift shop, a spa, and a museum are on the property. **Pros:** unique, homey lodging; quiet and low-key. **Cons:** not a white-sand beach; rooms are not luxurious. ⊠ *9400 Kaumualiʻi Hwy., Box 367, Waimea* ☎ *808/338–1625 or 800/992–4632* ⊕ *www.waimea-plantation.com* ⊅ *48 cottages* ♿ *In-room: no a/c, kitchen (some), Internet. In-hotel: restaurant, bar, pool, spa, beachfront, Internet terminal* ⊟ *AE, D, DC, MC, V.*

UNDERSTANDING KAUA'I

Vocabulary

HAWAIIAN VOCABULARY

Although an understanding of Hawaiian is by no means required on a trip to the Aloha State, a *malihini*, or newcomer, will find plenty of opportunities to pick up a few of the local words and phrases. Traditional names and expressions are widely used in the Islands. You're likely to read or hear at least a few words each day of your stay.

With a basic understanding and some uninhibited practice, anyone can have enough command of the local tongue to ask for directions and to order from a restaurant menu. One visitor announced she would not leave until she could pronounce the name of the state fish, the *humuhumunukunukuāpua'a*.

Simplifying the learning process is the fact that the Hawaiian language contains only eight consonants—H, K, L, M, N, P, W, and the silent *'okina*, or glottal stop, written '—plus one or more of the five vowels. All syllables, and therefore all words, end in a vowel. Each vowel, with the exception of a few diphthongized double vowels such as *au* (pronounced "ow") or *ai* (pronounced "eye"), is pronounced separately. Thus *'Iolani* is four syllables (ee-oh-la-nee), not three (yo-la-nee). Although some Hawaiian words have only vowels, most also contain some consonants, but consonants are never doubled.

Pronunciation is simple. Pronounce A "ah" as in *father*; E "ay" as in *weigh*; I "ee" as in *marine*; O "oh" as in *no*; U "oo" as in *true*.

Consonants mirror their English equivalents, with the exception of W. When the letter begins any syllable other than the first one in a word, it is usually pronounced as a V. *'Awa*, the Polynesian drink, is pronounced "ava," *'ewa* is pronounced "eva."

Almost all long Hawaiian words are combinations of shorter words; they are not difficult to pronounce if you segment them. *Kalaniana'ole*, the highway running east from Honolulu, is easily understood as *Kalani ana 'ole*. Apply the standard pronunciation rules—the stress falls on the next-to-last syllable of most two- or three-syllable Hawaiian words—and Kalaniana'ole Highway is as easy to say as Main Street.

Now about that fish. Try *humu-humu nuku-nuku āpu a'a*.

The other unusual element in Hawaiian language is the *kahakō*, or macron, written as a short line [¯] placed over a vowel. Like the accent ['] in Spanish, the kahakō puts emphasis on a syllable that would normally not be stressed. The most familiar example is probably *Waikīkī*. With no macrons, the stress would fall on the middle syllable; with only one macron, on the last syllable, the stress would fall on the first and last syllables. Some words become plural with the addition of a macron, often on a syllable that would have been stressed anyway. No Hawaiian word becomes plural with the addition of an *S*, since that letter does not exist in the language.

What follows is a glossary of some of the most commonly used Hawaiian words. Hawaiian residents appreciate visitors who at least try to pick up the local language.

'a'ā: rough, crumbling lava, contrasting with *pāhoehoe*, which is smooth.

'ae: yes.

aikane: friend.

āina: land.

akamai: smart, clever, possessing savoir faire.

akua: god.

ala: a road, path, or trail.

ali'i: a Hawaiian chief, a member of the chiefly class.

aloha: love, affection, kindness; also a salutation meaning both greetings and farewell.

'ānuenue: rainbow.

'a'ole: no.

'apōpō: tomorrow.

'auwai: a ditch.

auwē: alas, woe is me!

'ehu: a red-haired Hawaiian.

'ewa: in the direction of 'Ewa plantation, west of Honolulu.

hala: the pandanus tree, whose leaves (*lau hala*) are used to make baskets and plaited mats.

hālau: school.

hale: a house.

hale pule: church, house of worship.

ha mea iki or **ha mea 'ole:** you're welcome.

hana: to work.

haole: ghost. Since the first foreigners were Caucasian, *haole* now means a Caucasian person.

hapa: a part, sometimes a half; often used as a short form of *hapa haole*, to mean a person who is part-Caucasian.

hau'oli: to rejoice. *Hau'oli Makahiki Hou* means Happy New Year. *Hau'oli lā hānau* means Happy Birthday.

heiau: an outdoor stone platform; an ancient Hawaiian place of worship.

holo: to run.

holoholo: to go for a walk, ride, or sail.

holokū: a long Hawaiian dress, somewhat fitted, with a yoke and a train. Influenced by European fashion, it was worn at court, and at least one local translates the word as "expensive mu'umu'u."

holomū: a post–World War II cross between a *holokū* and a mu'umu'u, less fitted than the former but less voluminous than the latter, and having no train.

honi: to kiss; a kiss. A phrase that some tourists may find useful, quoted from a popular hula, is *Honi Ka'ua Wikiwiki:* Kiss me quick!

honu: turtle.

ho'omalimali: flattery, a deceptive "line," bunk, baloney, hooey.

huhū: angry.

hui: a group, club, or assembly. A church may refer to its congregation as a *hui* and a social club may be called a *hui*.

hukilau: a seine; a communal fishing party in which everyone helps to drive the fish into a huge net, pull it in, and divide the catch.

hula: the dance of Hawai'i.

iki: little.

ipo: sweetheart.

ka: the. This is the definite article for most singular words; for plural nouns, the definite article is usually *nā*. Since there is no *S* in Hawaiian, the article may be your only clue that a noun is plural.

kahuna: a priest, doctor, or other trained person of old Hawai'i, endowed with special professional skills that often included prophecy or other supernatural powers; the plural form is kāhuna.

kai: the sea, saltwater.

kalo: the taro plant from whose root *poi* (paste) is made.

kamā'aina: literally, a child of the soil; it refers to people who were born in the Islands or have lived there for a long time.

kanaka: originally a man or humanity, it is now used to denote a male Hawaiian or part-Hawaiian, but is occasionally taken as a slur when used by non-Hawaiians. *Kanaka maoli,* originally a full-blooded Hawaiian person, is used by some native Hawaiian rights activists to embrace part-Hawaiians as well.

kāne: a man, a husband. If you see this word on a door, it's the men's room. If you see *kane* on a door, it's probably a misspelling; that is the Hawaiian name for the skin fungus tinea.

kapa: also called by its Tahitian name, *tapa,* a cloth made of beaten bark and usually dyed and stamped with a repeat design.

kapakahi: crooked, cockeyed, uneven. You've got your hat on *kapakahi*.

kapu: keep out, prohibited. This is the Hawaiian version of the more widely known Tongan word *tabu* (taboo).

kapuna: grandparent; elder.

kēia lā: today.

keiki: a child; *keikikāne* is a boy, *keiki-wahine* a girl.

kona: the leeward side of the Islands, the direction (south) from which the *kona* wind and *kona* rain come.

kula: upland.

kuleana: a homestead or small plot of ground on which a family has been installed for some generations without necessarily owning it. By extension, *kuleana* is used to denote any area or department in which one has a special interest or prerogative. You'll hear it used this way: If you want to hire a surfboard, see Moki; that's his *kuleana*.

lā: sun.

lamalama: to fish with a torch.

lānai: a porch, a balcony, an outdoor living room. Almost every house in Hawai'i has one. Don't confuse this two-syllable word with the three-syllable name of the island, Lāna'i.

lani: heaven, the sky.

lau hala: the leaf of the *hala,* or pandanus tree, widely used in handicrafts.

lei: a garland of flowers.

limu: sun.

lolo: stupid.

luna: a plantation overseer or foreman.

mahalo: thank you.

makai: toward the ocean.

malihini: a newcomer to the Islands.

mana: the spiritual power that the Hawaiian believed inhabited all things and creatures.

manō: shark.

manuwahi: free, gratis.

mauka: toward the mountains.

mauna: mountain.

mele: a Hawaiian song or chant, often of epic proportions.

Mele Kalikimaka: Merry Christmas (a transliteration from the English phrase).

Menehune: a Hawaiian pixie. The *Menehune* were a legendary race of little people who accomplished prodigious work, such as building fishponds and temples in the course of a single night.

moana: the ocean.

mu'umu'u: the voluminous dress in which the missionaries enveloped Hawaiian women. Now made in bright printed cottons and silks, it is an indispensable garment. Culturally sensitive locals have embraced the Hawaiian spelling but often shorten the spoken word to "mu'u." Most English dictionaries include the spelling "muumuu."

nani: beautiful.

nui: big.

ohana: family.

'ono: delicious.

pāhoehoe: smooth, unbroken, satiny lava.

Pākē: Chinese. This *Pākē* carver makes beautiful things.

palapala: document, printed matter.

pali: a cliff, precipice.

pānini: prickly pear cactus.

paniolo: a Hawaiian cowboy, a rough transliteration of *español,* the language of the Islands' earliest cowboys.

pau: finished, done.

pilikia: trouble. The Hawaiian word is much more widely used here than its English equivalent.

puka: a hole.

pupule: crazy, like the celebrated Princess Pupule. This word has replaced its English equivalent in local usage.

pu'u: volcanic cinder cone.

waha: mouth.

wahine: a female, a woman, a wife, and a sign on the ladies' room door; the plural form is *wāhine.*

wai: freshwater, as opposed to saltwater, which is *kai.*

wailele: waterfall.

wikiwiki: to hurry, hurry up (since this is a reduplication of *wiki,* quick, neither W is pronounced as a V).

Note: Pidgin is the unofficial language of Hawai'i. It is a Creole language, with its own grammar, evolved from the mixture of English, Hawaiian, Japanese, Portuguese, and other languages spoken in 19th-century Hawai'i, and it is heard everywhere.

Travel Smart Kaua'i

WORD OF MOUTH

"I would recommend not renting a Jeep, as it turns out to be a rough ride and annoying if you are driving for any length of time. You will be driving primarily on regular roads, so I wouldn't bother with getting a Jeep."

–kangamom

GETTING HERE AND AROUND

■ AIR TRAVEL

Flying time is about 10 hours from New York, 8 hours from Chicago, and 5 hours from Los Angeles.

Some of the major airline carriers serving Hawai'i fly directly from the U.S. mainland to Kaua'i, allowing you to bypass connecting flights out of Honolulu. Although Līhu'e Airport is smaller and more casual than Honolulu International, it can also be quite busy during peak times. Allot extra travel time during morning and afternoon rush-hour traffic periods.

Plan to arrive at the airport approximately 60 minutes before departure for interisland flights and slightly longer than that for flights to the mainland.

Plants and plant products are subject to regulation by the Department of Agriculture, both on entering and leaving Hawai'i. Upon leaving the Islands, you'll have to have your bags X-rayed and tagged at one of the airport's agricultural inspection stations before you proceed to check-in. Pineapples and coconuts with the packer's agricultural inspection stamp pass freely; papayas must be treated, inspected, and stamped. All other fruits are banned for export to the U.S. mainland. Flowers pass—except for gardenias, rose leaves, jade vine, and mauna loa. Also banned are insects, snails, soil, cotton, cacti, sugarcane, and all berry plants.

You'll have to leave dogs and other pets at home. A 120-day quarantine is imposed to keep out rabies, which is nonexistent in Hawai'i. If specific pre- and post-arrival requirements are met, animals may qualify for a 30-day or 5-day-or-less quarantine.

Air Travel Resources in Hawai'i State of Hawaii Airports Division Offices (☎ 808/836–6417 ⊕ www.hawaii.gov/dot/ airports).

AIRPORTS

Honolulu International Airport (HNL) is the main stopover for most domestic and international flights. From Honolulu, there are interisland flights to Kaua'i departing regularly from early morning until evening. In addition, some carriers now offer nonstop service directly from the U.S. mainland to Līhu'e Airport (LIH) on a limited basis.

HONOLULU/O'AHU AIRPORT

Hawai'i's major airport is Honolulu International, on O'ahu, 20 minutes (9 mi) west of Waikīkī. To travel interisland from Honolulu, you can depart from either the interisland terminal or the commuter-airline terminal, located in two separate structures adjacent to the main overseas terminal building. A free bus service, the Wiki Wiki Shuttle, operates between terminals.

Information Honolulu International Airport (HNL) (☎ 808/836–6413 ⊕ www.hawaii.gov/ dot/airports).

KAUA'I

On Kaua'i, visitors fly into Līhu'e Airport, on the East Side of the island. Visitor Information Booths are outside each baggage-claim area. Visitors will also find news- and lei stands, an HMS Host restaurant, and a Travel Traders gift shop at the airport.

Information Līhu'e Airport (LIH) (☎ 808/246–1448 ⊕ www.hawaii.gov/dot/ airports).

GROUND TRANSPORTATION

Marriott Kaua'i and Radisson Kaua'i Beach Resort provide airport shuttles to and from the Līhu'e Airport. In addition, travelers who've booked a tour with Kaua'i Island Tours, Roberts Hawai'i, or Polynesian Adventure Tours will be picked up at the airport.

SpeediShuttle offers transportation between the airport and hotels, resorts, and time-share complexes on the island. There is an online reservation and fare quote system for information and bookings. Or, you can hire a taxi or limousine. Cabs are available curbside at baggage claim. Cab fares to locations around the island are estimated as follows: Po'ipū $35–$41, Wailua-Waipouli $17–$20, Līhu'e–Kukui Grove $10, Princeville-Hā'ena $72–$95. There are three limousine companies that service Līhu'e Airport: Any Time Shuttle, Custom Limousine, and Kaua'i Limousine.

Contacts Any Time Shuttle (☎ *808/927–1120*). **Custom Limousine** (☎ *808/246–6318*). **Kaua'i Limousine** (☎ *808/245–4855*). **SpeediShuttle** (☎ *877/242–5777*).

FLIGHTS

Alaska Airlines has a daily Seattle–Līhu'e flight. America West/US Airways flies into Līhu'e from San Francisco and Denver and also has flights into O'ahu, Maui, and the Big Island. American Airlines offers a daily, nonstop Los Angeles–Kaua'i flight, in addition to its service into Honolulu, Maui, and the Big Island. Continental flies into O'ahu (Honolulu). Delta has a Los Angeles–Līhu'e flight and also serves O'ahu (Honolulu) and Maui. United Airlines provides direct service to Līhu'e Airport from Denver, Los Angeles, and San Francisco. The carrier also flies into Honolulu, Maui, and the Big Island.

Airline Contacts American Airlines (☎ *800/433–7300* ⊕ *www.aa.com*). **America West/US Airways** (☎ *800/428–4322* ⊕ *www.usairways.com*). **Continental Airlines** (☎ *800/523–3273* ⊕ *www.continental.com*). **Delta Airlines** (☎ *800/221–1212* ⊕ *www.delta.com*). **Hawaiian Airlines** (☎ *800/367–5320* ⊕ *www.hawaiianair.com*). **Northwest Airlines** (☎ *800/225–2525* ⊕ *www.nwa.com*). **United Airlines** (☎ *800/864–8331* ⊕ *www.united.com*).

INTERISLAND FLIGHTS

Check local and community newspapers when you're on Kaua'i for deals and coupons on interisland flights, should you wish to visit neighboring islands. go! Mokulele Airlines, Hawaiian Airlines, and IslandAir offer regular service between the Islands. In addition to offering very competitive rates and online specials, all have free frequent-flier programs that will entitle you to rewards and upgrades the more you fly. Be sure to compare prices offered by all of the interisland carriers. If you are somewhat flexible with your days and times for island hopping, you should have no problem getting a very affordable round-trip ticket.

Interisland Carriers go! Mokulele Airlines (☎ *888/435–9462 or 808/426–7070* ⊕ *www.iflygo.com or www.mokuleleairlines.com*). **Hawaiian Airlines** (☎ *800/367–5320* ⊕ *www.hawaiianair.com*). **IslandAir** (☎ *800/652–6541* ⊕ *www.islandair.com*).

▪ BOAT TRAVEL

CRUISES

For information about cruises, see chapter 1, "Experience Kaua'i."

▪ BUS TRAVEL

On Kaua'i, the County Transportation Agency operates the Kaua'i Bus, which provides service between Hanalei and Kekaha. It also provides service to the airport and limited service to Kōloa and Po'ipū. The fare is $2 for adults, and frequent-rider passes are available.

Information Kaua'i Bus (☎ *808/241–6410* ⊕ *www.kauai.gov/OCA/Transportation*).

▪ CAR TRAVEL

The best way to experience all of Kaua'i's stunning beauty is to get in a car and explore. The 15-mi stretch of Nāpali Coast, with its breathtaking, verdant-green sheer cliffs, is the only part of the island that's not accessible by car. Otherwise, one main road can get you from Barking Sands Beach on the West Side to Hā'ena on the North Shore.

Asking for directions will almost always produce a helpful explanation from the locals, but you should be prepared for an island term or two. Instead of using compass directions, remember that Hawai'i residents refer to places as being either *mauka* (toward the mountains) or *makai* (toward the ocean) from one another. Hawai'i has a strict seat-belt law. Those riding in the front seat must wear a seat belt, and children under the age of 17 in the backseats must be belted. The fine for not wearing a seat belt is $92. Jaywalking is also very common in the Islands, so please pay careful attention to the roads. It also is considered rude to honk your horn, so be patient if someone is turning or proceeding through an intersection. While driving on Kaua'i, you will come across several one-lane bridges. If you are the first to approach a bridge, the car on the other side will wait while you cross. If a car on the other side is closer to the bridge, then you should wait while the driver crosses. If you're enjoying the island's dramatic views, pull over to the shoulder so you don't block traffic.

GASOLINE

You can count on having to pay more at the pump for gasoline on Kaua'i than on the U.S. mainland. There are no gas stations past Princeville on the North Shore, and no stations past Waimea on the West Side, so if you're running low, fuel up before heading out to the end of the road.

PARKING

On Kaua'i there are no parking meters, parking garages, parking tags, or paid parking. If there's room on the side of the road, you can park there. A good rule of thumb is if there are other cars parked in that area, it's safe to do the same.

ROAD CONDITIONS

Kaua'i has a well-maintained highway running south from Līhu'e to Barking Sands Beach; a spur at Waimea takes you along Waimea Canyon Drive to Kōke'e State Park. A northern route also winds its way from Līhu'e to the end of the road at Hā'ena, the beginning of the rugged and roadless Nāpali Coast. Opt for

a four-wheel-drive vehicle if dirt-road exploration holds any appeal.

ROADSIDE EMERGENCIES

If you find yourself in an emergency or accident while driving on Kaua'i, pull over if you can. If you have a cell phone with you, call the roadside assistance number on your rental-car contract or AAA Help. If you find that your car has been broken into or stolen, report it immediately to your rental-car company and an agent can assist you. If it's an emergency and someone is hurt, call 911 immediately and stay there until medical personnel arrive.

Emergency Services AAA Help
(☎ *800/222–4357*).

CAR RENTAL

Should you plan to do any sightseeing on Kaua'i, it is best to rent a car. Even if all you want to do is relax at your resort, you may want to hop in the car to check out one of the island's popular restaurants.

While on Kaua'i, you can rent anything from an econobox to a Ferrari. Rates are usually better if you reserve through a rental agency's Web site. It's wise to make reservations far in advance and make sure that a confirmed reservation guarantees you a car, especially if you're visiting during peak seasons or for major conventions or sporting events. Rates begin at about $25 to $35 a day for an economy car with air-conditioning, automatic transmission, and unlimited mileage, depending on your pickup location. This does not include the airport concession fee, general excise tax, rental-vehicle surcharge, or vehicle license fee. When you reserve a car, ask about cancellation penalties and drop-off charges should you plan to pick up the car in one location and return it to another. Many rental companies in Hawai'i offer coupons for discounts at various attractions that could save you money later on in your trip.

In Hawai'i you must be 21 years of age to rent a car, and you must have a valid driver's license and a major credit card. Those under 25 will pay a daily surcharge

Car Rental Resources

Automobile Associations		
U.S.: American Automobile Association	☎ 315/797–5000	⊕ www.aaa.com
National Automobile Club	☎ 650/294–7000	⊕ www.thenac.com; CA residents only
Major Agencies		
Alamo	☎ 800/462–5266	⊕ www.alamo.com
Avis	☎ 800/331–1212	⊕ www.avis.com
Budget	☎ 800/527–0700	⊕ www.budget.com
Hertz	☎ 800/654–3131	⊕ www.hertz.com
National Car Rental	☎ 800/227–7368	⊕ www.nationalcar.com
Thrifty Car Rental	☎ 888/400–8877	⊕ www.thrifty.com

of $15–$25. Request car seats and extras such as GPS when you book. Hawai'i's Child Restraint Law requires that all children three years and younger be in an approved child safety seat in the backseat of a vehicle. Children ages four–seven must be seated in a rear booster seat or child restraint such as a lap and shoulder belt. Car seats and boosters range from $5 to $8 per day.

In Hawai'i, your unexpired mainland driver's license is valid for rental for up to 90 days.

Since the road circling the island is two lanes mostly, be sure to allow plenty of time to return your vehicle so that you can make your flight. Traffic can be bad during morning and afternoon rush hour. Give yourself about two hours before departure time to return your vehicle.

LOCAL DO'S AND TABOOS

GREETINGS

Hawai'i is a very friendly place, and this is reflected in the day-to-day encounters with friends, family, and even business associates. Women often hug and kiss one another on the cheek, and men shake hands and sometimes combine that with a friendly hug. When a man and a woman are greeting each other and are good friends, it is not unusual for them to hug and kiss on the cheek. Children are taught to call any elders "auntie" or "uncle," even if they aren't related. It's a way to show respect and can result in a local Hawaiian child having dozens of aunties or uncles. It's also reflective of the strong sense of *'ohana* (family) that exists in the Islands.

When you walk off a long flight, perhaps a bit groggy and stiff, nothing quite compares with a Hawaiian lei greeting. The casual ceremony ranks as one of the fastest ways to make the transition from the worries of home to the joys of your vacation. Though the tradition has created an expectation that everyone receives this floral garland when he or she steps off the plane, the State of Hawai'i cannot greet each of its nearly 7 million annual visitors.

If you've booked a vacation with a wholesaler or tour company, a lei greeting might be included in your package, so check before you leave. If not, it's easy to arrange a lei greeting for yourself or your companions before you arrive into Līhu'e Airport. Kama'āina Leis, Flowers & Greeters has been providing lei greetings for visitors to the Islands since 1983. To be really wowed by the experience, request a lei of plumeria, some of the most divine-smelling blossoms on the planet. A plumeria or dendrobium orchid lei is considered standard and costs $19 to $22 per person.

Information Kama'āina Leis, Flowers & Greeters (☎ *808/836–3246 or 800/367–5183* ⊕ *www.alohaleigreetings.com*).

LANGUAGE

Hawai'i was admitted to the Union in 1959, so residents can be sensitive when visitors refer to their own hometowns as "back in the States." Remember, when in Hawai'i, refer to the contiguous 48 states as "the Mainland" and not as the United States. When you do, you won't appear to be such a *malahini* (newcomer).

English is the primary language on the Islands. Making the effort to learn some Hawaiian words can be rewarding, however. Despite the length of many Hawaiian words, the Hawaiian alphabet is actually one of the world's shortest, with only 12 letters: the five vowels, *a, e, i, o, u,* and seven consonants, *h, k, l, m, n, p, w.* Hawaiian words you're most likely to encounter during your visit to the Islands are *aloha, mahalo* (thank you), *keiki* (child), *haole* (Caucasian or foreigner, a derogatory term), *mauka* (toward the mountains), *makai* (toward the ocean), and *pau* (finished, all done). Hawaiian history includes waves of immigrants, each bringing its own language. To communicate with each other, they developed a sort of slang known as "pidgin." If you listen closely, you'll know what is being said by the inflections and by the extensive use of body language. For example, when you know what you want to say but don't know how to say it, just say, "You know, da kine." For an informative and somewhat hilarious view of things Hawaiian, check out Jerry Hopkins's series of books titled *Pidgin to the Max* and *Fax to the Max,* available at most local bookstores in the Hawaiiana sections.

ESSENTIALS

■ COMMUNICATIONS

INTERNET

If you've brought your laptop with you to Kaua'i, you should have no problem checking e-mail or connecting to the Internet. Most of the major hotels and resorts offer high-speed access in rooms and/or lobbies. You should check with your hotel in advance to confirm that access is wireless; if not, ask whether in-room cables are provided. In some cases an hourly charge will be posted to your room that averages about $15 per hour. If you're staying at a small inn or B&B without Internet access, ask the proprietor for the nearest café or coffee shop with wireless access.

■ HEALTH

In addition to being the Aloha State, Hawai'i is known as the Health State. The life expectancy here is 79 years, the longest in the nation. Balmy weather makes it easy to remain active year-round, and the low-stress aloha attitude certainly contributes to general well-being. When you are visiting the Islands, however, there are a few health issues to keep in mind.

The Hawai'i State Department of Health recommends that you drink 16 ounces of water per hour to avoid dehydration when hiking or spending time in the sun. Use sunblock, wear UV-reflective sunglasses, and protect your head with a visor or hat for shade. If you're not acclimated to warm, humid weather you should allow plenty of time for rest stops and refreshments. When visiting freshwater streams, be aware of the tropical disease leptospirosis, which is spread by animal urine and carried into streams and mud. Symptoms include fever, headache, nausea, and red eyes. If left untreated, it can cause liver and kidney damage, respiratory failure, internal bleeding, and even death. To avoid this, don't swim or wade in freshwater streams or ponds if you have open sores, and don't drink from any freshwater streams or ponds, especially after heavy rains.

On the Islands, fog is a rare occurrence, but there can often be "vog," an airborne haze of gases released from volcanic vents on the Big Island. During certain weather conditions such as "Kona Winds," the vog can settle over the Islands and wreak havoc with respiratory and other health conditions, especially asthma or emphysema. If susceptible, stay indoors and get emergency assistance if needed.

The Islands have their share of bugs and insects that enjoy the tropical climate as much as visitors do. Most are harmless but annoying. When planning to spend time outdoors in hiking areas, wear long-sleeved clothing and pants and use mosquito repellent containing deet. In very damp places you may encounter the dreaded local centipede. On the Islands they usually come in two colors, brown and blue, and they range from the size of a worm to an 8-inch cigar. Their sting is very painful, and the reaction is similar to bee- and wasp-sting reactions. When camping, shake out your sleeping bag before climbing in, and check your shoes in the morning, as the centipedes like cozy places. If planning on hiking or traveling in remote areas, always carry a first-aid kit and appropriate medications for sting reactions.

■ HOURS OF OPERATION

Even people in paradise have to work. Generally, local business hours are weekdays 8–5. Banks are usually open Monday–Thursday 8:30–3 and until 6 on Friday. Some banks have Saturday-morning hours.

Many self-serve gas stations stay open around the clock, with full-service stations usually open from around 7 AM until 9 PM.

U.S. post offices are open weekdays 8:30 AM–4:30 PM and Saturday 8:30–noon.

Most museums generally open their doors between 9 AM and 10 AM and stay open until 5 PM Tuesday–Saturday. Many museums operate with afternoon hours only on Sunday and close on Monday. Visitor-attraction hours vary throughout the state, but most sights are open daily, with the exception of major holidays such as Christmas. Check local newspapers upon arrival for attraction hours and schedules if visiting over holiday periods. The local dailies carry a listing of "What's Open/What's Not" for those time periods.

Stores in resort areas sometimes open as early as 8, with shopping-center opening hours varying from 9:30 to 10 on weekdays and Saturday, a bit later on Sunday. Bigger malls stay open until 9 weekdays and Saturday and close at 5 on Sunday. Boutiques in resort areas may stay open as late as 11.

∎ MONEY

Prices throughout this guide are given for adults. Substantially reduced fees are almost always available for children, students, and senior citizens.

CREDIT CARDS

Throughout this guide, the following abbreviations are used: **AE**, American Express; **D**, Discover; **DC**, Diners Club; **MC**, MasterCard; and **V**, Visa. It's a good idea to inform your credit-card company before you travel. Otherwise, the credit-card company might put a hold on your card owing to unusual activity—not a good thing halfway through your trip. Record all your credit-card numbers—as well as the phone numbers to call if your cards are lost or stolen—in a safe place, so you're prepared should something go wrong. Both MasterCard and Visa have general numbers you can call (collect if you're abroad) if your card is lost, but you're better off calling the number of your issuing bank, since MasterCard and Visa usually just transfer you

to your bank; your bank's number is usually printed on your card.

Reporting Lost Cards **American Express** (☎ 800/528–4800 ⊕ www.americanexpress. com). **Diners Club** (☎ 800/234–6377 ⊕ www. dinersclub.com). **Discover** (☎ 800/347–2683 ⊕ www.discovercard.com). **Master-Card** (☎ 800/627–8372 in the U.S. ⊕ www. mastercard.com). **Visa** (☎ 800/847–2911 ⊕ www.visa.com).

∎ PACKING

Hawai'i is casual: sandals, bathing suits, and comfortable, informal clothing are the norm. In summer, synthetic slacks and shirts, although easy to care for, can be uncomfortably warm.

One of the most important things to tuck into your suitcase is sunscreen.

As for clothing in the Hawaiian Islands, there's a saying that when a man wears a suit during the day, he's either going for a loan or he's a lawyer trying a case. Only a few upscale restaurants require a jacket for dinner. The aloha shirt is accepted dress in Hawai'i for business and most social occasions. Shorts are acceptable daytime attire, along with a T-shirt or polo shirt. There's no need to buy expensive sandals on the mainland—here you can get flip-flops for a couple of dollars and off-brand sandals for $20. Golfers should remember that many courses have dress codes requiring a collared shirt; call courses you're interested in for details. If you're not prepared, you can pick up appropriate clothing at resort pro shops. If you're visiting in winter, bring a sweater or light- to medium-weight jacket. A polar fleece pullover is ideal and makes a great impromptu travel pillow.

∎ SAFETY

Hawai'i is generally a safe tourist destination, but it's still wise to follow the same commonsense safety precautions you would normally follow in your own hometown.

Be wary of those hawking "too good to be true" prices on everything from car rentals to attractions. Many of these offers are just a lure to get you in the door for time-share presentations. When handed a flier, read the fine print before you make your decision to participate.

Safety Transportation Security Administration (⊕ www.tsa.gov).

▌ TAXES

There's a 4.16% state sales tax on all purchases, including food. As of July 2010, a hotel room tax, plus the state sales tax, add a 13.42% rate to your hotel bill. A $3-per-day road tax is also assessed on each rental vehicle.

▌ TIME

Hawai'i is on Hawaiian Standard Time, five hours behind New York and two hours behind Los Angeles for the winter months.

While the U.S. Mainland uses daylight saving time from March until November, Hawai'i does not, so add an extra hour of time difference between the Islands and U.S. Mainland destinations during that part of the year. You may also find that things generally move more slowly here. That has nothing to do with your watch—it's just the laid-back way called Hawaiian time.

▌ TIPPING

Tip cabdrivers 15% of the fare. Standard tips for restaurants and bar tabs run from 15% to 20% of the bill, depending on the standard of service. Bellhops at hotels usually receive $1 per bag, more if you have bulky items such as bicycles and surfboards. Tip the hotel room maid $1 per night, paid daily. Tip doormen $1 for assistance with taxis; tips for concierges vary depending on the service. For example, tip more for "hard-to-get" event tickets or dining reservations.

For single-day guided activities like a boat trip to the Nāpali, a ziplining tour, or surf lessons, you should tip each guide at least $10–$20 if you feel he or she enhanced your experience. Oftentimes, the tour company takes the bulk of your booking price, and the locals who are sharing their aloha with you are depending on your tips.

▌ TOURS

Globus has two Hawai'i itineraries that include Kaua'i, one of which is an escorted cruise on Norwegian Cruise Lines' *Pride of Aloha* that includes two days on the Garden Island. Tauck Travel offers an 11-night *Best of Hawai'i* tour that includes two nights on Kaua'i with leisure time for either relaxation or exploration.

EscortedHawaiiTours.com, owned and operated by Atlas Cruises & Tours, sells more than a dozen Hawai'i trips ranging from 7 to 12 nights operated by various guided-tour companies including Globus, Tauck, and Trafalgar. Several of these trips include two to three nights on Kaua'i.

Recommended Companies Atlas Cruises & Tours (☎ 800/942–3301 ⊕ www.EscortedHawaiiTours.com). **Globus** (☎ 866/755–8581 ⊕ www.globusjourneys. com). **Tauck Travel** (☎ 800/788–7885 ⊕ www. tauck.com).

SPECIAL-INTEREST TOURS
BIRD-WATCHING

Hawai'i has more than 150 species of birds that live in the Hawaiian Islands. Field Guides has a three-island (O'ahu, Kaua'i, and the Big Island), 11-day guided bird-watching trip for 14 birding enthusiasts that focuses on endemic land birds and specialty seabirds. While on Kaua'i, birders will visit Kōke'e State Park, Alaka'i Wilderness Preserve, and Kīlauea Point. The trip costs about $4,400 per person and includes accommodations, meals, ground transportation, interisland air, an eight-hour pelagic boat trip, and guided bird-watching excursions. Travelers must purchase their own airfare to

INTERNATIONAL TRAVELERS

CURRENCY

The dollar is the basic unit of U.S. currency. It has 100 cents. Coins are the penny (1¢); the nickel (5¢), dime (10¢), quarter (25¢), half-dollar (50¢), and the very rare golden $1 coin and even rarer silver $1. Bills are denominated $1, $5, $10, $20, $50, and $100, all mostly green and identical in size; designs and background tints vary. You may come across a $2 bill, but the chances are slim.

Customs Information U.S. Customs and Border Protection (⊕ www.cbp.gov).

DRIVING

Gas costs in Hawai'i range from $3 to $4 a gallon. Driving in the United States is on the right. Speed limits are posted in miles per hour, between 25–55 mph in the Islands. Watch for lower limits near schools (usually 20 mph). Hawai'i has a strict seat-belt law. Passengers in the front seats must be belted. Children under the age of three must be in approved safety seats in the backseat, and those ages four to seven must be in a rear booster seat or child restraint such as a lap and shoulder belt. Morning (between 6:30 and 9:30 AM) and afternoon (between 3:30 and 6:30 PM) rush-hour traffic around major cities on most of the Islands can be bad, so use caution. In rural areas, including almost all of Kaua'i, it's not unusual for gas stations to close early. If you see that your tank is getting low, don't take any chances; fill up when you see a station.

If your car breaks down, pull onto the shoulder and wait for help, or have your passengers wait while you walk to an emergency phone. If you have a cell phone with you, call the roadside assistance number on your rental car agreement.

ELECTRICITY

The U.S. standard is AC, 110 volts/60 cycles. Plugs have two flat pins set parallel to each other.

EMBASSIES

Contacts Australia (☎ 202/797–3000 ⊕ www.austemb.org). **Canada** (☎ 202/682–1740 ⊕ www.canadianembassy.org). **United Kingdom** (☎ 202/588–7800 ⊕ www.britainusa.com).

Australia Australian Consulate (✉ 1000 Bishop St., Honolulu ☎ 808/524–5050).

Canada Canadian Consulate (✉ 1000 Bishop St., Honolulu ☎ 808/524–5050).

New Zealand New Zealand Consulate (✉ 900 Richards St., Room 414, Honolulu ☎ 808/543–7900).

United Kingdom British Consulate (✉ 1000 Bishop St., Honolulu ☎ 808/524–5050).

EMERGENCIES

For police, fire, or ambulance, dial 911 (0 in rural areas).

HOLIDAYS

New Year's Day (Jan. 1); Martin Luther King Day (3rd Mon. in Jan.); Presidents' Day (3rd Mon. in Feb.); Memorial Day (last Mon. in May); Independence Day (July 4); Labor Day (1st Mon. in Sept.); Columbus Day (2nd Mon. in Oct.); Thanksgiving Day (4th Thurs. in Nov.); Christmas Eve and Christmas Day (Dec. 24 and 25); and New Year's Eve (Dec. 31).

MAIL

You can buy stamps and aerograms and send letters and parcels in post offices. Stamp-dispensing machines can occasionally be found in airports, bus and train stations, office buildings, drugstores, and convenience stores. U.S. mailboxes are stout, dark blue steel bins; pickup schedules are posted inside the bin (pull down the handle to see them). Parcels weighing more than a pound must be mailed at a post office or at a private mailing center. Within the United States a first-class letter weighing 1 ounce or less costs 44¢; each additional ounce costs 17¢. Postcards cost 28¢. A 1-ounce airmail letter to most countries costs 88¢, an airmail post-card costs 75¢; a 1-ounce letter or postcard to Canada or Mexico costs 75¢. To receive mail on the road, have it sent c/o General Delivery at your destination's main post office (use the correct five-digit ZIP code). You must pick up mail in person within 30 days, with a driver's license or passport for identification.

Contacts **DHL** (☎ *800/225–5345* ⊕ *www. dhl.com*). **Federal Express** (☎ *800/463– 3339* ⊕ *www.fedex.com*). **Mail Boxes, Etc./ The UPS Store** (☎ *800/789–4623* ⊕ *www. mbe.com*). **United States Postal Service** (⊕ *www.usps.com*).

PASSPORTS AND VISAS

Visitor visas aren't necessary for citizens of Australia, Canada, the United Kingdom, or most citizens of European Union countries coming for tourism and staying for fewer than 90 days. If you require a visa, the cost is $100, and waiting time can be substantial, depending on where you live. Apply for a visa at the U.S. consulate in your place of residence; check the U.S. State Department's special Visa Web site for further information.

Visa Information **Destination USA** (⊕ *travel.state.gov/visa/*).

PHONES

Numbers consist of a three-digit area code and a seven-digit local number. The area code for all calls in Hawai'i is 808. For local calls to businesses on the island where you are staying, you only need to dial the seven-digit number (not the 808 area code). If you are calling businesses on other neighboring islands, you will need to use "1-808" followed by the number.

Calls to numbers prefixed by "800," "888," "866," and "877"are toll-free and require that you first dial a "1," just like calls to any other area codes. For calls to numbers prefixed by "900" you must pay—usually dearly. For international calls, dial "011" followed by the

country code and the local number. For help, dial "0" and ask for an overseas operator.

Most phone books list country codes and U.S. area codes. The country code for Australia is 61, for New Zealand 64, for the United Kingdom 44. Calling Canada is the same as calling within the United States, whose country code, by the way, is 1. For operator assistance, dial "0." For directory assistance, call 555–1212 or occasionally 411 (free at many public phones). You can reverse long-distance charges by calling "collect"; dial "0" instead of "1" before the 10-digit number.

Instructions are generally posted on pay phones. Usually you insert coins in a slot (usually 25¢–50¢ for local calls) and wait for a steady tone before dialing. On long-distance calls the operator tells you how much to insert; prepaid phone cards, widely available in various denominations, can be used from any phone. Follow the directions to activate the card (there's usually an access number, then an activation code), then dial your number.

CELL PHONES

The United States has several GSM (Global System for Mobile Communications) networks, so multiband mobiles from most countries (except for Japan) work here. Unfortunately, it's almost impossible to buy a pay-as-you-go mobile SIM card in the U.S.—which allows you to avoid roaming charges—without also buying a phone. That said, cell phones with pay-as-you-go plans are available for well under $100. AT&T, T-Mobile, and Virgin Mobile offer affordable, pay-as-you-go service.

and from their gateway city. Field Guides has been offering worldwide birding tours since 1984.

Victor Emanuel Nature Tours, the largest company in the world specializing in birding tours, has two nine-day trips that include Kaua'i. The guide for both tours is Bob Sundstrom, a skilled birder with a special interest in birdsong who has been leading birding tours in Hawai'i and other destinations since 1989. *Kaua'i and Hawai'i* is the theme of the March birding trip, when seabird diversity on the island is at its peak. Birders will see the koloa (Hawaiian duck), one of Hawai'i's most endangered wetland birds; as well as Laysan albatrosses, red- and white-tailed tropic birds, red-footed boobies, wedge-tailed shearwaters, great frigate birds, brown boobies, and possibly even red-billed tropic birds. Participants in the *Fall Hawai'i* birding trip will visit O'ahu, Kaua'i, and the Big Island in October. Birders will see Kaua'i honeycreepers and Hawaiian short-eared owls at Koke'e State Park and Alaka'i Swamp and seabirds at the National Wildlife Refuges at Kīlauea and Hanalei. *Kaua'i and Hawai'i* costs about $3,300/person and *Fall Hawai'i* is priced at about $3,600/person. Both trips include accommodations, meals, interisland air, ground transportation, and guided excursions. Travelers must purchase their own airline ticket to and from their gateway city.

Contacts Field Guides (☎ 800/728–4953 ⊕ www.fieldguides.com). **Victor Emanuel Nature Tours** (☎ 800/328–8368 ⊕ www.ventbird.com).

CULTURE
Elderhostel, a nonprofit educational travel organization, offers several guided tours for older adults that focus on Hawaiian culture. With all the tours listed, travelers must purchase their own airline tickets to Hawaii. We've chosen a few of our favorite tours here, but more information on tour subjects can be found on the organization's Web site.

Best of Kaua'i's Natural and Cultural Wonders is a six-night tour presented in association with the Kaua'i Historical Consortium. You'll visit Hanalei, Kīlauea Point National Wildlife Refuge, Grove Farm Homestead Museum, Kaua'i Museum, and Kōke'e Natural History Museum. You'll learn *lauhala* weaving and other traditional arts and crafts and discover why the island truly is like no other. The cost of this tour starts at $1,475 per person and includes accommodations, meals, ground transportation, and admission fees.

Nature, History and Culture on Kaua'i and Hawai'i is a 10-night trip that includes 5 nights on each island. Presented in association with the Kaua'i Historical Consortium and University of Hawai'i, Hilo, the tour highlights include field trips to Kīlauea Point National Wildlife Refuge, Waimea Canyon, and the National Tropical Botanical Garden. Field interpreters from the Kaua'i Museum, Kaua'i Historical Society, and Grove Farm Homestead Museum will share the island's history and cultural traditions with travelers. Prices start at $2,471 per person and include accommodations, meals, ground transportation, admission fees, and interisland air travel between Kaua'i and the Big Island.

Contact Elderhostel (☎ 800/454–5768 ⊕ www.elderhostel.org).

ECOTOURS
Want to spend a week in Kaua'i hiking, snorkeling, surfing, and paddling? Kayak Kaua'i has a seven-day *Discovery Tour* where you will explore Kaua'i's peaks and canyons, rivers and coastlines, and discover lagoons with crystal-clear water and breathtaking waterfalls, sacred trails,

and miles of ivory-white sand beaches. Tours are offered every month and include accommodations, airport shuttles, van support during the week, communal gear, linens, all meals, guides, day tours, and activities. *Discovery Tour* is rated moderate but can be challenging at times, and participants should be in good physical condition. For two people, the cost is $2,500 per person; with a group of four or more, it is priced at $1,750 per person. Travelers must purchase their own airline tickets between their gateway cities and Kaua'i.

Contact **Kayak Kaua'i** (☎ *800/437–3507* or *808/826–9844* ⊕ *www.kayakkauai.com*).

HIKING

Hiking Hills, Swimming Seas is the theme of a weeklong trip to Kaua'i sponsored by Sierra Club Outings. In addition to daylong hikes of 5 to 9 mi through many of the trails in Koke'e State Park, participants will have opportunities for snorkeling and swimming at secluded beaches, as well as bird-watching. Hikers also will help in the maintenance of some of the trails. Accommodations are in shared cabins, and as with all Sierra Club Outings, participants are expected to help prepare some of the meals using only local, fresh ingredients. The trip costs about $1,300 per person and includes accommodations, meals, and ground transportation.

Hawai'i Three Island Hiker is a seven-night hiking tour to Kaua'i, Maui, and the Big Island. Included in the per-person price of about $3,700 are accommodations, meals, interisland air between the Islands, shuttle transportation, support vehicle, professional guides, a T-shirt, and a water bottle. Hikers will spend three nights on Kaua'i exploring Nāpali coast, including hikes to Hanakāpī'ai Falls and the Nu'lolo Cliffs/Awa'awapuhi Loop. Another highlight of the adventure is a cruise and snorkel trip along the North Shore. The trip is rated moderately easy to moderate. The World Outdoors has been organizing and leading adventure trips around the world for 20 years.

Timberline Adventures has a five-night, *Kaua'i: Waimea Canyon & the Nāpali Coast* tour. Participants will hike more than 25 mi total as they explore the rugged southern coastline on the Shipwreck Beach trail, the lush rain forests of Koke'e State Park, majestic Waimea Canyon, the incredible waterfalls and cliffs along Nāpali Coast and even the quiet Sleeping Giant. Included in the per-person price of about $2,195 are accommodations on the West Side and North Shore, meals and ground transportation.

Travelers must purchase their own tickets to and from their gateway city.

Contacts **Sierra Club Outings** (☎ *415/977–5500* ⊕ *www.sierraclub.org/outings*). **The World Outdoors** (☎ *800/488–8483* ⊕ *www.theworldoutdoors.com*). **Timberline Adventures** (☎ *800/417–2453* ⊕ *www.timbertours.com*).

LUXURY

For the ultimate luxurious adventure experience, you'll want to book one of the Pure Kaua'i vacations. Included in all of these high-end adventure and spa vacations are private accommodations at elegant estates and villas, all meals prepared by a personal chef, activities, and on-island transportation. There are *Family Adventure*, *Adventure Boot Camp*, *Learn to Surf/Yoga*, and *Romantic Getaway* programs. The company also can create customized vacations with itineraries of any length and theme. Vacationers must purchase their own air between Kaua'i and their gateway city.

Contact **Pure Kaua'i** (☎ *866/457–7873* or ⊕ *www.purekauai.com*).

▌ TRIP INSURANCE

Comprehensive trip insurance is valuable if you're booking a very expensive or complicated trip (particularly to an isolated region) or if you're booking far in advance. Comprehensive policies typically cover trip cancellation and interruption, letting you cancel or cut your trip short because of illness, or, in some cases, acts of terrorism in your destination. Such policies might also cover evacuation and medical care. Some also cover you for trip delays because of bad weather or mechanical problems as well as for lost or delayed luggage.

Another type of coverage to consider is financial default—that is, when your trip is disrupted because a tour operator, airline, or cruise line goes out of business. Generally you must buy this when you book your trip or shortly thereafter, and it's available to you only if your operator isn't on a list of excluded companies.

Always read the fine print of your policy to make sure that you're covered for the risks that most concern you. Compare several policies to be sure you're getting the best price and range of coverage available.

Insurance Comparison Info **Insure My Trip** (☎ 800/487–4722 ⊕ www.insuremytrip.com). **Square Mouth** (☎ 800/240–0369 ⊕ www.squaremouth.com).

Comprehensive Insurers **Access America** (☎ 800/284-8300 ⊕ www.accessamerica.com). **AIG Travel Guard** (☎ 800/826–4919 ⊕ www.travelguard.com). **CSA Travel Protection** (☎ 800/873–9855 or 800/711–1197 ⊕ www.csatravelprotection.com). **Travelex Insurance** (☎ 888/228–9792 or 888/457–4602 ⊕ www.travelex-insurance.com). **Travel Insured International** (☎ 800/243-3174 ⊕ www.travelinsured.com).

❚ VISITOR INFORMATION

Before you go, contact the Kaua'i Visitors Bureau for a free travel planner that has information on accommodations, transportation, sports and activities, dining, arts and entertainment, and culture. You can also take a virtual tour of the island that includes great photos and helpful planning information.

The Hawai'i Tourism Authority's Travel Smart Hawaii site offers tips on everything from packing to flying. Also visit the Hawai'i State Vacation Planner for all information on the destination, including camping.

ONLINE TRAVEL TOOLS
The Hawai'i Department of Land and Natural Resources has information on hiking, fishing, and camping permits and licenses; online brochures on hiking safety and mountain and ocean preservation; and details on volunteer programs. The Kaua'i Visitors Bureau has Kaua'i-specific information on everything from activities to lodging options and organizes it by geographic regions on the island.

ALL ABOUT KAUA'I
Resources **Hawai'i Beach Safety** (⊕ www.hawaiibeachsafety.org). **Hawai'i Department of Land and Natural Resources** (⊕ www.state.hi.us/dlnr). **Kaua'i Vacation Explorer** (⊕ www.kauaiexplorer.com). **Kaua'i Visitors Bureau** (⊕ www.kauaidiscovery.com).

INDEX

PHOTO CREDITS

1, Douglas Peebles/Aurora Photos. 2, *Douglas Peebles/eStock Photo.* 5, *Mark A. Johnson/Alamy.* **Chapter 1: Experience Kaua'i:** 8-9, *SIME s. a.s/eStock Photo.* 10-12, *Kaua'i Visitors Bureau.* 13, James Michael Kruger/iStockphoto.15, *SuperStock/age fotostock.* 16 (left), *Robert Coello/Kaua'I Visitors Bureau.* 16 (top right), *Greg Vaughn/ Alamy.* 16 (bottom center), *Lee Foster/Alamy.* 16 (bottom right), *Starwood Hotels & Resorts.* 17 (top left), *Andre Jenny/Alamy.* 17 (bottom left), *Photo Resource Hawaii/Alamy.* 17 (right) and 18, *Ty Milford/Aurora Photos.* 19 (left), *Chad Ehlers/Alamy.* 19 (right), Photo Resource Hawaii/Alamy. 20, Jess Moss. 21, Jay Spooner/iStockphoto. 22, iStockphoto. 23, Stephanie Horrocks/iStockphoto. 24, *Kaua'i Visitors Bureau.* 25 (left), *Starwood Hotels & Resorts.* 25 (right), *Mark A. Johnson/Alamy.* 27, iStockphoto. 29, Katja Govorushchenko/iStockphoto. 30, *Photo Resource Hawaii/Alamy.* 31, nicole waring/iStockphoto. 32, James Michael Kruger/iStockphoto. 33, *Kaua'i Visitors Bureau.* 34, *Photo Resource Hawaii/Alamy.* 35, *iStockphoto.* 36 Travis Rowan/Alamy. 37, *Travis Rowan/Alamy.* **Chapter 2: Exploring Kaua'i:** 37, *Douglas Peebles Photography/Alamy.* 39, *Douglas Peebles/Aurora Photos.* 47, *Chad Ehlers/Stock Connection/Aurora Photos.* 48-50 and 51 (top), *Douglas Peebles Photography.* 51 (bottom), *iStockphoto.* 52 and 53 (top), *Photo Resource Hawaii/Alamy.* 53 (bottom), *SuperStock/age fotostock.* 54, *Mark A. Johnson/Alamy.* 55 (top), *Photo Resource Hawaii/Alamy.* 55 (bottom), *Dallas & John Heaton/age fotostock.* 57, *Cornforth Images/Alamy.* 61, *Steve Vidler/eStock Photo.* 63, *Roger Fletcher/Alamy.* 67, John Sigler/iStockphoto. 74-75, *Tom Till/Alamy.* 77, *Ron Dahlquist/Kaua'i Visitors Bureau.* 79, *Andre Jenny/Alamy.* 81, *Images Etc. Ltd/Alamy.* 84-86, Russ Bishop / Alamy. 88, Junko Kubota/iStockphoto. 93, Joe Vogan / Alamy. 95, Jess Moss. 96, *Grant Studios/eStock Photo.* 101, Mark Pinkerton/iStockphoto. **Chapter 4: Water Sports & Tours:** 103, *Mark A. Johnson/Alamy.* 107, *Photo Resource Hawaii/Alamy.* 112, *Ty Milford/Aurora Photos.* 119, *Pacific Stock/SuperStock.* 121, Ron Dahlquist/HVCB. 122, *Pacific Stock/SuperStock.* 125, *David Fleetham/Alamy.* 126, jarvis gray/Shutterstock. 128, Robert Plotz/iStockphoto. **Chapter 5: Golf, Hiking & Outdoor Activities:** 131, *Douglas Peebles/eStock Photo.* 135, *Mark A. Johnson/Alamy.* 137, *Luca Tettoni/viestiphoto.com.* 138, *Kaua'i Visitors Bureau.* 139 (bottom), Jack Jeffrey. 141, *Giovanni Simeone/SIME/eStock Photo.* 142, *Douglas Peebles Photography/Alamy.* 145, Greg Vaughn/Alamy. 146, Pacific Stock/SuperStock. 150, *Douglas Peebles Photography/Alamy.* 153, Princeville Ranch Adventures. **Chapter 6: Shops & Spas:** 155, *Dana Edmunds.* 163 (top), *Linda Ching/HVCB.* 163 (bottom), *Sri Maiava Rusden/HVCB.* 164, *Michael Soo/Alamy.* 165 (top), *leisofhawaii.com.* 165 (2nd from top), *kellyalexanderphotography.com.* 165 (3rd, 4th, and 5th from top), *leisofhawaii.com.* 165 (bottom), *kellyalexanderphotography.com.* 167 (all), *Grand Hyatt Kaua'i Resort and Spa.* **Chapter 7: Entertainment & Nightlife:** 171, *Douglas Peebles Photography/Alamy.* 173, *Danita Delimont/Alamy.* 176, *Hawaii Visitors & Convention Bureau.* 177, *Thinkstock LLC.* 179, *Hawaii Visitors & Convention Bureau.* **Chapter 8: Where to Eat:** 183, *Douglas Peebles/Alamy.* 185, Jess Moss. 187, Princeville Resort. 193, Ray Kachatorian/Starwood Hotels & Resorts. 196, muhawi001/Flickr. 201, *Polynesian Cultural Center.* 202 (top), *Douglas Peebles Photography.* 202 (top center), *Douglas Peebles Photography/Alamy.* 202 (center), *Dana Edmunds/Polynesian Cultural Center.* 202 (bottom center), *Douglas Peebles Photography/Alamy.* 202 (bottom), *Purcell Team/Alamy.* 203 (top, top center, and bottom center), *HTJ/HVCB.* 203 (bottom), *Oahu Visitors Bureau.* 208-09, Beach House Restaurant. **Chapter 9: Where to Stay:** 211 and 229 (top and bottom left), *Grand Hyatt Kaua'i Resort and Spa.* 229 (bottom right), *Douglas Peebles Photography/Alamy.*

ABOUT OUR WRITERS

Lois Ann Ell is a freelance journalist and food writer who lives on Kaua'i. She writes a weekly food and restaurant column for the *Garden Island* newspaper, and her work has appeared in other regional publications.

Michael Levine, a relative newcomer to the Hawaiian Islands, is a staff writer and assistant news editor for the *Garden Island*, Kaua'i's only daily newspaper. He has covered court cases, county and state government, and many other local stories.

Charles E. Roessler is a long-time Kaua'i resident who was an editor for the *Japan Times* and the *Buffalo News* after teaching English and journalism for 10 years. He regularly contributes to the *New York Times* as a stringer/freelancer and loves Kaua'i, especially playing tennis and swimming daily at 'Anini Beach.

Kim Steutermann Rogers lives on Kaua'i, where she hikes the mountains in her backyard and paddles the ocean's waters in her front yard. She volunteers for numerous organizations, including Kīlauea Point National Wildlife Refuge, Kaua'i Search and Rescue, Hawaiian Monk Seal Conservation Hui, and ReefCheck. She is the editor of OutriggerHawaii.com.